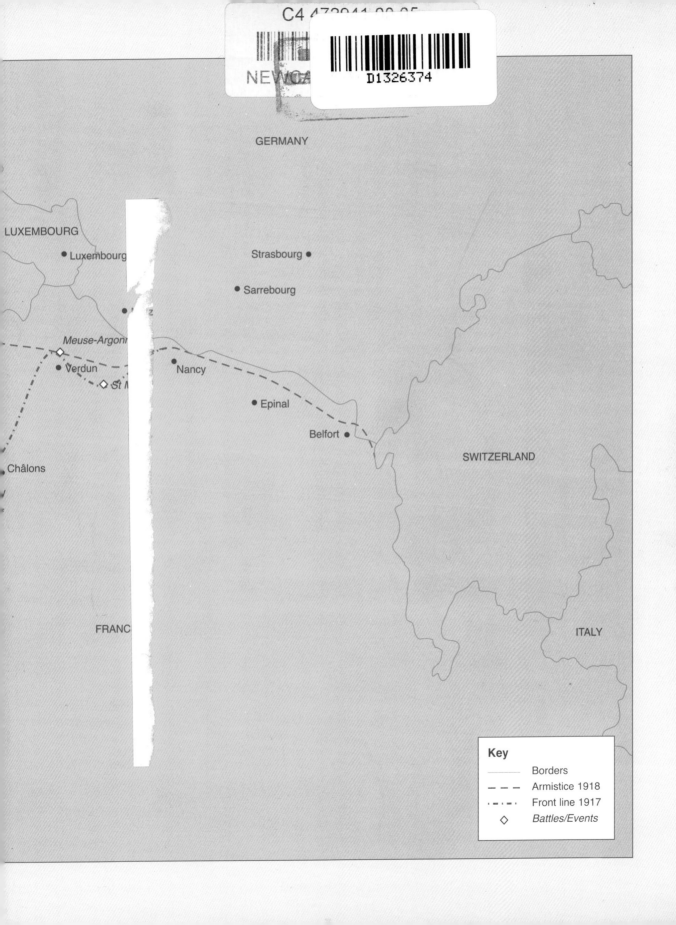

GERMANY

LUXEMBOURG

• Luxembourg

Strasbourg •

• Sarrebourg

Meuse-Argonn

◇
• Verdun

◇ *St M*

• Nancy

• Epinal

Belfort •

Châlons

SWITZERLAND

FRANC

ITALY

Key

——	Borders
– – –	Armistice 1918
–·–·–	Front line 1917
◇	*Battles/Events*

THE WESTERN FRONT
1917–1918

THE HISTORY OF WORLD WAR I

THE WESTERN FRONT
1917–1918

FROM VIMY RIDGE TO AMIENS AND THE ARMISTICE

ANDREW WIEST

FOREWORD BY PROFESSOR GARY SHEFFIELD

amber
BOOKS

To my London parents Ben and Ruby Buckle, to whom

This edition first published in 2008

Published by
Amber Books Ltd
Bradley's Close
74–77 White Lion Street
London N1 9PF
United Kingdom
www.amberbooks.co.uk

ISBN: 978-1-906626-20-0

Series Commissioning Editor: Charles Catton
Editorial: Ilios Publishing, Oxford, UK
Picture Research: Terry Forshaw and Susannah Jayes
Design: Jerry Williams
Indexer: Alison Worthington

For editorial or picture enquiries please contact editorial@amberbooks.co.uk

Printed in Dubai

MAP SYMBOLS KEY

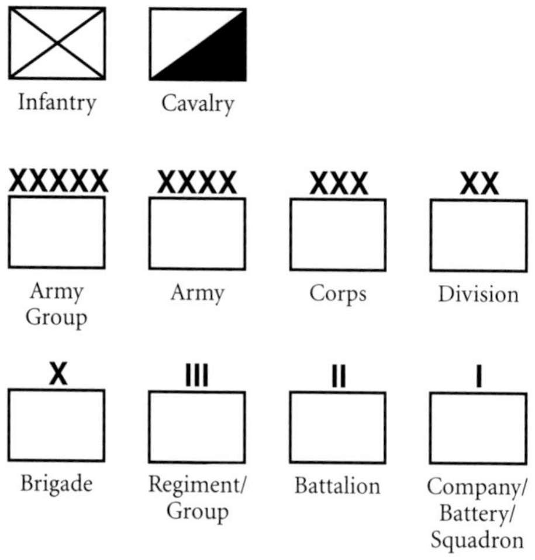

Infantry

Cavalry

XXXXX — Army Group

XXXX — Army

XXX — Corps

XX — Division

X — Brigade

III — Regiment/Group

II — Battalion

I — Company/Battery/Squadron

List of nationalities:

ALLIED FORCES

BL Belgium
FR France
GR Greece
IT Italy
RO Romania
RU Russia
SE Serbia
US United States

BRITISH EMPIRE
AN ANZAC
AU Australia
BR British
CN Canada
IN India

CENTRAL POWERS

AH Austro-Hungary
BU Bulgaria
GE Germany
OT Ottoman Empire

OTHER NATIONALITIES

PO Poland

E.g.

GE

Contents

Foreword

When the Berlin Wall came down in 1989, it triggered the beginning of the end of a period of history that began with the assassination of Archduke Franz Ferdinand in Sarajevo 75 years earlier. The death of the heir to the thrones of Austria-Hungary fanned the smouldering embers of international rivalry into life, and within six weeks most of Europe was at war. World War I destroyed the existing international balance; brought down mighty empires; created the conditions that led to the rise of fascism and communism; made a second global conflagration likely, if not inevitable; and even sowed the seeds of the Cold War. When, after the collapse of the Soviet Union in 1991, historians looked back, they readily identified 1914, the outbreak of World War I, as the beginning of the 'Short Twentieth Century', the bloodiest period in history.

Such a critical era demands to be properly understood, and I am delighted that such a distinguished Anglo-American team of historians – all of them acknowledged experts in their fields – have written a series of admirably accessible books on the war. As it happens, all of them are colleagues, past or present. They have succeeded magnificently in presenting accounts of the key campaigns that skilfully interweave narrative with some incisive analysis incorporating up-to-date research. This is grown-up history for the 21st century.

Gary Sheffield
Professor of War Studies
Centre for First World War Studies
University of Birmingham

A British prisoner of war.

INTRODUCTION

Pause for Breath

After three years of brutal warfare on the Western Front, and after the twin bloodlettings of Verdun and the Somme, the combatant nations paused to take stock of the strategic situation at the beginning of 1917. Fearing a repetition of the horrible attritional battles, each of the belligerent powers would gamble everything on victory in 1917 but would fall short.

The carnage of Verdun and the Somme had a pervasive effect on World War I as a whole and on the Western Front in particular. The twin battles shattered lives, ended some military careers and advanced others, toppled governments and altered strategic planning. At the most personal level, Verdun and the Somme had fundamentally altered the lives of their soldier participants. Far from the quick and glorious victories that many had expected in 1914, the titanic battles for many had instead epitomized slow, senseless slaughter and the sacrifice of a generation. German lieutenant Ernst Jünger spoke for many:

German troops pass through a French village as part of Germany's strategic retreat on the Western Front in 1917. The withdrawal, meant to shorten German lines to allow for the accumulation of much-needed reserves, threw complicated Allied plans for attack in 1917 into disarray.

Field Marshal Paul von Hindenburg (centre), who had risen to fame first at the Battle of Tannenberg, and then as the overall commander of the Eastern Front, in 1916 took control of Germany's overall military policy, working in tandem with General Erich Ludendorff.

'For I cannot too often repeat, a battle was no longer an episode that spent itself in blood and fire; it was a condition of things that dug itself in remorselessly week after week and even month after month. What was a man's life in this wilderness whose vapour was laden with the stench of thousands upon thousands of decaying bodies? Death lay in ambush for each one in every shell-hole, merciless, and making one merciless in return. … There it was [at the Somme] that the dust first drank the blood of our trained and disciplined youth. Those fine qualities which had raised the German race to greatness leapt once more in dazzling flame and then slowly went out in a sea of mud and blood.'

At the strategic level, Junger's commander, General Erich Ludendorff, who along with Field Marshal Paul von Hindenburg had effectively taken control of the German war effort, had to come to terms with the legacy of 1916. Admitting in his memoirs that the battles of Verdun and the Somme had left Germany 'completely exhausted on the Western Front', Ludendorff summarized the strategic implications of the resulting situation:

'The Supreme Army Command had to bear in mind that the enemy's great superiority in men and material would be even more painfully felt in 1917 than in 1916. It was plainly to be feared that early in the year "Somme fighting" would burst out at various points on our fronts, and that even our troops would not be able to withstand such attacks indefinitely, especially if the enemy gave us no time for rest and for the accumulation of material. Our position was unusually difficult, and no way of escape was visible. … The future looked dark.'

Although Field Marshal Sir Douglas Haig, in command of the British Expeditionary Force, and General Joseph Joffre, who led the French forces on the Western Front, were fully conscious of the fearsome butcher's bill that their nations had paid during the fighting of 1916, they interpreted Verdun and the Somme as costly victories. Working within that military analytical framework, on 16 November 1916, Haig and Joffre met at the Chantilly Conference to begin work on the strategic plan for the coming year and were primarily concerned with maintaining an unrelenting pressure on the Germans in both France and Flanders. Joffre explained his plan for 1917 rather bluntly: 'I have decided to seek the rupture of the enemy's forces by a general offensive executed between the Somme and the Oise at the same time as the British Armies carry out a similar operation between Bapaume and Vimy.'

It also became clear at Chantilly that, due to the price of Verdun, Britain would have to shoulder an ever-increasing military load on the Western Front. The changed Allied strategic balance, coupled with instructions from Prime Minister Herbert Asquith regarding the pivotal value of the German submarine bases on the Belgian coast, prompted Haig to press Joffre to agree that a British offensive in Flanders form the first part of Allied planning for the coming year, to

British wartime Prime Minister Herbert Asquith, whose indecisive wartime leadership led to the fracture of the Liberal Party and the rise of a coalition government under the fiery and fractious David Lloyd George. Asquith's eldest son, Raymond, was killed at the Battle of the Somme.

Industrial War

World War I was the first major conflict after the industrial revolution, which provided Western nations with the economic and technological strength first to arm millions of men and then to keep them in the field for years on end.

By 1914, due to advancements in both agriculture and industry, seven countries were able to field armies numbering in excess of one million men, which meant that World War I would not pit professional army against professional army; rather it would pit nations, their militaries, their populations and their economies, against nations in total war. Dwarfing all that came before, the twin battles of the Somme and Verdun best personified the new and terrible era of total war. Together the two battles lasted 16 months and cost two

million casualties. During the two battles, both sides fired off 35 million artillery shells and in excess of 60 million machine-gun bullets, a feat of industrial production never before witnessed. In addition to this, the men involved in the Somme and Verdun also consumed vast amounts of additional industrial and agricultural goods, ranging from food to gas respirators, which in the end meant that the two great battles of 1916 cost more than the gross national products of the vast majority of countries in the world. For nations to survive in the world of modern, total war, their populations had to accept great sacrifice, a fact that would also serve to transform World War I into a massive engine of both social and cultural change.

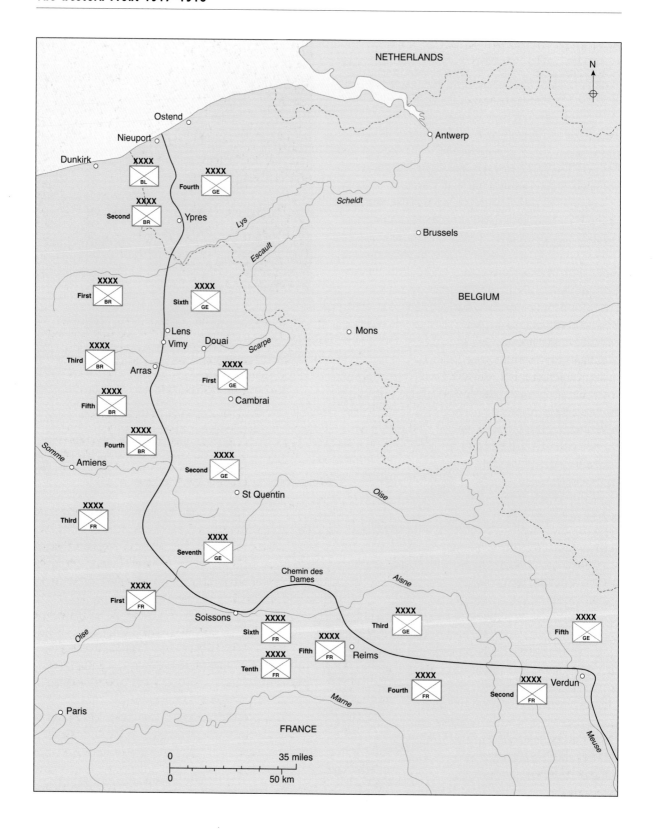

The Western Front at the beginning of 1917. Following grievous losses at Verdun and the Somme, the Germans felt unable to defend their holdings in France, which followed a circuitous route from the English Channel to the Swiss border, and chose instead to opt for a strategic withdrawal.

which Joffre reluctantly agreed. Joffre and Haig's desire doggedly to pursue strategic victory on the Western Front, as well as their interpretations of Verdun and the Somme as victories, however, resulted in immediate conflict with their own governments, who defined both the experience of 1916 and the most effective military route to victory quite differently.

Even as Haig was presenting his revised plan to Joffre, a seismic shift took place in British politics. Unhappy both with the tactical direction of the war and the indecisive leadership of Asquith, a coalition of Liberals, Conservatives and Labour took control of the House of Commons and elevated David Lloyd George to the position of Prime Minister. Haig had little in common with his new political master. Indeed the two were often at odds, with Haig regarding the Prime Minister as 'shifty and unreliable', while Lloyd George judged Haig to be but an 'arid strategist'. In matters of strategy, Lloyd George had long favoured shifting Britain's military might away from the Western Front to other, possibly more profitable, theatres of war. As such, the new Prime Minister's continuing devotion to the 'easterner' school of thought ran contrary to Haig's unwavering belief that the Allies had to destroy the might of the German Army in France and Flanders. Differing strategic visions set the two men on a collision course, for Lloyd George believed that the planning of Haig and Joffre would only result in another Somme; he later recalled in his memoirs:

General Robert Nivelle, who had risen to fame at the Battle of Verdun, by 1917 had taken command of French forces on the Western Front. His overconfidence and continued devotion to the power of the offensive resulted in disaster and mutiny in the ranks of the French military for much of 1917.

A lieutenant, serving with the elite French Escadrille No. 3, Groupe de Chasse 12. This squadron, known as the 'storks', was home to Georges Guynemer, one of the top French air aces of World War I who achieved 53 victories before his death in September 1917.

'The possibility never entered into the computation of these master minds that the survivors [of another Somme] might sooner or later object to this method of 'forming fours' by taking their turn in the slaughter house from which such multitude of their comrades never emerged. … Was there any other chance left except once more to sprinkle the western portal of the temple of Moloch with blood from what remained of the most valiant hearts amongst the youth of France and Britain? I decided to explore every possibility before surrendering to a renewal of the horrors of the West.'

The spectre of 1916 also haunted the halls of power in France. In December, the once unassailable General Joffre, who had always had a stormy relationship with the French parliament, fell from grace. Blaming him for failing adequately to prepare for the German attack on Verdun, Prime Minister René Viviani quietly removed Joffre from command by kicking him upstairs and promoting him to marshal of France. As a replacement, the French Government chose General Robert Nivelle, one of the heroes of Verdun.

Confident, articulate and effusive, Nivelle remained a devotee of the offensive, and believed that he had struck on a plan for certain victory in 1917. Rejecting the agreement that had been reached in Chantilly, Nivelle reopened the strategic debate by advocating a new plan designed finally to crush the German defensive lines. The scheme called for a diversionary British attack near Arras to distract German attention while the French gathered their strength for the climactic battle in the area of the Chemin des Dames Ridge.

NIVELLE'S PROPOSED OFFENSIVE

In mounting the main attack Nivelle proposed to use the same tactics that had won him such stirring victories at Verdun, but on a greater scale. Thorough artillery preparation, followed by a precise creeping barrage, would, he claimed, preface an attack of 'violence, brutality and rapidity' that would rupture the German front lines in at most 48 hours, leading to a pursuit of a defeated enemy into Germany. Most important to politicians wary of a repeat of Verdun or

Nursing

Female nurses from each belligerent nation served heroically in and near the front lines. An American nurse, known as 'Mademoiselle Miss', collected and published her letters home in an effort to educate the public concerning the role of nurses in war. In one letter, she attempted to outline her daily routine:

'Ever since I began my work I have been watching for a chance to sketch for you at least one day in detail, that you may have some vague idea of this unique and inexpressible life.

'At quarter to six A.M., I am up and sponged and well flesh-brushed. My good old lady gives me a huge bowl of coffee and four lumps of sugar, bread and butter, and a boiled egg, for 12 cents, an extravagance which I indulge in to avoid the probable consequence of the long walk to the Hospital on an empty stomach through the mists of the Marne, which are thick and weird enough in the early morning. It is a devious way through mud and mist, and almost anything is likely to cross your path, a bent, white-capped old woman like a stray from some old Dutch painting; a black cat, lean and rusty (everything is hungry about here); an aeroplane wheeling about on the watch for Taubes [German aircraft] which are frequent and fiery these days; a convoy of automobiles driving at top speed to the trenches; the dim wraith of a funeral procession disappearing in the distance.

'When I get to my pavilion, there is sure to be "Grandpa", my treasured old orderly, busy at brushing out the entrance. He immediately drops his broom, and holds out his good brawny hand to hope that his "Mademoiselle Miss" (the name I am generally known by) has slept well, and will not work too hard during the coming day. Grandpa is my Eternal Vigilance, always on hand, always ready to do every bidding, and zealous to spare me every possible fatigue. Last week he and my other orderlies were ill, he and Karbiche, the merry faithful clown, with bronchitis, and Loupias with tonsilitis and a bad bone-felon and I had to carry my patients to the surgical dressings room myself. He nearly wept with chagrin.

'The first thing I do, after a word of greeting to each of the 34 children, is to review the ward and see that it is well washed, in order, and no spoons or bottles out of place, and to start instruments boiling. After that begin the temperatures. Along with the temperatures go face-washing and mouth-rinsing, generally engineered by faithful Grandpa. About half-past eight, the doctor makes his appearance. When he has made the tour of the ward, I am left complete mistress of the scene for the

the Somme, though, was Nivelle's pledge to end his attack within two days if it had not achieved success. Desperate for a ray of hope in such dark times, the French Government approved Nivelle's scheme, over the objection of several important French military figures including General Henri Philippe Pétain and General Ferdinand Foch, who predicted that the offensive would end in disaster.

Only the British remained to be convinced. Realizing that Haig still supported a British offensive in Flanders, in January 1917, Nivelle took his case directly to Lloyd George, who was in Paris on the way home from an Allied strategic conference in Rome at which he had vainly pressed the case for shifting the emphasis of the war away from the Western Front. Aboard Lloyd George's train car while stopped at the Gare du Nord, Nivelle unfolded his plan. Unlike the notoriously tongue-tied Haig, Nivelle was a glib conversationalist and quite comfortable in the company of politicians. Apart from his social ease and fluent English, Nivelle offered Lloyd George a near-perfect military scenario. There would be no repeat of the slaughter and seemingly senseless sacrifice of the Somme. Making the offer even more irresistible, Nivelle's plan promised a victorious campaign in which the French would run the greatest risk and pay the highest cost. Eager to shift the strategic reality of a war he judged to be going wrong, Lloyd George

rest of the day, with 34 lives in my hand more than half of which hang in the balance. If there is anything critical, I send for the big surgeon, and he always comes graciously, which is a great mark of confidence.

'About 9 A.M. I begin the dressings, unless there are anti-tetanus injections to give for those who may have arrived in the night, or someone is dying, or there is an urgent operation. But we shall suppose an uninterrupted day. I begin with the important dressings, which are often long and dangerous, and I can do but three or four before the bell rings for soup at 10.45 A.M.

'I think you would sicken with fright if you could see the operations that a poor nurse is called upon to perform, the putting in of drains, the washing of wounds so huge and ghastly as to make one marvel at the endurance that is man's, the digging about for bits of shrapnel. I assure you that the word responsibility takes a special meaning here. After the soup for the wounded, comes that of the nurses, when all crowd into a tiny plank hut, and stuff meat and potatoes as fast as we can between disjointed bits of gossip. Immediately after lunch I spend an hour or so setting to rights the surgical dressings routine, doing little services, and distributing cakes or bonbons. It is amazing how a bit of peppermint will console a soldier when a smile goes with it!

'Dressings all the afternoon until it is time for temperatures; then soup for the soldiers; and mine, which is soon finished; then the massage for those that need it, etc., after which I prepare my soothing drinks and give the injections. It is the sweetest time of the day, for then one puts off the nurse and becomes the mother; and we have such fun over the warm drinks. They are nice and sweet and hot, and the soldiers adore their "American drinks".

'When this is done, I go around and stuff cotton under weary backs and plastered limbs, bid all the children good-night, polish my instruments, clean out the surgical dressings room, and hurry home through the frosty night.

'This is the rough outline of an ordinary day, and into that let your fancy weave all that is too holy or terrible, too touching or humorous to put into words: the last kiss a soldier gives you for his family he will never see; the watches with the priest when all is still and dark, but for the light of my little electric lamp and a bit of moonlight through the window; the agonies and heroisms; the wit and affection that play like varied lights and darks along the days.'

French soldiers in action on the Chemin des Dames, the dominating ridge line the capture of which formed the centrepiece of Nivelle's offensive plan in 1917 – a controversial scheme that resulted in a nearly unbearable strain within the Allied command structure.

quickly fell under the spell of Nivelle's charm. In writing to his mistress Frances Stevenson, Lloyd George made clear his preference for the plan of the dashing Nivelle over that of Haig stating: 'Nivelle has proved himself to be a Man at Verdun; and when you get a Man against one who has not proved himself, why, you back the Man!'

The acquiescence of Lloyd George ensured that Nivelle would have his chance at victory. However, even as planning for the offensive progressed, political manoeuvring continued that not only greatly damaged Allied unity but also shook the foundations of the British military command. Although he believed that he had succeeded in avoiding another Somme battle in 1917, Lloyd George did not trust his generals in the least. As Haig made preparations for an assault near Arras, as called for in Nivelle's plan, Lloyd George decided to utilize the occasion of Nivelle's offensive to assert his complete authority over the British military in matters of strategy and tactics.

At a February conference at Calais regarding logistic and transportation difficulties, Lloyd George

Siegfried Sassoon (1886–1967)

Born in 1886, Siegfried Sassoon enjoyed a privileged upbringing and had begun to build a budding career as a poet until World War I interrupted his life. Full of the patriotic fervour that so epitomized his generation, Sassoon volunteered for war, eventually joining the Royal Welch Fusiliers and seeing service in France. An exemplary officer, Sassoon won the Military Cross for bringing wounded back to the lines under enemy fire, and even earned the sobriquet 'Mad Jack' from his men, due to his fearless nature in battle. However, Sassoon's experience in battle left both him and his poetry changed forever. While convalescing in Britain after being wounded, Sassoon decided that

he could not return to such a wasteful war, and published 'A Soldier's Defiance' in a newspaper stating: 'I have seen and endured the sufferings of the troops, and I can no longer be party to prolonging these sufferings for ends which I believe to be evil and unjust'. Rather than prosecute Sassoon, whose poetry was already becoming well known, the military authorities had him declared unfit for service and sent to Craiglockhart Mental Hospital, where he received treatment for shell shock and befriended one of Britain's other most influential war poets, Wilfred Owen. Sassoon eventually returned to battle, only to be wounded again, after which time he spent the remainder of the war in Britain. In the inter-war years, Sassoon became one of Britain's best-known writers, and his anti-war poetry and prose became emblematic of Britain's desire never to fight such a war again.

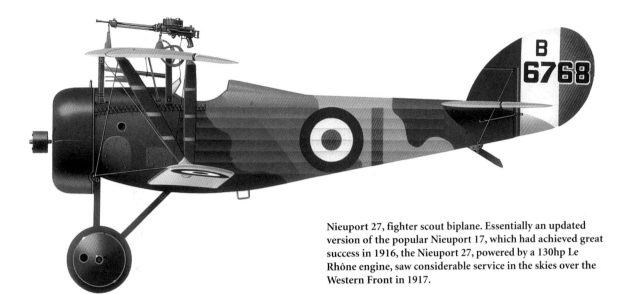

Nieuport 27, fighter scout biplane. Essentially an updated version of the popular Nieuport 17, which had achieved great success in 1916, the Nieuport 27, powered by a 130hp Le Rhône engine, saw considerable service in the skies over the Western Front in 1917.

unveiled secret plans to restructure the Allied system of command on the Western Front. Maurice Hankey, the War Cabinet Secretary, later recalled that the plan: 'fairly took my breath away, as it practically demanded the placing of the British army under Nivelle; the

> 'Farewell, comrades of the Somme! The earth which drank your blood is upheaved and torn asunder … it is turned into a desert, and your graves are made free from the dwellings of men. Those who tread it, your desert, will be greeted by our shells.'
>
> German journalist Georg Querl on the withdrawal to the Hindenburg Line

appointment of a British "chief of staff" to Nivelle, who had powers practically eliminating Haig as his Chief of the General Staff, the scheme reducing Haig to a cypher'. Shocked, Haig recorded that he 'would rather be tried by court-martial than betray the Army by agreeing to its being placed under the French'.

Tempers flared, threatening to lead to a breakdown of the conference and the resignation of much of the command structure of the BEF before cooler heads prevailed. The compromise agreement eventually reached at the Calais Conference placed Haig under Nivelle's overall command for only the duration of the coming offensive. The underlying causes of the crisis in command, though, remained. Lloyd George had been frustrated in his attempt to seize strategic control of the conflict, while Haig became ever more wary of the meddling of civilian amateurs in tactical matters best left to the military. The Calais Conference had strained British civil–military relations to the breaking point and, as the war neared a point of great crisis, relations between the government and the military in Britain remained characterized by mistrust and animosity.

THE GERMAN WITHDRAWAL

Even as the British command machine sputtered and coughed, the Germans intervened and greatly complicated the strategic picture on the Western Front, threatening to scuttle all Allied planning. Under great pressure from the British blockade, Germany was hard pressed both to feed its population and to provide adequately for its massive military efforts. A single army corps on a monthly basis consumed 453,592kg

German troops pass through the ruins of a French village during their withdrawal on the Western Front. Hoping to delay French and British pursuit, the Germans laid waste to the villages, farms and transportation network in the area of the retreat.

(one million pounds) of meat, 660,000 loaves of bread, 85,729kg (189,000lb) of fat and 33,112kg (73,000lb) of coffee. The XVIII Corps, for example, estimated that it needed 1000 wagons extending for 15km (nine miles) to haul its monthly stores of bread; it also slaughtered 1320 cows, 1100 pigs and 4158 sheep per month. Since no one in power had foreseen a long war, the massive supply needs of the military reduced the home front to ever-stricter forms of rationing. By the winter of 1916, the situation had become critical, with one observer remarking that the optimism of 1914 was long gone: 'Now one sees faces like masks, blue with cold and drawn by hunger, with the harassed expression common to all those who are continually speculating as to the possibility of another meal.'

Concerned by the state of German morale, and echoing Haig's appraisal of Verdun and the Somme as hard-fought victories, Ludendorff despaired of Germany's ability to survive another year of attrition

and want. In a desperate measure, the German command team ordered the evacuation of the German salient between Arras and Soissons and the withdrawal to a specially constructed defensive network, later dubbed by the Allies the Hindenburg Line. The withdrawal allowed for the accumulation of much-needed reserves and was also designed to buy Germany valuable time for the nation's greatest ever military gamble.

The strategic situation had become so grave that the German Government had decided to launch unrestricted submarine warfare in the Atlantic in an effort to starve the British into submission. Ludendorff and his command compatriots fully realized that unleashing the U-boats would result in an American entry into the conflict, but, with the German military so sorely pressed on the Western Front, the German command team judged the U-boat offensive to be worth the risk. Achieving victory through the submarine war in Ludendorff's words was of the 'highest importance' and the withdrawal to the Hindenburg Line was thus designed 'to postpone the struggle in the West as long as possible to allow the submarine campaign to produce decisive results'.

In February 1917, even as the German U-boats made their first kills, the German Army on the Western Front began its withdrawal to powerful new defensive lines that had already been under construction for five months. Under Ludendorff's orders, German troops carried out the evacuation with great ruthlessness, resulting in the destruction of most of the towns and villages in the salient. Ernst Jünger recalled the scene:

'The villages we passed through as we marched … had the appearance of lunatic asylums let loose. Whole companies were pushing walls down or sitting on the roofs of the houses throwing down the slats. Trees were felled, window-frames broken, and smoke and clouds of dust rose from heap after heap of rubbish. In short, an orgy of destruction was going on. The men were chasing

BELOW **German troops clearing dead from a shell-hole during the Battle of Verdun in 1916. The prodigious slaughter in the signature battles of 1916, Verdun and the Somme, caused each of the combatant powers on the Western Front to take strategic gambles in 1917.**

ABOVE **A wounded French soldier is carried from the battlefield at Verdun. It was General Robert Nivelle's promise that he would not allow his 1917 offensive to degenerate into another repetition of the Somme or Verdun that won approval for his planning.**

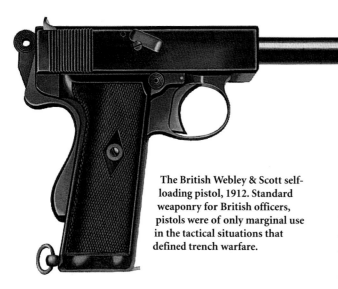

The British Webley & Scott self-loading pistol, 1912. Standard weaponry for British officers, pistols were of only marginal use in the tactical situations that defined trench warfare.

round with incredible zeal, arrayed in the abandoned wardrobes of the population, in women's dresses and with top hats on their heads. ... Every village up to the Siegfried Line [the German name for the Hindenburg Line] was a rubbish heap. Every tree felled, every road mined, every well fouled, every water course dammed, every cellar blown up or made into a death-trap with concealed bombs, all supplies or metal sent back, all rails ripped up, all telephone wire rolled up, everything burnable burned. In short the country over which the enemy were to advance had been turned into utter desolation.'

NO MORE VERDUNS

The German withdrawal took place in the very area in which Nivelle had proposed to attack, which both greatly disrupted French forward movement and made logistical preparations exceedingly difficult. Making matters worse, Nivelle's attack now faced a much more formidable German defensive network. In late March, a new French governmental team, Premier Alexandre Ribot and Minister of War Paul Painlevé, requested that Nivelle reconsider his planning in light of the changed tactical situation. Nivelle, though, stood his ground, considering the German withdrawal merely an inconvenience. Nivelle assured the sceptical politicians of impending victory and informed them that if he no longer held their confidence they should

appoint a successor. With the British slated soon to begin their attack at Arras, Painlevé feared that a cancellation of the offensive would be injurious to Allied unity, and possibly precipitate a crisis that would bring down the government. Although grave doubts remained, Painlevé had been defeated and had no choice but to allow Nivelle his chance at victory.

Although Nivelle had, in the end, failed to win the lasting support of his own government for his offensive, he had been able to convince his men and his nation that victory was at hand. He promised the war-weary troops that there would be no more Verduns and no more wasting of men's lives for minimal gain. No, his attack would be different, and French élan and firepower would win the day at last. To a nation tiring of sacrifice, Nivelle's words were a tonic. Morale soared, and as a result the spring of 1917 resembled that of 1914. Nivelle had raised French hopes to a new height – only to bring them crashing down to a disastrous low.

With almost criminal carelessness, Nivelle had informed several politicians, many newspapers and countless battalion and company commanders of the outlines of his military plan. Across France all of the talk was about the great offensive that would win the war. Everyone seemed to know the dates of the attack and its general goals, and the Germans could scarcely avoid taking notice of the rumours and publicity surrounding Nivelle's preparations.

Even worse, in both January and March German trench raids had succeeded in capturing detailed plans revealing the French dispositions and targets for the forthcoming attack. The German commanders, Hindenburg and Ludendorff, knew full well what the French were planning and arranged their defences and reserves accordingly, ensuring that the French offensive along the length of the Chemin des Dames Ridge would receive a very rude reception indeed.

The area affected by Operation Alberich, the code name for the German withdrawal on the Western Front. The move back to the strongly constructed fixed defences of the HIndenburg Line disrupted the planning for the Allied joint offensive of spring 1917.

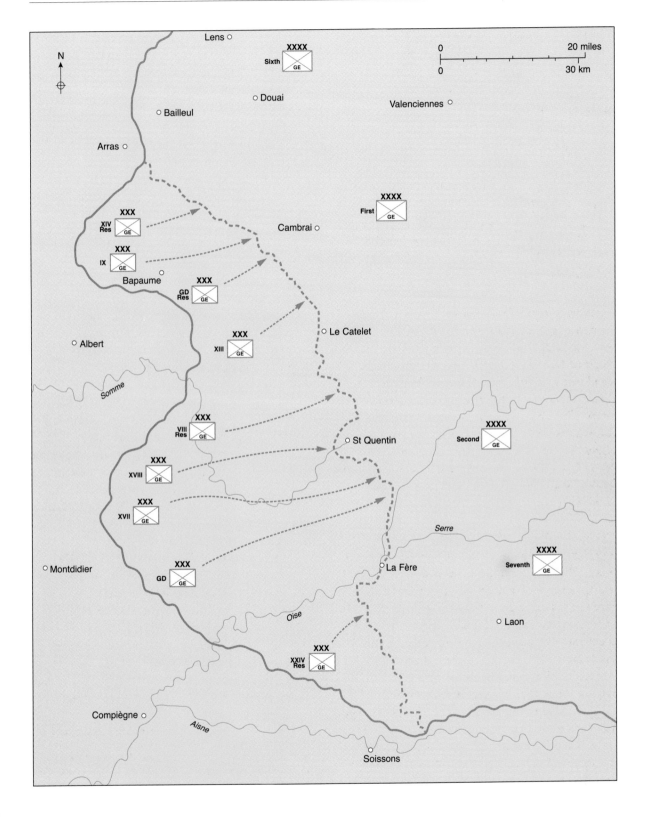

N

Lens ○

XXXX
Sixth | GE

○ Douai

Valenciennes ○

○ Bailleul

Arras ○

XXXX
First | GE

XXX
XIV Res | GE

Cambrai ○

XXX
IX | GE

Bapaume

XXX
GD Res | GE

○ Albert

Le Catelet ○

XXX
XIII | GE

Somme

XXX
VIII Res | GE

St Quentin ○

XXXX
Second | GE

XXX
XVIII | GE

XXX
XVII | GE

Serre

○ Montdidier

XXX
GD | GE

La Fère ○

XXXX
Seventh | GE

Oise

○ Laon

XXX
XXIV Res | GE

Compiègne ○

Aisne

Soissons ○

0 ____ 20 miles
0 ____ 30 km

CHAPTER 1

Nivelle's Folly

Having secured governmental approval for his scheme for a war-winning offensive, General Robert Nivelle raised the hopes of the French people and military to heights not seen since 1914. Instead of delivering a quick victory, though, his offensive produced only futility, driving the French Army into mutiny and changing the strategic balance on the Western Front.

The main British effort as part of Nivelle's overall offensive scheme for 1917 involved an attack on German lines near Arras, where six divisions of the German Sixth Army, commanded by General von Falkenhausen, faced 14 divisions of the British First Army, under the command of General Sir Henry Horne, Third Army, under the command of General Sir Edmund Allenby, and the Fifth Army, under the command of General Sir Hubert Gough. South of the river Scarpe, which bisected the battlefield, the Germans held the important high ground of the Monchy Spur, which formed part of the vaunted Hindenburg Line. North of the Scarpe

French soldiers work to prepare barbed-wire defences on the Chemin des Dames. It was bitter fighting around the heavily fortified German defences on the dominating ridge that caused the failure of the Nivelle Offensive.

LEFT General William Birdwood, commander of I ANZAC Corps, which bore the brunt of the brutal fighting around Bullecourt in the Battle of Arras.

RIGHT The British offensive at Arras, with its dramatic seizure of the Vimy Ridge, demonstrated the effectiveness of limited, bite-and-hold tactics. The British Third Army, under General Sir Edmund Allenby, attacked in the centre, whilst the First Army, spearheaded by the Canadian Corps under General Sir Julian Byng, attacked to the north. Fifth Army, under General Sir Hubert Gough, held the southern end of the line.

were the imposing heights of the Vimy Ridge, which was six kilometres (four miles) long, running from northwest to southeast, and honeycombed with German defences.

The most important feature of the battlefield, though, was the historic fortress town of Arras, the centre of which was only 1829m (2000 yards) from the front-line trenches. The proximity of the town offered Allenby and the Third Army a distinct advantage, for underneath Arras ran a network of tunnels, from which stone had once been quarried, and an extensive sewer system. Allenby's men expanded and linked the tunnels and sewers, even adding electric lighting and an underground light railway. The extensive labyrinth was capable of enabling 30,000 men to move up to

their jumping-off points for the attack in safety and secrecy. North of Arras, near the Vimy Ridge, the First Army and Canadian Corps achieved similar results by digging 12 massive tunnels, the longest stretching 1722m (1883 yards) into the chalky soil, which allowed assault forces to assemble free from German observation.

South of the Scarpe, the Hindenburg Line relied on new defence-in-depth techniques perfected in the later stages of the Battle of the Somme. Wherever possible the Germans situated their defences on the reverse slopes of hills, thus denying observation to the attacker. Bristling with machine-gun nests, the front-line defences were only thinly manned, and were made up of a system of mutually supporting strongpoints designed to cause maximum carnage to the attacker, while exposing the least number of defending troops to artillery fire. After exacting a heavy toll, the defending forces would then fall back and draw the attackers, bloodied and exhausted, forwards to their doom in the form of massive counterattacks from the second line of defences, known as the battle zone. The German defensive advancements, though, were only

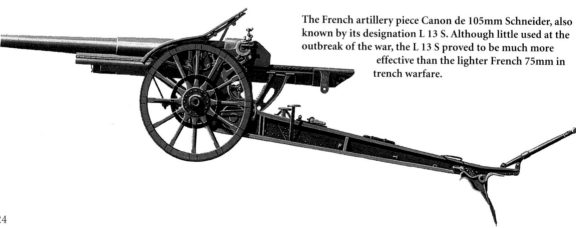

The French artillery piece Canon de 105mm Schneider, also known by its designation L 13 S. Although little used at the outbreak of the war, the L 13 S proved to be much more effective than the lighter French 75mm in trench warfare.

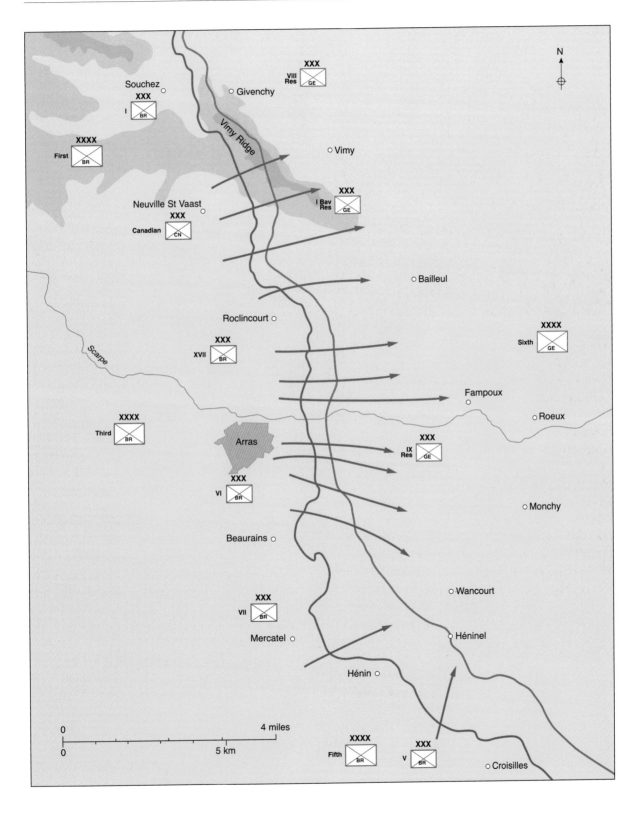

Souchez
Givenchy
XXX
VIII
Res
GE
XXX
I
BR
First
XXXX
BR
Vimy Ridge
Vimy
XXX
I Bav
Res
GE
Neuville St Vaast
Canadian
XXX
CN
Bailleul
Scarpe
Roclincourt
XVII
XXX
BR
Sixth
XXXX
GE
Fampoux
Roeux
Third
XXXX
BR
Arras
IX
Res
XXX
GE
VI
XXX
BR
Monchy
Beaurains
Wancourt
VII
XXX
BR
Héninel
Mercatel
Hénin
Fifth
XXXX
BR
V
XXX
BR
Croisilles

0   4 miles

0   5 km

N

A Canadian artillery team in action at Vimy Ridge during the Battle of Arras. The artillery barrage that accompanied the British attack at Arras was three times stronger than that utilized on the disastrous first day of the Battle of the Somme in 1916.

unevenly applied, and, as a result, to the north of the Scarpe and on Vimy Ridge, the German trenches were located on the forward slope, heavily manned and well within range of the coming British bombardment. Additionally, in this region German reserve formations were located too far to the rear to have an immediate effect on the battle.

The preparation for the Battle of Arras, which fell mainly to Horne and Allenby, demonstrated that the BEF had learned much in its trials during the Somme, especially in artillery planning. British artillerists were now technologically adept professionals instead of gentlemen amateurs who, though there remained a certain amount of trial and error, took great care in their planning, especially against the defences of Vimy

Ridge. The exact length of trench to be assailed had been calculated, and the appropriate artillery assigned to the task at hand. Heavy guns concentrated on German rear positions, bombarding the German artillery and any attempts at reinforcement, while medium guns dealt with German wire and trenches. At the moment of attack, the artillery would provide a creeping barrage augmented by a secondary barrage of machine-gun bullets and light howitzer shells, which gave the advancing infantry such effective protection that one sergeant informed his men:

'All you have got to do is to hang on to the back wheel of the barrage, just as if you were biking down the Strand behind a motor bus; carefully like, and not in too much of a hurry; and then when you come to Fritz, and he holds up his hands, you send him back to the rear.'

Scientific advances in gunnery also improved counterbattery work, while industrial advances on the home front meant that the quality of British munitions had risen markedly since the Somme, which provided

Artillery

The artillery of World War I was prodigiously strong, with the largest pieces, including the British 12in siege howitzer, firing shells that weighed nearly 456kg (1000lb) to a range of 14km (nine miles). However, at first artillerymen did not know how the conditions around them could affect the flight of their shell. Later studies, as artillerists learned their craft, indicated the price paid through such ignorance. If a gun utilizing indirect fire in 1916 fired 100 shells at a stationary target, 50 of those shells would miss the target entirely. The remaining 'hits' would fall into a zone 37m (40 yards) long and five metres (five yards) wide. The value of such 'hits', though, was quite limited, considering the fact that trenches were only a metre in width and machine-gun nests only a bit larger. Thus, even the vast majority of 'hits' had but little effect on entrenched defenders. Of the 100 shells fired, only two would be direct hits on such a small target, and only a very tiny percentage of those direct hits would be so accurate as to penetrate the trench and destroy a bunker under it. Add to this the fact that one of those direct hits was likely to be a dud round, and the ineffectiveness of artillery from 1915 to 1917 becomes easier to understand.

the artillerists with much more sensitive and effective fuses and many fewer dud rounds. Finally, though, sheer numbers told the true story of artillery success at Arras. The attacking forces had 2827 guns, of which 963 were of heavy calibre, to cover an attack frontage of 21km (13 miles). At Vimy Ridge, the Canadian Corps had 377 heavy guns on a front of just over six kilometres (four miles), or one heavy gun for every 18m (20 yards) of front. Because of the military and industrial advances, the artillery barrage that accompanied the Arras attack was three times as strong as that employed on the first day of the Somme, in addition to being much more accurate and lethal.

The British attack at Arras not only had to be powerful enough to draw German attention away from the French preparations further south, but also, as part of a wider Allied plan to achieve ultimate

Defensive works at Vimy Ridge. Unlike other areas of the Arras battlefield, where the main defences were positioned to the rear, the German defences at Vimy Ridge were located too far forwards and did not rely on defence-in-depth techniques, making them vulnerable to attack.

victory, had to aim at a breakthrough that would augment and complement Nivelle's own planned rupture of the German defences along the Chemin des Dames. The resulting plan called for the First Army to guard the flank of the offensive by seizing Vimy Ridge, while the Third Army attacked towards Cambrai. Haig held an infantry corps and cavalry units in reserve to exploit any success.

Although Horne and Allenby advocated a whirlwind bombardment, Haig intervened in favour of a longer artillery barrage, which, in five days, fired over two and a half million shells into the German lines. Although the steady bombardment indicated

Men of the Cameronians (Scottish Rifles) advance to the attack. Although losses remained high, the success of the BEF in the early stages of the Battle of Arras indicated that the infantry was returning to a prominent place on the World War I battlefield.

that a major British offensive was in the offing, due to the massing of attacking forces under cover of the tunnel networks at Arras and near Vimy Ridge, the Germans remained unaware of the timing of zero hour until the British and Canadian infantry were nearly across no man's land.

ATTACK AT ARRS

In the north, the Canadian Corps, under the capable command of General Sir Julian Byng, achieved one of the most notable successes to date of the entire war. Backed by devastating support from nine heavy artillery groups and covered by an effective machine-gun barrage, the Canadians burst forth from their concealment and assaulted Vimy Ridge, which had withstood multiple French attacks in 1915 and had been the site of some of the war's most bitter fighting. Having rehearsed their assault in painstaking detail,

Royal Aircraft Factory SE 5a. One of Britain's most successful fighter aircraft of the Great War, the SE 5a was powered by a 150hp engine, and carried a Vickers machine gun that was timed to fire through the whirling blades of the propeller.

the Canadians surged forward, unperturbed by a late season snowstorm. The 3rd and 4th divisions on the Canadian left advanced so quickly that the attacking soldiers were into the German trenches before the German machine-gunners had even manned their weapons. Surprise was so complete that the 2nd Canadian Mounted Rifles captured 150 Germans who were only half dressed, and many still had their shaving cream on their faces. Many Canadian soldiers actually advanced beyond their final objective, because the German trench line that marked their halt point had been so thoroughly obliterated by the artillery barrage as to be unrecognizable.

On the Canadian right flank, surviving German strongpoints, including an especially troubling German machine-gun nest that cut down the Canadians even as they emerged from the exit of the Tottenham Tunnel, slowed the advance of the 1st and 2nd divisions. Demonstrating tactical flexibility, Byng's men utilized combined infantry and artillery attacks to neutralize the troublesome defensive emplacements and captured the German defensive redoubt of Hill 135 in heavy and sometimes hand-to-hand fighting. Gathering momentum, the Canadians burst forward into the German artillery lines, and in one case men of the Canadian 1st Brigade captured German guns that had been abandoned so quickly that the luncheons in the officers' dugout were still

Strategic Bombing

On 31 May 1915, a new era of modern warfare had begun when the German Zeppelin LZ38 flew over London and dropped its cargo of high explosive. In total Germany mounted 53 Zeppelin raids on Great Britain, dropping over 5700 bombs and killing 556 civilians. However, the Zeppelins were slow moving, carried few bombs and proved extremely vulnerable to anti-aircraft defences. By 1917, though, the Germans had developed the Gotha bomber, which was capable of carrying a heavier bomb load to strike at the United Kingdom. The first Gotha raid took place on 13 June 1917, in which 20 bombers dropped 72 bombs near Liverpool Street Station in London. Casualties in the raid reached 162 dead (including 18 children when a bomb struck a school) and 432 wounded. The raids continued through August 1917, dropping a total of 33,112kg (73,000lb) of bombs and causing 1364 casualties before British anti-aircraft defences forced the Germans to bomb only at night. Although the raids were limited in character, the panic that they caused led many inter-war thinkers to believe that more effective and numerous bombers might well prove decisive in war.

A British 18-pounder field gun in action at Arras. The standard field gun of the BEF during the Great War, the 18-pounder had a range of 5966m (6525 yards). As denoted by the stockpile of ammunition to the left, by 1917 British industry had made possible the lavish use of firepower.

warm and untouched on the table. On another occasion the City of Winnipeg Battalion came across a German artillery battery that opened fire when the Canadians were only 46m (50 yards) from it. Raising a cheer, the Winnipeggers charged down the slope and either bayoneted or captured the German gunners.

On the Canadian left, at 3.15pm, men of the Nova Scotia Highlanders moved to attack the last German holdout positions atop Hill 145, the highest point of Vimy Ridge, hoping to seize the dominating position before nightfall. Due to communications problems, the Highlanders never received word that their brigadier

had called off their artillery cover as being too dangerous. The tide of Canadian victory was so complete, though, that even without the protective barrage, the Highlanders quickly overran the hill, taking a number of German prisoners, and completing the capture of Vimy Ridge.

The seizure of Vimy Ridge in a single day was, in many ways, a testament to the strength of Canadian arms and will, one so significant that it remains celebrated as a landmark event in the birth of the Canadian nation. At a cost of 11,000 casualties, the Canadians had seized a German position that had hitherto been impregnable; they had also taken 3600 prisoners and captured 36 artillery pieces in the process. However, the fighting at Vimy Ridge was but a part of the wider offensive at Arras, where further to the south advances by British and Australian forces demonstrated that the entire BEF both had become more professional and had undertaken a considerable military learning curve since the bitter fighting at the Somme.

To the south of Vimy Ridge, Allenby's Third Army, in an operation that rivalled that of the Somme in both attack frontage and in the number of divisions involved, achieved a level of success that even exceeded that of the Canadian Corps; a success judged by Cyril Falls, the official historian of the battle, as, 'from the British point of view one of the great days of the War. It witnessed the most successful British offensive hitherto launched … [and was] among the heaviest blows struck by British arms in the Western theatre of war.'

In the British centre, benefiting from the proximity of the tunnels of Arras, where one battalion diarist remarked that it was possible to 'get from the crypt of the [Arras] Cathedral to under the German wire without braving one shell in the open', VI Corps enjoyed the support of nine heavy artillery groups, and faced the traditional German forward defences rather than the more sophisticated defence-in-depth fortifications. Having achieved tactical surprise in the wake of thorough artillery preparation, VI Corps advanced under cover of a creeping barrage and smokescreen and quickly achieved all of its goals. Moving forwards nearly three kilometres (two miles), men from the 12th and 15th (Scottish) divisions achieved the summit of Observation Ridge and found themselves looking upon Battery Valley below. In the words of the official historian:

'As they swept down the eastern slope of the Observation Ridge, a dramatic scene of a type rare in this theatre of war unfolded. The whole of Battery Valley was dotted with German artillery: some batteries already abandoned; some, having got their teams up, making off as fast as they could; but several others firing point-blank at the British Infantry at ranges of only a few hundred yards. Their blood up … [they] advanced by short rushes. … Pushing on the Essex took nine guns and the R. Berkshire no less than 22, as well as a number of prisoners.'

The Dead

In World War I, offensives often gained only little ground while lasting for months, leaving little time to gather the wounded or bury the dead. As the battles progressed, soldiers were left to fight among, live among and dig new trenches through the bodies of their one-time foes and their own deceased comrades. The stench of the battlefields was nauseating, and Private Thomas McIndoe recalled:

'There was a dead Frenchman once. I saw him. His body was decomposed. And it nearly made me sick. There was his arm … he'd been on the receiving end of something fairly big. And as I saw him I thought, "Christ! We could bury him. We could cover him over", which eventually we did. And this bloody great rat ran out of his arm here after supping up, he'd been feeding on his arm here, see? Bloody great thing ran out there, nearly made me sick. I thought to myself, "Oh, filthy things! Oh Dear!"'

With its heightened lethality and static nature, the Western Front was characterized by battlefields strewn with the dead and dying. Many veterans likened battle in World War I to fighting in an open graveyard.

The greatest gains of the day, though, fell to XVII Corps to the north of the river Scarpe. Following in the wake of a punishing barrage, the 9th Division quickly pressed on to its final objective, and later allowed the 4th Division to pass through, which achieved an advance of six kilometres (three and a half miles), the largest gain made by any belligerent force on the Western Front since the onset of trench warfare. In several places British forces had broken through the German line of defences, demonstrating the BEF mastery of the set-piece battle. The advance, which had seized the high ground and allowed British forces to overlook open and undefended territory beyond, seemed to offer a fleeting opportunity for exploitation. If any opportunity did exist, though, the cavalry had been held too far behind the lines to play a substantial role in the fighting.

Although the seizure of Vimy Ridge and the advance of XVII Corps were cause for optimism, difficulties on other sectors of the front tempered the British victory. On the right flank of the Third Army, VII Corps attacked the northern extremities of the Hindenburg Line. Facing the brunt of the German defences, especially around Telegraph Hill, and with many of its supporting tanks bogged down in terrain ruined in the German withdrawal and further churned up by artillery fire, VII Corps made only sporadic gains, a sobering example of the capabilities of the new German form of defence amidst a day otherwise marked by unmarred Allied success.

THE ATTACK SLOWS

Careful artillery and infantry preparation had enabled substantial, though imperfect, British and Canadian gains on the first day of the attack at Arras. However, the bitter tactical reality of battle on the Western Front was that

General Robert Nivelle's ambitious plan in 1917 called for a British diversion at Arras to allow the main French assaults entirely to dislocate the German defences on the Western Front, which would result in the restoration of a war of movement and the eventual collapse of the German position.

the very tools that made an advance possible lost much of their value after the opening round of an offensive. After the initial advance, the artillery, on which so much of any successful attack depended, had to move forwards, along with prodigious supplies of artillery shells – slow and laborious tasks made all the more difficult by the fact that the artillery had destroyed much of the ground that it now had to traverse. Since the attackers lacked a weapon of exploitation to maintain the momentum of an advance, as the artillery struggled forwards, German reinforcements rushed to the scene, and created new defences that again required careful preparations to overthrow. It was indeed the central riddle of World War I. Defenders could react more quickly to developments than could attackers, causing offensives to stall.

Because of the inexorable tactical logic of World War I, the British and Canadian assaults on 10 April met with diminishing returns. The all-important artillery barrage and covering fire, which had done so much to make the gains of the previous day possible, were much more limited in both weight and accuracy as the artillery struggled forwards. With minimal covering fire and facing new German defensive positions, the exhausted British and Canadian infantry made few additional gains against gathering German

A French infantry sergeant carrying the 8mm Chauchat M1915 light machine gun. Promised quick victory by their new commander, General Robert Nivelle, French infantry instead suffered through another seemingly futile assault at the Chemin des Dames, and morale crumbled.

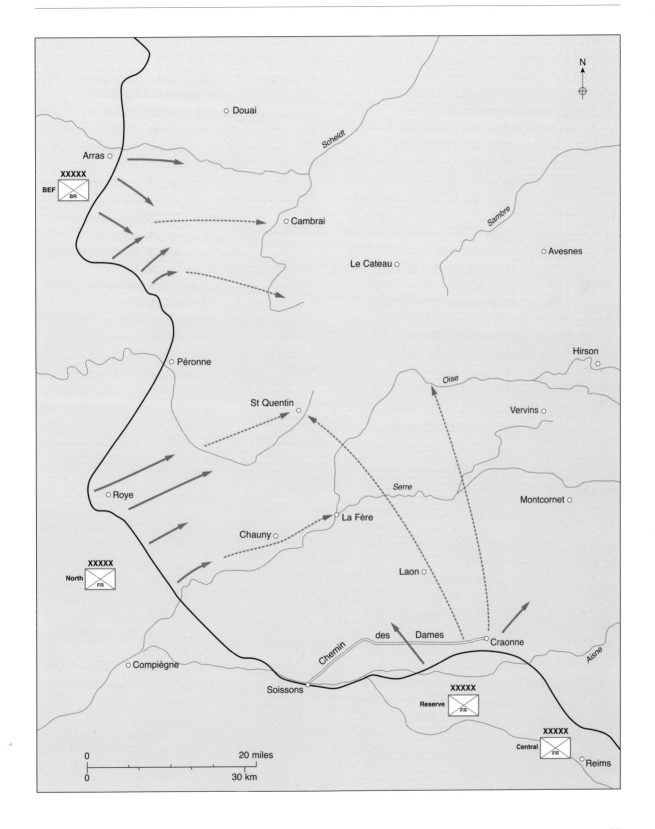

Douai

Scheldt

Arras

BEF **XXXXX** BR

Cambrai

Le Cateau

Sambre

Avesnes

Péronne

Hirson

St Quentin

Oise

Vervins

Serre

Roye

Montcornet

Chauny

La Fère

North **XXXXX** FR

Laon

Craonne

Aisne

Compiègne

Chemin des Dames

Reserve **XXXXX** FR

Soissons

Central **XXXXX** FR

Reims

0		20 miles
0		30 km

N

reserves. Allenby, though, knew little of the failure of the renewed attack. Denied information from spotter aircraft due to worsening weather, Allenby mistakenly declared to his commanders that, 'Third Army is now pursuing a defeated enemy and risks must be freely taken'. The orders sent British and Canadian forces forward again on 11 April, including cavalry efforts at exploitation that were two days too late. Although British forces did succeed in capturing the defended village of Monchy-le-Preux, the once-promising attack had stalled.

While initial advances in the centre and north of the British line portended well for the future, in the far south of the area of operations, greater difficulties had emerged, where the Fifth Army, under Gough, faced the might of the Hindenburg Line proper and depended on a tenuous logistic network that stretched through the area of desolation left behind after the German withdrawal. Since Gough's operation was

British troops coming out of the line after the Battle of Arras. Benefiting from elaborate planning, the initial British advances were stunning. However, the battle soon stagnated, indicating that breaking through enemy trench systems remained impossible.

subsidiary to that of Allenby, Fifth Army received the least weight of shell in its artillery preparation, which left much of the German's barbed wire uncut and their defences intact. With the twin objectives of capturing the strongpoint of Bullecourt and aiding Third Army in its rupture of the German lines, Gough initially put off his assault due to the poor artillery preparation. However, the nearly uniform success enjoyed by Allenby's forces at the outset of his attack left Gough anxious to play his role in what seemed to be a great victory, an enthusiasm that served to dampen his justifiable fears.

Believing that the Germans on his front would withdraw due to the successes achieved by Third Army, and convinced that the relatively few tanks on hand could deal with the wire left uncut by the artillery, Gough gave the go ahead for the attack, over the objections of General William Birdwood, whose I ANZAC Corps would bear the brunt of the coming battle. The tanks, though, were late in arriving, necessitating a further postponement of the operation until 11 April. Even with the extra time, the tanks proved to be unreliable: several broke down or were put out of action by German fire and none made it to

A section of a German defensive network. In response to the heavy bloodlettings of the Somme and Verdun, the Germans developed an intricate defence-in-depth system, designed first to tire and then to shatter Allied attacks. This system worked as designed against the Nivelle Offensive.

but because the BEF had to continue to play its ongoing role to take German pressure off Nivelle's climactic offensive further to the south.

NIVELLE'S OFFENSIVE

General Robert Nivelle had enjoyed a meteoric rise since August 1914, beginning the war as a colonel in the artillery and achieving the command of a division in February 1915. Instrumental in the development of the creeping barrage, by December Nivelle had received promotion to corps commander. After distinguishing himself at Verdun, in May 1916 Nivelle took command of the Second Army and, by the end of the year, assumed command of all armies in northern and northeastern France. The French Government had placed its future in the hands of a 'can do' optimist who arguably had already been promoted beyond his ability. As all others around him, including even the notoriously optimistic Haig, were coming to terms with the weakness of the attack and beginning to

the German front lines, leaving the Australian infantry alone to breach the intact German wire. Amazingly, the Australians persevered, and on much of a three-kilometre (two-mile) front captured the German front line, with some units even achieving a foothold in the German second line of defences. However, the Germans mounted fierce counterattacks and, with sparse artillery cover and ammunition running low, the Australians withdrew from their meagre gains with heavy losses. The 4th Australian Brigade indeed had almost been destroyed, losing 2258 out of 3000 men involved in the attack.

The Battle of Arras had seemingly run its course, demonstrating not only the power of attackers to achieve a 'break-in' to defensive networks but also the difficulties of ever achieving a 'breakthrough' amid the tactical and logistical realities that formed the strategic centre of World War I. Haig would have been well served to stop the offensive after 12 April; however, he did not. The attack would continue into the month of May, not because Haig had any faith that continued assaults near Arras would achieve substantial gains,

'Again the Canadians have "acquired merit."
In the capture of Vimy Ridge on April 9th … they have shown the same high qualities in victorious advance as they displayed in early days in desperate resistance on many stricken fields.'

Canadian War Records Office, April 1917

understand World War I in terms of limited advances and attrition, Nivelle remained the last true proponent of decisive battle – the last worshipper at the altar of the cult of the offensive. Nivelle's bold hope was to rupture the German lines within 48 hours and then destroy the German reserves in open battle. He wrote to his subordinates: 'The objective is the destruction of the principle mass of the enemy's forces on the

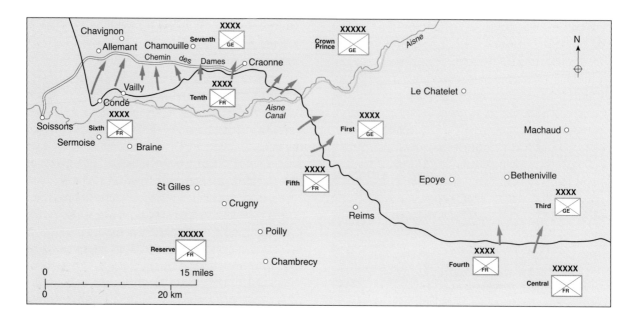

While the ground gained during the Nivelle Offensive actually compared favourably to attacks of previous years, Nivelle's scheme fell far short of its stated goals, leading to a crisis of confidence in the French military and the ability of the generals to win the war.

Western Front. This can be attained only by a decisive battle, delivered against the reserves of the adversary and followed by intensive exploitation.'

Nivelle's final plan called for both the Central Army Group and the Northern Army Group to undertake supporting attacks, while the Reserve Army Group, under the command of General Alfred Micheler, carried out the main assault against the German defences on the Chemin des Dames. Micheler had the Sixth Army on his left and the Fifth Army on his right to make his assault, while the Tenth Army was held in close reserve to pass between the two attacking armies after they had broken through the German lines.

Although Nivelle remained convinced that the 'violence, brutality and speed' of the French attack would overcome any German defensive network, Micheler developed severe doubts about the wisdom of the planned offensive. In a letter to Nivelle, Micheler pointed out that the original plan had called for the Reserve Army Group to attack what had been comparatively weak German defences. However, the

retreat to the Hindenburg Line meant that the Reserve Army Group would instead attack into the teeth of the most advanced defensive system on the Western Front, located atop the dominating high ground of the 183m-high (600ft) Chemin des Dames. Unknown to Micheler was the fact that the Germans were expecting the coming assault, and had moved 21 divisions into the front-line system, as well as holding a further 17 in reserve. Regardless of Micheler's warning, Nivelle stood firm, confident that his artillery and the élan of the French military would prevail.

Along a front of nearly 40km (25 miles), the Reserve Army Group had massed a staggering total of 5350 artillery pieces, including 1650 heavy guns. Artillery preparation for the battle began in earnest on 9 April, and, by 5 May, the French artillery had fired 11 million rounds, two and a half million of which were heavy rounds. However, poor weather limited the effectiveness of the barrage, while German command of the air made it difficult to adjust fire, especially on the German positions located out of sight on the reverse slope of the Chemin des Dames. The situation was so bad that one artillery liaison officer with the front-line troops reported that the barrage had hardly damaged the German defences and warned that the infantry should expect to face 'strong resistance'.

When the infantry advanced on 16 April, it faced largely intact German defences and murderous fire. The commander of II Colonial Corps, tasked with the seizure of the crest of the Chemin des Dames, described the assault of his unit against the German defence-in-depth system:

'At H-hour, the troops approach in order the first enemy positions. The geographic crest [of the Chemin des Dames] is attained almost without losses. ... Nevertheless, our infantry advances with a slower speed than is anticipated. The rolling barrage is unleashed and almost immediately and steadily moves ahead of the first waves, which it quickly ceases to protect. A few machine guns on the plateau do not halt the ... infantrymen, who are able to descend the northern side of the plateau to the edge of the steep slope descending into the valley [on the reverse slope]. There, they were welcomed and fixed in place by the deadly fire of numerous machine guns that, located on the slope, outside the reach of our projectiles, have remained undamaged.

'A few groups ... succeed in descending the slope. But in general, the troops suffered considerable losses in a few minutes, particularly in leaders, and not succeeding in crossing this deadly zone, halt, take cover, and at some points withdrew to the first trench to their rear.

'The enemy's reserves are in effect almost intact. Well protected in holes on the northern slope or in very strong dugouts, they have not suffered from the bombardment.'

The remaining forces of the Fifth and Sixth armies met with similar fates. On the right flank, Fifth Army achieved limited gains, and in some areas succeeded in entering the German second line of defences. Even where its attack had been most successful, though, Fifth Army ended the day short of the line that it was to have reached by 9.30am. On the left, the Sixth Army, including II Colonial Corps, initially made substantial gains, which, though they had heartened the attackers, were a function of the German defence-in-depth system designed to draw attackers forward

An artist's rendition of the French assault on the Chemin des Dames, a painting that juxtaposes the bravery of the French soldier with the seeming futility of the fighting in the Great War, a sense of futility that played a major role in the onset of the French Army mutiny.

only to subject them to counterattack by fresh German reserve formations.

Having failed to achieve a breakthrough, Nivelle hoped to salvage the deteriorating situation by ordering Fifth Army to attack more towards the northeast. However, as the offensive continued on 17 April, and French artillery cover became even less effective, the Fifth and Sixth armies made only extremely limited gains. During the night of 17 April, though, the Germans chose to withdraw from a vulnerable salient in their lines near Condé, which resulted in the left flank of Sixth Army moving forwards with great rapidity, covering nearly six kilometres (four miles) and capturing 5300 prisoners

and vast stocks of munitions before regaining contact with the new German lines on 20 April. Meanwhile, though, the remainder of Sixth Army and the entirety of Fifth Army hardly moved forwards at all. In an attempt to restore forward momentum, and both to save his cherished offensive and his career, on 19 April Nivelle ordered the Tenth Army into the fray, to little avail.

By 20 April, it had become obvious to all that Nivelle's effort to rupture the German lines and score a decisive victory had failed. Instructed by the French Government to avoid further losses, Nivelle lowered the sights of his offensive to a limited attack aimed only at the seizure of the remainder of the Chemin des

Shell Shock

War, and its attendant killing, along with the constant risk of mutilation or violent death, often inflicts severe mental trauma upon the soldiers called upon to take part in the conflict. The scale of the industrialized slaughter of World War I, coupled with its static nature that often placed the living and dead in intimate proximity for months on end, ensured that mental casualties would be at an all-time high. Although cases of 'soldier's heart' were not unknown in the American Civil War, psychiatric battle casualties, known by the term 'shell shock', became much better known during the Great War, symptoms of which ranged from paralysis, through aimless wandering to loss of bladder and bowel control. Although many looked upon shell shock victims as deserters or cowards, the losses due to the phenomenon were so high, with the United States alone having 159,000 soldiers put out of action due to psychiatric problems, that every belligerent nation searched for both the cause of shell shock and its cure. Psychiatrists initially believed that the concussion of exploding shells compressed the brain, causing symptoms that closely mimicked those of genuine psychiatric cases. Only later in the war did most nations come to believe that the effects of battle in fact

The Great War, with its bloody, static battles and grim landscape of corpses, resulted in an unprecedented number of psychiatric casualties among its combatants.

did have true psychiatric consequences. Even then, though, the prognosis for shell shock victims remained grim, with the Austrians even choosing to employ electric shock therapy as a possible cure.

Dames. Even with the change in strategic aim, the French Army as a whole had lost faith in Nivelle's leadership. As subordinate commanders, including Micheler and Pétain, raised objections to Nivelle's plan to continue a limited assault on the defences of the Chemin des Dames, the French Government wrestled with how best to rid itself of Nivelle. After some confusion, on 29 April the politicians appointed General Henri Pétain as chief of staff of the French Army, and slowly eased Nivelle from power.

In late April and early May, French operations at the Chemin des Dames slowly drew to a close. In ground gained, the Nivelle Offensive compared favourably to those launched by Joffre, and actually had resulted in one of the greatest French forward movements to date in the conflict, in the wake of the German withdrawal from the Condé Salient. Additionally, French forces had captured 28,500 prisoners and 187 artillery pieces. However, the cost had been high, including 30,000 killed, 100,000 wounded and 4000 captured. Indeed the Nivelle Offensive might have been trumpeted as a great success earlier in the war; however, Nivelle had sealed his own doom by convincing the French soldiery of the imminence of climactic and cathartic

The battlefields of World War I were dominated by indirect artillery fire, and this ensured that observation and communication were key. The Germans wisely sited their defensive networks on the high ground, giving them a singular advantage over the Allies in many areas.

victory. Morale in the military and the nation had soared on the expectation that the great trials and suffering of the war would soon be things of the past. What Nivelle had delivered instead of decisive victory, though, had been more of the same: more futility, more suffering, more losses, more Verduns. Although it had yet to become fully apparent, Nivelle's failure to achieve victory caused French military and national morale to plummet to new lows, which very nearly cost France the war.

CONTINUED OPERATIONS AT ARRAS

As Nivelle's offensive floundered and the French Government struggled to decide whether to jettison its commander-in-chief, the diversionary British offensive at Arras continued. Although surprise was no longer possible, and operations at Arras had arguably passed the point at which any substantial gains beckoned, Haig had to continue the offensive as

The Lewis gun. Designed by Samuel Maclean, the weapon was of American origin and could fire 450–500 rounds per minute. Light and portable, the Lewis gun was adopted into widespread service in the BEF, and provided the infantry with renewed firepower.

part of the overall Allied scheme to pin the German defenders in place and deny the enemy military resources for use against the French along the Chemin des Dames. On 14 April, Allenby issued orders for a renewal of the offensive by elements of the Third Army in two days' time, but on the advice of many of his subordinates, Haig ordered a postponement to allow time to prepare for an attack on a larger scale. At the Somme, Haig had learned the price to be paid by mounting piecemeal, uncoordinated attacks and refused to make such a mistake at Arras.

Although the goals for the renewed assault at Arras were strictly limited, and both effective artillery fire and a number of tanks supported the assault, the attack that resulted on 23 April entailed some of the most difficult maneuvres of the war for the men of the BEF. Half of the British units involved in the attack had been engaged in earlier fighting at Arras and had not had adequate time to recover, while for their part the Germans had worked feverishly not only to rush fresh reserves and artillery to the scene but also to overhaul their defensive strategy. Sensing imminent danger, the German high command had sent defensive specialist Colonel Fritz von Lossberg to Arras, who altered the German defences there more closely to resemble the defence-in-depth scheme employed by the Hindenburg Line, which had brought the Nivelle Offensive to grief.

The results of the renewed offensive were mixed. Due in part to the nature of the German defensive scheme, units on the British right flank initially moved forwards well, only to face stern resistance in the battle zone, where several companies that had advanced more quickly than their brethren were cut off and surrounded. Although the fighting was bitter, VII Corps advanced over a kilometre and achieved most of its objectives, while VI Corps achieved similar gains.

On the British left flank, the experiences of XVII and XIII corps typified the ebb and flow of the difficult

A British 9.2in howitzer. Much more powerful than field guns (the 9.2 could throw a 132kg (29lb) shell almost 10km (six miles)), howitzers were ideal for trench warfare. However, howitzers were very difficult to move forwards, which often resulted in attacks losing their momentum.

A German surrenders outside his defensive fortification during the latter stages of the Battle of Arras. Without surprise, and facing strong German defences, the British assault at Arras stagnated into bitter attritional fighting as the battle lingered.

struggle. Backed by especially heavy artillery fire, the 63rd (Royal Naval) Division achieved one of the most notable successes of the day in its seizure of the heavily defended village of Gavrelle. However, the attackers had failed to seize some of the most important of their tactical goals, including the critical village of Roeux. After a pause in the fighting, British units moved forwards again on 28 April, but the failure of the attack, launched on a narrow frontage, was best illustrated by the experience of the 10th Battalion of the Lincolnshire Regiment. The barrage covering the advance of the Linconshires into Roeux was too weak, and resulted in what their official history termed, 'the most disastrous action ever fought by the 10th Lincolnshires'. The claim was of considerable importance, considering that in

1916, the unit had been involved in some of the worst fighting on the first day of the Battle of the Somme, suffering 59 per cent casualties. In the attack on Roeux, though, the Lincolnshires lost a staggering 67 per cent casualties.

As the fighting around Arras continued, the Allied strategic situation became increasingly and tragically muddled as it slowly became clear to Haig that Nivelle was falling from grace. In a private meeting with Nivelle on 24 April, Haig, who had always favoured an

Soldiers' Songs

Like soldiers in every war, the fighting men of World War I invented songs, some ribald and others touching, both to sing while on march and as a not so subtle form of protest. Many of the songs became quite well known, including a BEF standard, 'Fred Karno's Army' (named after a popular comedian and sung to the tune of 'The Church's one Foundation'):

> *We are Fred Karno's army,*
> *The ragtime infantry,*
> *We cannot fight, we cannot shoot,*
> *What bloody use are we?*
> *And when we get to Berlin,*
> *The Kaiser he will say,*
> *'Hoch, hoch, Mein Gott,*
> *What a bloody fine lot,*
> *Are Fred Karno's infantry.'*

Other songs were more sombre, including 'The Old Barbed Wire':

> *If you want to find the sergeant,*
> *I know where he is, I know where he is,*
> *If you want to find the sergeant,*
> *I know where he is,*
> *He's lying on the canteen floor,*
> *I've seen him, I've seen him,*
> *Lying on the canteen floor.*
>
> *If you want to find the sergeant-major,*
> *I know where he is, I know where he is,*
> *If you want to find the sergeant-major,*
> *I know where he is,*
> *He's boozing up the privates' rum,*
> *I've seen him, I've seen him,*
> *Boozing up the privates' rum.*
>
> *If you want to find the C.O.,*
> *I know where he is, I know where he is,*
> *If you want to find the C.O.,*
> *I know where he is,*
> *He's down in the deep dug-outs,*
> *I've seen him, I've seen him,*
> *Down in the deep dug-outs.*
>
> *If you want to find the old battalion,*
> *I know where they are, I know where they are,*
> *If you want to find the old battalion,*
> *I know where they are,*
> *They're hanging on the old barbed wire,*
> *I've seen 'em, I've seen 'em,*
> *Hanging on the old barbed wire.*

attack in Flanders, sought assurances that his attacks at Arras in adherence to the Allied strategic scheme were not misguided. Haig recorded in his diary:

'I requested him [Nivelle] *to assure me that the French Armies would continue to operate energetically, because what I feared was that, after the British Army had exhausted itself in trying to make Nivelle's plan a success, the French Government might stop the operations. I would then not be able to give effect to the other plan, viz. that of directly capturing the northern ports.'*

With his mind already wandering to the potentialities of a British offensive in Flanders aimed at seizing the Belgian coast, and amid the uncertainty of the French command situation, Haig made his worst mistake of the battle. For several reasons, which included seizing tactically dominant ground near Arras, encouraging the French and maintaining a level of attrition on the Germans that could advantage future offensive operations, Haig decided to continue limited operations at Arras – even after the fighting in late April had demonstrated both that the Germans were ready and waiting and that hope for a meaningful victory in the area had long since passed.

On 3 May, the British advanced on a frontage of 22km (14 miles), in an attack that the British official historian of the battle referred to as, 'a ghastly failure, some thought the blackest day of the war'. Although the attack was mercifully cancelled after only 24 hours, it was followed by continuation of a subsidiary assault by the Fifth Army under General Gough aimed at the seizure of Bullecourt.

In their initial assault on Bullecourt on 3 May, V Corps and I ANZAC Corps achieved only limited gains into the German defensive network, which was part of the Hindenburg Line. Faced with the decision between abandoning the very vulnerable lodgements in the German lines, or pressing the attack to the seizure of the entirety of Bullecourt, Haig chose the latter, in part to keep German attention away from Flanders. The result was a bloody battle of two weeks' duration, which succeeded in its dubious goals but greatly strained Anglo-Australian relations. The seesaw nature of the battle, involving brutal fighting concentrated on a very narrow frontage, resulted in a situation in which the dead of both sides covered the landscape, while the living clambered over and around the bodies to prosecute the battle. One witness remarked that in no other battle of the war were the living and the unburied dead in such close proximity for so long and that the nauseating stench made him wonder how 'any human beings could hold and fight under these conditions'.

The fighting at Arras, which had cost both sides over 100,000 casualties, resulted in quite mixed results for Haig and the BEF. Careful planning, increasing professionalism in both the artillery and the infantry and tactical surprise had resulted in great gains on the first day of the offensive. Indeed, Haig's army was much more tactically advanced than it had been 12 months previously at the Battle of the Somme. The BEF had proven that it could effect a break-in to even the most advanced German defensive systems; however, a breakthrough remained ever elusive. Although there were extenuating circumstances in the need to continue the fighting at Arras as part of the overall Nivelle scheme, Haig had once again demonstrated a propensity to continue offensives long after real hopes for substantial gains had passed, indicating that the BEF and its commander-in-chief still had much to learn. Even as the BEF began to codify and disseminate the tactical and strategic lessons of Arras, it soon became clear that the process was of the greatest urgency. In the wake of the failed Nivelle Offensive the French Army faced a crisis of morale, one that left the bulk of the fighting in 1917 to an improving but still flawed BEF.

British troops pass through a ruined French village on their way to the front lines during the Battle of Arras. While the first stage of the battle had been cause for optimism, a strategic gain had again eluded the BEF as the fighting degenerated into an attritional struggle.

CHAPTER 2

Mutiny and Messines

In the wake of Nivelle's failed offensive, the French Army dissolved into mutiny, threatening the Allied position on the Western Front. Against all odds, General Henri Philippe Pétain rescued the French military from the brink. Field Marshal Sir Douglas Haig launched the first phase of his planned offensive in Flanders, a limited assault on the Messines Ridge.

T he nearly three years of bitter struggle, much of which had taken place on its own soil and had devastated vast swathes of once productive countryside, had left France very nearly broken. Dashed hopes, futile offensives and the slaughter of Verdun, especially when combined with raucous governmental and Allied squabbles, had seriously compromised French civilian and military morale. Indeed, a growing sense of war weariness became noticeable within the French military even before the onset of offensive actions at the Chemin des Dames. While the erosion of morale had concerned Nivelle, he was certain that he knew its

Troops from the 11th Leicester Regiment advance to the front. As mutiny stalked the exhausted French Army, more and more of the fighting on the Western Front would fall to the BEF.

45

lamentable source. In a letter to the French Government before he unleashed his climactic offensive, Nivelle placed the blame for the decline in morale on civilian pacifist agitators:

'I have the honour to inform you that I have reported the following pacifist intrigues to the Minister of the Interior. Faced with this grave threat to the morale of the troops, I am persuaded that serious measures must be taken. … For more than a year, there have been pamphlets – pacifist brochures and papers – getting into the hands of the troops. Their distribution has now reached epidemic proportions. … While on leave, a certain number of soldiers attend meetings where … the leading trade unionists and anarchists air their pacifist theories. When they return to the trenches, the soldiers repeat to their comrades the arguments they have heard.'

A French tank unit awaits orders. Serving what they believed to be an uncaring command structure, in the wake of the failure of the Nivelle Offensive, the morale of the French infantry began to crack and incidents of what became known as 'collective indiscipline' began to break out.

Nivelle went on to recommend that the 'pacifist propaganda [should be] smashed' and the laws more strictly enforced, which, he claimed, would put an end to the crisis.

Although the rather chaotic version of wartime democracy that characterized the French home front doubtless complicated the issue of military morale, Nivelle need not have looked beyond the policies of the French military to locate the problem's true source. Having expected a quick victory in 1914, the military simply had not built up the kind of infrastructure required properly to look after many of the basic needs of its soldiery in a prolonged war. French soldiers received the lowest pay of any Allied force on the Western Front. Their food was often of poor quality and their rations meagre, but, more importantly to the average French *poilu*, their wine was often poor and in short supply.

Of greatest concern, though, was that home leave was almost unheard of; even British soldiers who had to cross the Channel to return home had more.

Indeed, by the close of the Nivelle Offensive, many French soldiers had not received any home leave for 18 months, instead spending what little 'rest' time they had in squalid rear area camps. Even when a French soldier did receive precious leave time, he found that he had to fend for himself on his journey home, wasting valuable time waiting for trains and spending what little money he had on overpriced wayside accommodations and food.

While the upper echelon of the French command structure comfortably placed the blame for teetering morale on the actions of 'trade unionists and anarchists', evidence collected by the postal authorities, who censored letters home from the front, begged a different conclusion. In the weeks before the launching of the Nivelle Offensive the soldiers' complaints in their letters home included: 'bad food, lack of clothing, sustained fatigue, unskilled or indifferent leaders, [and] length of inaction'. After years of toil and bloodshed, many within the French military simply believed that their sacrifice was

French Morale

Although the French Army mutinies have become a part of the public historic consciousness of World War I, what is less known is the fragile state of French public morale during the trying months of 1917. Especially in Paris, many were worried that France was nearing a state of revolution. One Parisian wrote:

'Everybody is complaining, in Paris and elsewhere. People are on strike over the price rises and over the lack of fuel, and this winter the poor will have nothing to use for heating. Can't you just hear the rising strains of revolution! This winter, when the destitute are dying of cold or starving to death in their garrets because of the lack of foresight on the part of our ruling classes who do nothing to avert the danger, the mob will take to the streets, and will burn our furniture to keep warm, which will only be fair. But don't think for a moment that the deputies in parliament are likely to sacrifice their salaries to come to the aid of the poor!'

underappreciated and that they had been ill used by an uncaring military elite.

The same postal authorities took note of the great surge in morale that accompanied Nivelle's lavish claims of impending victory before the assault on the Chemin des Dames. As the failure of the offensive became clear, though, the censors catalogued a rapid decline in morale as the soldiers' letters home described the attack in the following terms: 'fiasco, lynching, botched, misfire, massacre, butchery, failure'. In the minds of many French soldiers, the bloody offensive transformed the nature of their military leadership from merely uncaring to criminal. Morale plummeted. Even what was arguably the best news of the month, the United States' entry into the conflict, failed to give the soldiers hope. The postal authorities reported that, 'Many think that the entry of America into the war, while giving us numerous advantages, will prolong the war at least a year and, by the relief of workers [who will be replaced by Americans], send thousands of Frenchmen to their deaths.'

The French Army slowly descended into a state of disarray in the wake of the Nivelle Offensive, and from late April through to May, there were 72 outbreaks of 'collective indiscipline'. Although locally quite serious, at the outset the incidents were sporadic, lacked overall political goals and were devoid of organized leadership. Initially the indiscipline often took the form of small groups of soldiers simply shouting, 'Down with the war!' or, 'We are through with the killing!'

The situation worsened with the 29 April report of the first true mutiny, the nature of which came to typify much of the coming national ordeal. The 2nd Battalion of the 18th Infantry Regiment had been in the forefront of Nivelle's attack on 16 April and penetrated German lines to a depth of nearly 400m (437 yards) before being shattered on the German second line of defence. Scattered groups of the unit succeeded in making it back to French lines, where the next morning it became clear that only 200 survivors remained from the 600 men who had taken part in the assault. Only a few officers and non-commissioned officers remained to take the remnants of the unit to a rest area near Soissons. Although rumours abounded that the battalion would be disbanded, new drafts soon arrived to bring it back up to strength. The next

step was to send the battalion off to a quiet area of the front for recuperation and training. Suddenly, though, the new officers of the unit ordered the men to pick up their gear and fall into formation. Only two weeks removed from its futile sacrifice, the rebuilt 2nd Battalion was going back into the front line to renew the attack on the Chemin des Dames. Shocked by the news the men refused the order, took over their encampment and quickly consumed the entire wine ration on hand. After midnight, a military police platoon confronted the now sober mutineers who belatedly and sullenly made their way toward the front. Five of the supposed 'ringleaders' of the incident were sentenced to death.

THE MUTINIES SPREAD

What began as an isolated incident soon spread like a disease through the demoralized French Army. The outbreaks of indiscipline were so spontaneous and disorganized that even the best among the French commanders were caught unaware. General Paul Maistre, in command of Sixth Army, reported to his superiors that XXI Corps was steadfast and could be entrusted with offensive operations. Barely two days later, though, he wrote, 'The operation must be postponed … We risk having the men refuse to leave the assault trenches. … They are in a state of wretched morale.'

The Fusil Mitrailleur FM 1915 'Chauchat' light machine gun. Weighing 9kg (20lb), and capable of firing 250 rounds per minute, the Chauchat was easy to manufacture, but was notoriously inaccurate and temperamental. Still, it remained in service throughout the Great War.

The mutinies, though, were especially virulent in rest camps where men had access to copious amounts of alcohol, and often flared when veteran units received orders to return to the front lines. On one such occasion in late May, ringleaders of the 370th Infantry Regiment of XXI Corps urged their brethren not to board their troop transports to the front. After a number of wine-sodden speeches, large numbers of soldiers made their way to the nearest railway station where they promptly stormed an available locomotive. Chanting slogans and firing rifles into the air, the 370th Infantry Regiment commandeered the train and departed for Paris, bent on overthrowing the government and ending the war. The mutineers, though, had to halt the train near Villers-Cotterets, because a loyal cavalry unit had blocked the tracks with fallen trees. Now sober, most of the mutineers surrendered peacefully, while those who resisted were shot on the spot. From late May, railways became a focus of mutinous activity as several units sought to make their way to Paris, while others simply took over trains to get home and see their families.

A French firing squad in action. Faced with military indiscipline on a grand scale, the French, under the leadership of General Henri Philippe Pétain, sentenced 554 mutineers to death, only 55 of whom actually were executed. Many others served long prison sentences.

Minister of War Paul Painlevé had occasion to visit troops at a rest camp near Prouilly and described the topics of the harangues of mutinous leaders:

'*Some spoke of the exhaustion of the troops; others, of the scandalous privileges of the* embusqués [shirkers] *in the rear echelons; still others, of the incapacity of the staffs, who accepted honours and privileges but failed to give the troops the victory which each day had been promised them; and, finally, other orators spoke of the news from Russia* [where troops were nearing a state of rebellion] *and pointed to the Russian soldiers as an example.*'

Even though the futile Nivelle Offensive, assumed to be the immediate cause of the problem, had drawn to a close, the mutinies actually, for a number of reasons, worsened and reached their most dangerous stage during the first week of June. Although the

attack on the Chemin des Dames had ceased, the underlying factors of poor pay, squalid conditions and inadequate leave remained. Most frightening, though, was the fact that the mutinies intellectually had begun to coalesce. As in Russia, mutineers began to form soldiers' councils that identified closely with far left political parties that stood in opposition to the continuation of the war.

Perhaps the most disturbing incident among the new wave of mutinies involved the 298th Infantry Regiment, the men of which, in what had become almost standard fashion, had informed their commanding officers that they would not return to the front lines. When the officers rejected their demands the soldiers rose up and captured the town of Missy-aux-Bois. Electing their own new officers, the mutineers established a revolutionary government for the village and set up defensive lines to resist attacks from loyal troops. Soon a cavalry unit arrived and cut

An engraving by Leon Ruffe, entitled 'The Rumbling Discontent', portrays the results of the harsh life of trench warfare and the Nivelle Offensive on the long-suffering French infantryman. This lack of concern for the well–being of the French *poilu* was to have serious results.

off the small town and successfully starved the mutineers into submission. Even then, though, the men of the 298th maintained 'revolutionary discipline' and paraded out of the town to offer a formal surrender.

The more organized qualities of the mutinies, along with their more ambitious revolutionary goals, greatly worried both the French military and political leadership. In a letter to a member of the French parliament, General Franchet d'Espérey gave voice to the fears of many:

'There exists an organized plot to dissolve discipline. … The ringleaders among the troops are in contact with suspicious elements in Paris. They scheme to seize a *railway station so that they may transport themselves to Paris and raise the populace in insurrection against the war. The Russian Revolution has served as their model. … The troops are in a continual state of excitation kept up by the newspapers, which are filled with details of the events in Russia, by parliamentary criticism of the generals and by the exaggeration of pessimists. … Why do you close your eyes to this? … Unless it is stopped we will have no Army and the Germans can be in Paris in five days!'*

ENTER PÉTAIN

It was one of the pivotal moments of the conflict on the Western Front, for the valiant French military appeared to be disintegrating. Mutinies of varying severity had affected up to 50 divisions, and as many as 30,000 soldiers had deserted. French commanders and politicians, understandably keeping the information of the growing indiscipline to themselves and away from enemy and ally alike, despaired that in its present condition the French Army could not even defend against a German attack, much less persevere to victory in a long war. Even more frightening was the seemingly very real possibility that France could succumb to the same type of revolution that had engulfed Russia. Desperate measures were required to avoid defeat and to avoid revolution; France needed a hero.

To some, including Sir Douglas Haig, the May 1917 shift to Pétain as commander of the French armies, while General Ferdinand Foch became Chief of the

Mata Hari (1876–1917)

Mata Hari was the stage name for the Dutch exotic dancer and courtesan Margaretha Zelle. Born in 1876 in the Netherlands, Zelle eventually gained fame as a flirtatious dancer, as well as for her scanty and extravagant costumes. Since the Netherlands remained neutral in World War I, Zelle was able to pass European borders freely and continue her career, wooing both Allied and German officers and businessmen alike. In her unique position, Zelle almost certainly worked as a double agent, uncovering and selling secrets for both the Allies and the Central Powers. In the charged wartime atmosphere, the actions of Mata Hari could not have gone unnoticed. In January 1917, French intelligence intercepted a German message, which lauded the efforts of a spy code-named H-21, and was able to deduce that the spy in question was in fact Mata Hari. Oddly, the code used to transmit the information about H-21 was one that the Germans knew to be compromised, which has led some historians to conjecture that the Germans wanted Mata Hari to be caught, because she was in fact working for the Allies. Regardless, on 13 February 1917, French authorities arrested Mata Hari, accusing her of treason. Although there was precious little

Margaretha Zelle, dressed in one of the elaborate and seductive costumes that helped her to gain fame as Mata Hari.

evidence against her, with French morale at a critically low level, Mata Hari was convicted and sentenced to death, and on 15 October 1917 she was executed by firing squad.

General Staff, had seemed to be a dangerous gamble. White haired and aged 61, Pétain had only three years earlier been but an obscure colonel. He had risen to fame at Verdun, but had since been branded as a pessimist. Having reached the pinnacle of his military career amid the aftermath of Nivelle's failed offensive, Pétain took stock of the situation only to find a French Army that was in ruins. 'They call me only in catastrophes,' he later remarked. One of his subordinates recorded the grim nature of Pétain's first few days in command:

'I do not know a more horrible sensation for a commander than to suddenly learn that his army is breaking up. I saw the initial disaster at Verdun and the day following [the Italian defeat at] Caporetto, but on these occasions I always sensed that with some reserves and a little imagination it would be possible to caulk up the front. But there had never been anything like May 20! We seemed absolutely powerless. From every section of the front the news arrived of regiments refusing to man the trenches. … The slightest German attack would have sufficed to tumble down our house of cards and bring the enemy to Paris.'

Pétain set about the urgent project of rebuilding French military morale with both boundless energy and great urgency. Unlike so many of his predecessors, Pétain did not simply blame the mutinies on outside agitators or on cowardice; instead he recognized that many of the soldiers' basic complaints were valid. He worked feverishly to improve conditions at rest camps and to make certain that all soldiers enjoyed a uniform and high level of training. He also announced a pay raise and ordered the provision of fresh fruit and vegetables for field kitchens close to the front lines. Most importantly, though, he issued more liberal policies regarding leave, allowing every soldier to take 10 days of leave every four months, and made certain that soldiers were well cared for during their leave.

Having risen to fame during the Battle of Verdun, General Henri Pétain took over command of the French Army on the Western Front at its nadir in the wake of Nivelle's offensive. Tasked both with rebuilding the army and winning the war, Pétain quipped, 'They call me only in catastrophes.'

Pétain also sought to cement a closer bond between the officers of the French Army and their men, and he directed that the officers undertake weekly meetings with those under their command, contending that, 'by explaining, one achieves understanding and arrives quickly at a community of ideas, the basis of cohesion'. Practising what he preached, Pétain visited and spoke to the men of 90 divisions. During his visits he spoke of the overall strategic situation and contended that American entry into the conflict had made victory inevitable. Besides utilizing his enormous credibility with the common soldier to rebuild morale by eating and speaking with them, Pétain published a series of articles entitled 'Why We Are Fighting', which attempted to reconnect the soldiers to the sacrifices of the past. One pamphlet read:

'We fight because we have been attacked by Germany.
We fight to drive the enemy from our soil …
We fight with tenacity and discipline, because these are essential to obtain victory.'

French soldiers (here pictured disembarking for the front) received little home leave, and the lowest pay of any Allied force, contributing factors to the mutiny that Pétain worked to ameliorate. When many of these basic complaints began to be addressed, morale started to rise.

Pétain once again treated the French *poilu* with dignity and respect, and the results were nearly instantaneous. However, the new commander also leavened his kindness with firm discipline. Armies cannot stand for mutiny, and there had to be retribution. Pétain first warned his officers not to tolerate further disruptions of discipline and empowered them to take firm control of the matter by issuing the following order on 5 June:

'At the time of some recent incidents, officers have not always seemed to do their duty. Certain officers have concealed from their superiors the signs of adverse spirit which existed in their regiments. Others have not, in their repression, displayed the desired initiative or energy. ... Inertia is equivalent to complicity. The Commander in Chief has decided to take all necessary action against these weaklings. The Commander in Chief will protect with his authority all those who display vigour and energy in suppression.'

In the end the French Army convicted 3427 soldiers of offences during the mutinies and sentenced 554 to death, only 55 of whom actually were executed, with the remainder serving long prison sentences. Considering the widespread nature of the mutinies, the retribution was slight. Pétain realized that, since many of the grievances of the French soldiers were genuine, if discipline were too harsh, morale might suffer further decline and the mutinies continue. Explaining his motives Pétain remarked in June, 'I have pressed hard for the repression of these grave acts of indiscipline; I will maintain this pressure with firmness but without forgetting that it is applied to soldiers who, for three years, have been with us in the trenches and are "our soldiers".'

Of the greatest importance to the rebuilding of French military morale, though, was Pétain's eschewing of vain efforts at achieving decisive victory in favour of attacks aimed only at limited and achievable objectives. Pétain quickly made it clear that under his leadership no longer would French soldiers throw their lives away for the vain hopes of floundering commanders. Indicative of his philosophy

German 'walking wounded' and stretcher cases. In World War I, as in most other conflicts, the number of military wounded (over 20 million) outnumbered the more infamous number of military deaths (estimated at nearly 10 million).

of war, one of Pétain's first strategic memorandums read in part:

'*The equality of the opposing forces does not for a moment permit us to envisage the rupture of the front.* … [It does not make sense] *to mount great attacks in depth on distant objectives, spreading our initial artillery preparations over* [enemy] *defences, resulting in bombardment so diluted that only insignificant results are obtained.* … [Future attacks will be mounted] *economically with infantry and with a maximum of artillery.*'

ALLIED PLANNING

The prospect of limited offensives in which lives were not going to be wasted eventually proved a tonic to the morale of the French Army. However, in June 1917, even Pétain remained unsure of whether the French Army could hold against a concerted German

Wounded

The industrialized slaughter of World War I produced not only record numbers of dead but also of wounded, often men with horrific wounds, who, due to advancements in medicine, were kept alive but often had only no real chance of ever again leading a normal life. With reconstructive surgery in its infancy, the worst such cases involved head wounds. An orderly at a London hospital recalled:

'To talk to a lad who, six months ago, was probably a wholesome and pleasing specimen of English youth, and is now a gargoyle, and a broken gargoyle at that ... is something of an ordeal. You know very well that he has examined himself in a mirror. That one eye of his has contemplated the mangled mess that is his face. ... He has seen himself without a nose. Skilled skin grafting has reconstructed something which owns two small orifices that are his nostrils; but the something is emphatically not a nose. He is aware of just what he looks like: therefore you feel intensely that he is aware that you are aware, and that some unguarded glance of yours might cause him hurt. ... Suppose he is married or engaged to be married ... could any woman come near that gargoyle without repugnance? His children. ... Why a child would run screaming from such a sight. To be fled from by children. That must be a heavy cross for some souls to bear.'

offensive aimed at Paris, for he needed time to rebuild his shattered forces and for his reforms to take effect. The results of the mutiny, thus, in the short term altered the strategic balance of the war and required Pétain to advocate continued British action on the Western Front to thwart any potential German efforts to assail the wounded French Army. In the long term, the results of the French Army mutinies foretold a scenario in which more and more of the fighting would fall both to the BEF and later to the Americans.

While his own offensive around Arras wound down, and it became increasingly obvious that French failures at the Chemin des Dames spelled the doom of the Nivelle's plan to achieve decisive victory, Haig's thoughts turned to the possibility of major operations in Flanders. For a variety of reasons the British commander-in-chief had long favoured an attack from the salient around Ypres. The Germans held the high ground around the constricted Ypres Salient, making the area one of the most deadly on the Western Front for the BEF. Relatively modest gains would push the Germans off the ridges and make the British salient much safer and more defensible. Greater gains would threaten the vital German communications hub of Roulers, some 40km (25 miles) east of Ypres, the capture of which would threaten German logistics in the area and possibly force a German evacuation of the coast to Ostend. Such gains would be of the utmost strategic importance to Britain, for in the midst of a submarine war that was going increasingly badly, the Admiralty agonized over the naval threat that emanated from the German bases in occupied Belgium. Indeed, a forward movement in Flanders seemed of more strategic value than anywhere else on the Western Front. In a letter to Nivelle shortly before his fall, Haig made his desires clear:

'I feel sure you realize the great importance to all of the Allies of making a great effort to clear the Belgian coast

> "[T]he state of the French army is now very good, but at the end of May there were 30,000 "rebels" who had to be dealt with. ...This shows how really bad the condition of the French army was after Nivelle's failure."
>
> Diary of Field Marshal Haig

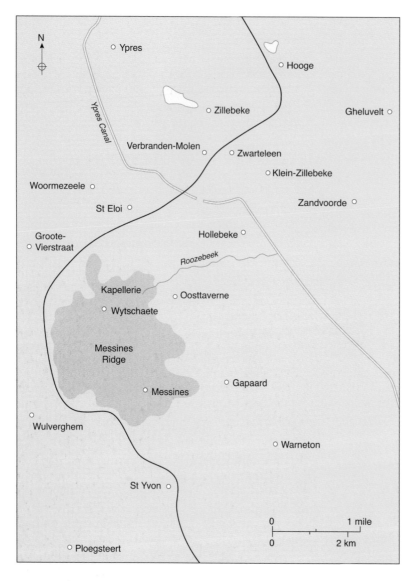

N

Ypres

Hooge

Zillebeke

Gheluvelt

Ypres Canal

Verbranden-Molen

Zwarteleen

Klein-Zillebeke

Woormezeele

Zandvoorde

St Eloi

Groote-Vierstraat

Hollebeke

Roozebeek

Kapellerie

Oosttaverne

Wytschaete

Messines Ridge

Gapaard

Messines

Wulverghem

Warneton

St Yvon

0   1 mile
0   2 km

Ploegsteert

The British sector of the Western Front in 1917 was dominated by German positions on the high ground near Messines and to the east of Ypres, overlooking the salient. It was this patch of high ground in Flanders that was to be the target of the British Second Army, under General Sir Herbert Plumer, during the Battle of Messines.

military. Once it had become clear that Pétain, not Nivelle, controlled French strategy, though, the situation quickly sorted itself out, for Haig and Pétain had similar goals, though both guarded their counsel and refused to be entirely honest with each other. For his part Haig strongly desired to launch an attack in Flanders, but realized that he would need French cooperation in the attack, lest Lloyd George veto the operation for fear that it could become another Somme. Pétain, on the other hand, had to walk a strategic tightrope. Although he never fully believed in Haig's plan, he desperately required a British offensive to ensure that the Germans would not attack the vulnerable French Army. Pétain knew that the state of French morale was so perilous that he could offer but little aid to any British offensive in Flanders, but he had to promise enough aid to make certain that Haig received the approval of the British Government for his Flanders plan. Such is the nature of imperfect alliances.

Having undertaken preliminary planning for operations in Flanders in 1916, Haig already had a general outline of offensive there in mind even before the Nivelle Offensive and the fighting at Arras had ended. In May Haig had informed his army commanders of his intention to shift the bulk of BEF offensive operations to Flanders, but to facilitate his goal, Haig's plan called for several wearing-down

this summer. The enemy's submarine operations have become such a serious menace to the sea communications, on which all the Allies are so dependent for many of their requirements, that the need to deprive the enemy of the use of the Belgian ports is of the highest importance and demands a concentration of effort.'

That Haig wrote initially to Nivelle demonstrates that the British knew little regarding the seismic shift in the French command system. Although they received disturbing snippets of intelligence, the British knew even less regarding the perilous state of the French attacks, including continued action at Arras. An assault on the Messines Ridge, which dominated the area around Ypres, would follow on 7 June 1917. After the completion of the Messines operation, the main assault would take place in the neighbourhood of Ypres.

Even at this early stage, Haig's strategic scheme seemed at cross-purposes and contained inconsistencies that conspired to doom his cherished Flanders offensive to seeming futility. Haig had learned much from the first years of World War I. Fighting at Arras and the latter stages of the Somme had indicated both that the BEF was proficient at set-

piece battles aimed at limited gains and that offensive operations achieved diminishing returns over time. However, Haig firmly believed that the German Army had a breaking point, and overly optimistic information provided by BEF intelligence chief, Brigadier-General John Charteris, indicated that the German breaking point was in fact drawing near. The

Australian troops grab what rest they can, while their machine guns remain at the ready. It was the machine gun, with its lethal rapid fire, that came to epitomize the Great War. It was, however, artillery fire that caused the majority of the casualties.

lessons of past offensives, coupled with the hope of a collapse of German morale, left Haig in a quandary. Should the coming offensive in Flanders be limited in nature, or should it aim to achieve something more decisive? Fatally, perhaps, Haig chose both.

In a 16 May memorandum to Chief of the Imperial General Staff, General Sir William Robertson, Haig made it clear that he planned for operations in Flanders to take the form of limited, set-piece battles similar in nature to the first phase of operations at Arras:

'I have already decided to divide my operations for the clearance of the Belgian coast into two phases, the first of which will aim only at capturing certain dominating positions in my immediate front, possession of which will be of considerable value subsequently, whether for offensive or defensive purposes.

'Preparations for the execution of this first phase [an attack on the Messines Ridge] *are well advanced and the action intended is of a definite and limited nature, in which a decision will be obtained a few days after the commencement of the attack.*

'A second phase is intended to take place several weeks later, and will not be carried out unless the situation is sufficiently favourable when the time for it comes.

'It will be seen, therefore, that my arrangements commit me to no undue risks, and can be modified to meet any developments in the situation.'

Haig also made it quite clear to his army commanders, though, that he hoped that the hammer blows by the BEF, while limited in nature, would result in a collapse of the German lines, and result in the 'possession of the Belgian coast up to the Dutch frontier, or, failing this, to dominate the Belgian ports now in the hands of the enemy to an extent that will make them useless to him for naval purposes'. Haig's scheme, then, had a fatal flaw: although the attacks themselves were to be limited in nature, they would take on a life of their own, continuing in the vain hope

Although the nation fought on, by 1917, stricken by constant war and the effects of the British blockade, Germany was suffering from shortages of all types, including shortages of horses, as indicated by this photo of German artillery being led by cattle.

that the next limited victory would cause German resilience to falter.

While planning progressed, Haig received word that Lloyd George would not approve the Flanders offensive unless the French agreed to launch major supporting operations. The news was distressing to Haig, who had just received word from his trusted confidant in Paris, Lord Esher, that the French under Pétain 'have agreed upon a so-called military policy, the basis of which is (however it may be wrapped up in jam), to wait for the Americans'. Both to divine the intentions of the French, and to ensure the support of his own government for his planning, on 18 May Haig met with Pétain at a conference in Amiens.

Although he feared that Haig's plan was overly optimistic and reminiscent of the Somme, Pétain wanted Haig to undertake an offensive, partly to reduce pressure on the demoralized French Army. However, Pétain could not tell Haig about the mutiny, for the French commander-in-chief knew that approval of the British offensive depended on French aid and that any sign of French weakness could only delay Haig's operation or result in its cancellation.

At the conference, then, Pétain assured Haig that he would 'fight and support the British in every possible way'. Although the goals of his operations would be strictly limited, Pétain agreed to undertake four attacks in the areas around the Chemin des Dames and Verdun to take pressure off British operations in Flanders. Pétain also promised that French forces would operate on the left flank of the main British attack around Ypres. Pétain's statements of support impressed Haig, who now had the assurances he needed to calm Governmental fears over his Flanders campaign. For his part, Pétain knew full well that he had made promises to Haig that he would have difficulty keeping, but he did so in the best interests of France. Haig had needed assurances of French support

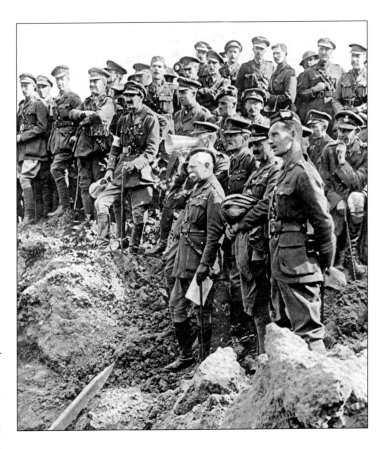

General Sir Herbert Plumer (centre). One of Britain's most able generals during World War I, Plumer was an advocate of bite-and-hold, limited offensives, leading the BEF to notable successes at Messines and during the second phase of the Third Battle of Ypres.

before he could attack, and that is exactly what Pétain gave him.

Soon after, however, reports of the French Army mutinies began to trickle in to Haig's headquarters, which severely damaged the value of Pétain's promises. On 25 May Charteris first noted the existence of indiscipline in the French ranks, and bemoaned the fact that the French had decided to grant each man 10 days' leave every four months, which meant that a quarter of a million French troops would be out of the front lines at any one time. Charteris passed the distressing intelligence on to Haig with the note, 'that we cannot expect any great help from the French this year'.

News concerning the French Army mutinies became so widespread that Pétain could no longer keep the truth of the situation from his British allies. On 2 June, only eight days before the first French attack scheduled in support of Haig's Flanders offensive, Pétain admitted to Haig that a state of indiscipline existed in certain parts of the French Army, which precluded any French attacks until at least July. Pétain then went on to request that the BEF proceed with offensive actions, to keep German pressure off the reeling French military. Pétain's entreaties had the desired effect on Haig, who later

that day told Winston Churchill of his belief that Britain needed to launch a powerful blow against the German lines because he doubted 'whether our French allies would quietly wait and suffer for another year'.

The news that the French would be unable to offer meaningful military support to the Flanders offensive threatened to derail Lloyd George's reluctant approval of Haig's planning. At the same time, though, General Sir Henry Wilson, who served as the British liaison officer with Pétain and was trusted by Lloyd George, began to piece together the severity of the situation in the French military, recording in his diary the belief that, 'it will be impossible to keep the French in the war for another 12 or 18 months waiting for America without a victory of some sort'. On the advice of Wilson, and more to safeguard the beleaguered French

British troops moving forward carrying supplies in 'Yukon packs'. Allowing the wearer to carry 23–27kg (50–60lb) of supplies comfortably over rough territory, Yukon packs were critical to Plumer's plan to keep his forward lines well supplied during the Battle of Messines.

A German observation post. Usually enjoying positions on the high ground, the Germans were often able to oversee Allied lines. The advantage enabled the Germans accurately to predict several Allied offensives.

military than out of faith in the judgment and planning of Haig, Lloyd George gave his grudging approval only to the first phase of the Flanders offensive, a strictly limited assault on the Messines Ridge.

MESSINES

Atop a spine of high ground, the German positions at Messines Ridge dominated the southern flank of the Ypres Salient. Haig realized that the capture of the ridge was an essential precursor to launching the main operation from Ypres, and entrusted the important operation to General Sir Herbert Plumer in command of Second Army. Plumer enjoyed a unique familiarity with the area, the Second Army having been stationed there for more than two years. With ample time to prepare his offensive, Plumer planned a very limited advance, along the lines of what the Canadians had achieved at Vimy Ridge, under the cover of a massive artillery barrage. Enjoying a close relationship with his men, based on 'trust, training and thoroughness', Plumer left little to doubt amid a meticulous build-up to battle. A hint at the level of preparedness of Second Army lies in the fact that water pipes had been laid that

A British 18-pounder field gun. Serving as the main British field gun for the duration of the war, the 18-pounder was mobile, but packed a comparatively small punch. The guns were often used to cut enemy barbed wire and to move forward rapidly to cover any gains made in battle.

could deliver up to 2,271,247 litres (600,000 gallons) per day, while light railways enabled the stockpiling of 130,634 tonnes (144,000 tons) of ammunition for the army's guns. In addition, each unit scheduled to take part in the offensive practised every movement that it was to undertake on the day of the attack on a large model of the ridge constructed behind British lines. Nothing had been left to chance.

Plumer had also hatched an ingenious scheme designed to blow the German defences of the Messines Ridge sky high. For nearly two years Second Army had been involved in the digging of 24 long tunnels beneath the German lines, tunnels that ranged from 183 to 1830m

Mining

Both the Germans and the Allies recruited for work on the Western Front professional miners, who had the backbreaking and dangerous task of fashioning tunnels beneath enemy defensive emplacements. Labouring in 12-hour stretches, the miners utilized only picks and light shovels and excavated their tunnels by hand, passing the soil in bags or buckets to the man behind them in line. Although under constant threat from collapsing tunnels and poison gas, the greatest fear for the miners was discovery by enemy forces while underground. Constantly on the lookout, defenders dug countermines, and employed listening equipment, ranging from sensitive microphones to simply pressing an ear to an overturned bucket, to discern the location and direction of enemy miners. Once an attacking mine was located, the defenders tunnelled as close as possible to the attacking force and then set off a small charge, called a camouflet, designed to collapse the enemy tunnel and entomb the attacking miners deep underground. On some occasions, though, the defenders got too close and the

Not only did miners in the Great War endure backbreaking labour but also they were often faced with fighting a brutal underground war with enemy miners.

mines converged, resulting in close-quarter underground fighting with picks and spades. The victors would take possession of the mine, while the losers had literally dug their own graves.

(200 to 2000 yards) in length, and were packed with an average of 21,772kg (48,000lb, 24 tons) of ammonal, a particularly lethal high explosive. The largest single explosive charge was the 43,363kg (95,600lb) of ammonal put in place by the Canadian Tunneling Company at the end of a 503m (1650ft) tunnel, 38m (125ft) beneath St Eloi.

Even as the final touches were put on the mines, on 26 May the preliminary barrage began in earnest, as a total of 2266 guns, including 756 heavy guns organized into 40 bombardment and counterbattery groups, opened fire on German lines. The preparatory bombardment was methodical, involving a sophisticated fire plan like that used at Arras. Air reconnaissance had located many of the German gun emplacements, which allowed the counterbattery teams to harass the German gunners with both high explosive and gas, which kept German artillery fire

during Second Army's advance to a minimum. A German machine-gunner remembered the effectiveness of the British barrage:

This is far worse than the Battle of Arras. Our artillery is left sitting and is scarcely able to fire a round … the sole object of every arm that enters the battle is to play itself out, in order to be withdrawn as quickly as possible.

By 7 June, as Plumer's men made ready to go 'over the top', the British artillery had fired over three and a half million shells into the German lines at Messines.

The Germans had long realized that their positions on Messines Ridge were vulnerable to mining, and that any British assault in Flanders would have the ridge as its main focus. General Hermann von Kuhl, chief of staff to Crown Prince Rupprecht, suggested that it would be better to evacuate the Messines Ridge and withdraw five kilometres (three miles) to more defensible positions. Local commanders, led by General von Laffert in command of XIX Corps, however, overruled Kuhl's suggestion, contending that the positions on the Messines Ridge were fully up to date and comprised a defence-in-depth scheme that would withstand any British attack.

At 3.10am on 7 June the mines beneath the Messines Ridge detonated. Norman Gladden, a young infantryman with the 23rd Division, remembered:

'With a sharp report a rocket began to mount into the daylit sky. A voice behind me cried, 'Now'. It was the hour, and that enemy light never burst upon the day. The ground began to rock. My body was carried up and down as though by the waves of the sea. In front the earth opened and a large black mass mounted on pillars of fire to the sky, where it seemed to remain suspended for some seconds while the awful red glow lit up the

British troops take what rest they can while holding a strong natural defensive position against the Germans. Amid the nearly continuous shellfire of battle, soldiers on both sides quickly mastered the ability to rest where and when they could.

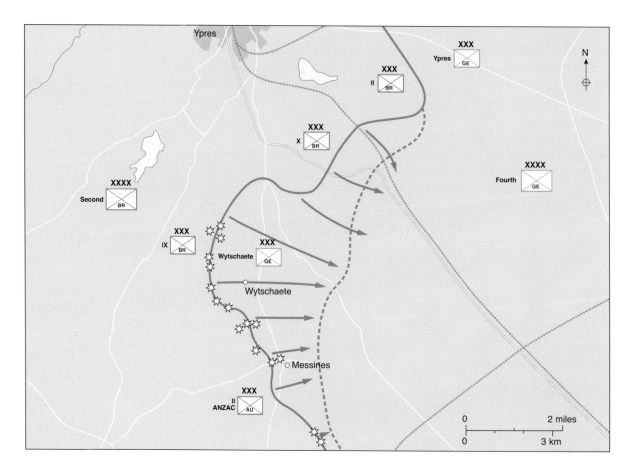

surrounding desolation. No sound came. My nerves had been so keyed to sustain a noise from the mine so tremendous as to be unbearable. For a brief spell all was silent, as though we were so close that the sound itself had leapt over us like some immense wave. Almost simultaneously a line of men rose from the ground a short distance in front and advanced away towards the upheaval, their helmets silhouetted and bayonets glinting in the unearthly redness.'

A Belgian priest who witnessed the explosions from some miles away recorded, 'I suddenly witnessed the most gigantic and at the same time chillingly wonderful firework that ever has been lit in Flanders, a true volcano, as if the whole southeast was spewing fire.'

On the day before the battle, Plumer's chief of staff, General Tim Harrington, had remarked, 'I do not know whether we shall change history tomorrow, but

At the Battle of Messines, Plumer's forces seized nearly all of their objectives, helped by the explosion of a series of huge mines, with only few losses, demonstrating the practicality of limited offensives in the Great War.

we shall certainly alter the geography.' His words were prophetic. The series of explosions ripped the top off much of the Messines Ridge, destroying the German front-line trenches and killing as many as 10,000. The force of the explosions was so great that it was felt in London, 208km (130 miles) away. The craters left by the mines were on average 69m (76 yards) wide and 24m (26 yards) deep, large enough to hold a five-storey building. Although the mines had been a marvellous success, for tactical reasons three had not been detonated. Somehow forgotten for years, one of the massive mines exploded during a thunderstorm in 1955, while two remain armed and ready to fire beneath the Messines Ridge to this very day.

In the wake of the devastating blasts, 80,000 British and Australian infantrymen of nine divisions moved forward to undertake their carefully rehearsed tasks under the cover of a smokescreen, a covering artillery barrage and a creeping barrage of machine-gun bullets. Utilizing grenades, light machine guns and the support of 72 tanks, the advancing forces flanked and destroyed the ubiquitous concrete pillboxes that made up the German forward line of defence and seized their first objectives within 35 minutes. Next the attackers entered the battle zone, where German reserve formations and their counterattacks had brought so many previous offensives, including that of Nivelle at the Chemin des Dames, to grief. However, the effects of the mines and the accurate covering barrage kept German resistance to a minimum, and by 7am II ANZAC Corps had seized the village of Messines, and all along the front the attackers had gained the crest of the ridge and overthrown the German second line of defence. The advance then

German reinforcements move toward the front lines. At Messines, as they had at Vimy Ridge, the Germans held their reserves too far to the rear to have a meaningful effect on the initial outcome of the battle.

halted under the cover of an additional protective barrage, to bring up reserve formations and prepare for additional expected German counterattacks. None, though, were forthcoming. In the words of the British official history:

'The German garrison had been defeated in detail. The front battalions had been overrun in the first rush, and few had escaped. Their support battalions [in the battle zone] had then been overwhelmed before the reserve battalions could reach them in any strength. Elements of the reserve battalions had come through and shared the fate of the support battalions; but the majority had remained lying out in shell-holes on the eastern slope of the ridge awaiting events.'

As they had at Vimy Ridge, the German had held their reserve divisions too far back to make an immediate effect on the fighting and in the words of one Australian officer, the next few hours were 'more like a picnic than a battle'. Behind the advance was only desolation, innumerable small shell holes created by the barrage and the gaping craters that were the only memory of the mines. To the front was only green grass and trees of the reverse slope of Messines Ridge. The few German reserves that were available were gathering

out of sight, feverishly moving vulnerable artillery pieces and constructing new lines of defence to contain the imminent British breakthrough rather than attempting a futile counterattack.

In the early afternoon, reserve forces passed through the British front-line troops and pushed toward the Oosttaverne Line of rearward German defences. On this occasion, though, Plumer had been if anything too methodical. The pause atop the Messines Ridge not only enabled the Second Army both to gather its reserves and to prepare the critical next phase of the artillery barrage, but also allowed the Germans to reinforce and dig in behind the Oosttaverne Line. Even so, the renewed advance, beginning at 3.10pm made substantial gains, even seizing the first trench of the Oosttaverne Line, and capturing 48 German artillery pieces.

As German resistance predictably began to stiffen while reserves rushed to the scene from other portions of the Western Front, Plumer brought his offensive to

a halt. It was a stirring victory. After months of intense planning, the Second Army had overthrown one of the most powerful German defensive positions on the Western Front and seized the entire Messines Ridge at a cost of only 24,562 casualties. Revealingly the German casualties during the battle numbered 25,000, including 10,000 missing. It was the first time on the Western Front since the advent of trench warfare that attacking forces had so evened the odds that battlefield losses were roughly equal.

As the weight of the Allied war effort shifted towards the British in the wake of the French Army mutinies, Plumer's successful assault on the Messines Ridge boded well for the future. As it had at Arras, the BEF had again proven adept at utilizing overwhelming firepower to achieve limited objectives even against the strongest German defences. After the conclusion of the battle, Plumer informed Haig that he would need three days to reorganize his forces to face a more northerly direction before undertaking a second limited offensive aimed at the seizure of the Gheluvelt Plateau, which would herald the main British advance from Ypres. For good reasons, though, Haig demurred; he wanted a longer period of preparation for the coming assault, something that had been so important to Plumer's own victory, and critical Governmental support for operations in Flanders unexpectedly began

> ‘When the crash came the bravest trembled. The very ground seemed to be opening at their feet. Hills were thrown into the air; trees blown sky-high; guns and men and concrete all buried together.’
>
> Max Pemberton, *The War Illustrated*, 23 June 1917

to waver. Although Haig's decision was both required by political realities and was in many ways tactically sound, it was one of his most fateful of the entire war, an unheralded moment of change that would almost undo Haig's career. Given time for rumination, instead of relying on the methodical and successful Plumer to continue the assault around Ypres, the ever-optimistic Haig turned to another commander who he hoped would be more aggressive if the limited attacks in Flanders indeed offered the chance of a greater success.

The desolation of war: a supply train passes an abandoned German trench, which, though pockmarked and battered, withstood the worst of the British artillery fire. Note the stick grenades left on the parapet, ready for use.

CHAPTER 3

Passchendaele

After the success of Messines, Field Marshal Sir Douglas Haig had to win support for his wider Flanders offensive from a reluctant British Government. After a furious debate, Lloyd George relented and the Third Battle of Ypres began. While the second stage of the battle achieved marked success, the fighting stagnated into grim futility in the mud around the village of Passchendaele.

As the BEF offensive at the Messines Ridge ran its successful course, Lloyd George began to get strategic cold feet regarding the continuation of Haig's broader Flanders campaign. Even though the Prime Minister had strongly supported his commander-in-chief in his initial planning discussions with Pétain in May, Lloyd George judged that the strategic situation had changed so much since then as to warrant a thorough review of the entire Allied war effort. Russian societal collapse and French military disarray meant that any BEF effort to assail the might of German defences on the

During the Third Battle of Ypres, better known as Passchendaele, incessant shelling shattered the delicate drainage systems of low-lying Flanders, converting the battlefield into a nearly impassable quagmire, as represented by these British gunners wrestling their piece forwards.

Western Front in 1917 would take place almost unaided, while, on the other hand, the United States' entry into the conflict boded well for the strategic balance of 1918, when the Americans would be able finally to unleash their latent military might. Perhaps, reasoned Lloyd George, it would be best to stand on the defensive on the Western Front, and not risk a major battle, while awaiting the arrival of the Americans. Apart from strategic considerations, Lloyd George had other, more personal, reasons to question the wisdom of Haig's Flanders planning. Political fallout from the Battle of the Somme had destroyed the career of Prime Minister Herbert Asquith, a drama in which Lloyd George had played the major role. Leader of a tenuous alliance between elements of the Liberal Party and the Conservative Party in the House of Commons, Lloyd George was unsure of his grip on power. Another major attritional struggle on the Western Front, whether tactically warranted or not, might strain Lloyd George's coalition to the breaking point and cause his own downfall, something that the Welsh politician could not countenance.

While he pondered his strategic and political options, in order both to streamline the British Government's conduct of the war and to review war policy as a whole, Lloyd George created the War Policy Committee, which consisted of Lloyd George, General Jan Christian Smuts, Lord Milner, Lord Curzon, Arthur Balfour and Andrew Bonar Law. Holding its first formal meeting on 11 June, the War Policy Committee represented a bid by Lloyd George to wrest strategic control of the conflict from what he judged to be a military cabal formed by Haig as Commander-in-Chief and Robertson as Chief of the Imperial General Staff.

STRATEGIC DEBATE

At the meeting Lloyd George gave the members of the committee their mandate: they were to review all aspects of military and naval policy in all theatres of war. Based on their findings the committee would then dictate strategic policy. Lloyd George made his own feelings known that it would be a mistake to assail the German lines in France and argued that Allied

British Prime Minister David Lloyd George. The fiery Welsh politician sought to seize the strategic leadership of the Great War, and hoped to shift British emphasis away from the stalemated Western Front – a policy that led to an ongoing struggle with the leadership of the British military.

policy should hinge on a defensive strategy in the west pending the arrival of American support, while attacking in Italy, which he considered a more profitable theatre of war. Impressed with the reasoning of the amateur strategist, the War Policy Committee agreed to place military planning for the remainder of 1917 on hold pending a meeting with Haig and Robertson.

Although they were never on the best of social terms (Haig was from a gentlemanly background while the gruff Robertson had risen from the ranks), Haig and Robertson together formed one of the most potent alliances in British military history. While Haig was something of a natural optimist and Robertson was much more cautious in his military reasoning, the two men were staunch believers in the primacy of the Western Front and argued that allowing the initiative there to slip to the Germans would be a grave mistake. Based in London, Robertson immediately took note of the danger posed by the War Policy Committee and wrote to Haig expressing his desire to present a unified military front to the politicians in favour of continued operations in Flanders. Although Robertson had little hope that an offensive near Ypres would result in more than an important attritional victory, he put his own doubts aside and warned Haig:

'What I do wish to impress on you is this: Don't argue that you can finish the war this year, or that the German is already beaten. Argue that your plan is the best plan – as it is – that no other would be safe let alone decisive, and then leave them to reject your advice and mine. They dare not do that.'

On 19 June Haig journeyed to London to put his planning before the War Policy Committee, demonstrating troop movements on a raised map. As instructed by Robertson, Haig portrayed his planning as aimed at limited, methodical gains that would both keep the pressure on the Germans and seize important tactical positions in the area around Ypres. He also characterized the Belgian coastline as the only area on the Western Front where any greater results would be of immeasurable strategic value. Foreseeing another Somme and fearing for his political life, Lloyd George

Admiral Sir John Jellicoe. As First Sea Lord, Jellicoe worried that the Royal Navy would not be able to defeat the German submarine threat, and gave critical support to the military plan to attack from Ypres and seize the German submarine bases on the Belgian coast.

Amphibious Landing Plan

It had long been a hallmark of British strategy to utilize the great strength and mobility of the Royal Navy to strike at Continental enemies through amphibious operations.

Soon after World War I had settled down into static fighting, Winston Churchill, then First Lord of the Admiralty, advocated landing British troops on the Belgian coast, behind the German lines, stating to the military command, 'Here at last you have their flank – if you care to use it. … There is no limit to what could be done [using amphibious operations].'

For years, first Field Marshal Sir John French and then Field Marshal Sir Douglas Haig, as commanders of the BEF, made amphibious operations designed to turn the German flank in Belgium part of their overall planning for an offensive in Flanders. During the Third Battle of Ypres, in 1917, the amphibious operation, which planned to land up to three divisions on the Belgian coast utilizing innovative, flat-bottomed landing craft (the precursors to the landing craft of World War II) was held in constant readiness. However, Haig hoped to use the landing as a *coup de grâce* finally to crush the German lines in Belgium, a moment that never came, in part due to the onset of bad weather, which stalled the promising British victories of September and early October.

was livid and fixated on Haig's broader strategic goals, recording in his memoirs:

'When Sir Douglas Haig explained his projects to the civilians, he spread on a table or desk a large map and made a dramatic use of both his hands to demonstrate how he proposed to sweep up the enemy – first the right hand brushing along the surface irresistibly, and then came the left, his outer finger ultimately touching the German frontier with the nail across.'

Lloyd George immediately questioned Haig's planning and contended that the Allies had neither the preponderance in troops nor artillery to ensure a successful offensive. Citing a growing manpower shortage, the Prime Minister argued that Haig's attack, if unsuccessful, could also leave Britain very weak and cede leadership within the Allied camp to the Americans. Although the assembled committee members agreed with Haig that an offensive in Flanders provided the best chance for achieving a meaningful victory, the majority concurred with the reasoning of Lloyd George and leaned toward a defensive stand on the Western Front pending an infusion of American military might. Haig's Flanders plan seemed in serious jeopardy.

It is a time-honoured British military strategy not to allow a major land power to dominate the Continental coastline of the English Channel. However, in 1914 the Germans had captured the Belgian coastline of the Channel up to the area of Nieuport. From the beginning of the war the Admiralty and the Royal Navy had fretted over the German-dominated Channel ports and had demanded their recapture. Then First Lord of the Admiralty Winston Churchill first sounded the alarm after the initial fall of the ports of Antwerp, Ostend and

A pilot of the Royal Flying Corps in France in 1917. Facing the danger of being shot down behind enemy lines, pilots were usually armed with a pistol for their protection.

Zeebrugge in October 1914, and wrote to Field Marshal Sir John French:

'But my dear friend, I do trust that you will realize how damnable it will be if the enemy settles down for the winter along lines that comprise Calais, Dunkirk or Ostend. There will be continual alarms and greatly added difficulties. We must have him off the Belgian coast!'

In support of military operations designed to retake the Belgian coastline, the Admiralty offered the firepower of the Royal Navy and the option of an amphibious landing to turn the German seaborne flank. While such considerations, along with concern about the security of cross-Channel communications vital to the survival of the BEF, were in the forefront of the military planning of both French and Haig, other battles and considerations had always intervened.

The advent of German unrestricted submarine warfare in February 1917, though, had infused Admiralty demands concerning the strategic nature of the Belgian coast with greater urgency. Elevated from command of the Grand Fleet to the position of First Sea Lord in order to deal with the submarine threat, Admiral Sir John Jellicoe found the Royal Navy and Britain's seaborne trade routes to be in grave peril. During April alone Allied and neutral shipping lost to submarine attacks reached 860,592 tonnes (847,000 tons), with an additional 325,135 tonnes (320,000 tons) of shipping damaged so badly that it needed to be taken out of service, totals that far exceeded German forecasts of losses required to starve Britain into submission. Although, due mainly to the belated introduction of the convoy system, Allied shipping losses fell to 609,628 tonnes (600,000 tons) in May, the

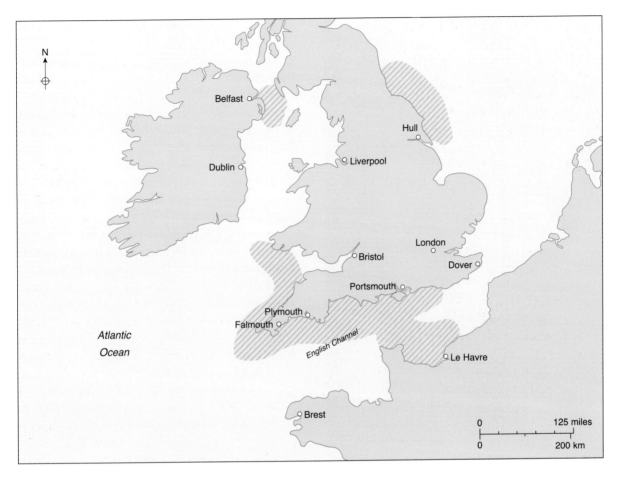

German U-boats concentrated their efforts around British ports, hoping to sink ships as they slowed to enter the harbours. Initially the Germans met with great success, until the introduction of the convoy system. This diagram shows the principal area of British shipping losses in late 1917.

wastage rate remained so high that Jellicoe despaired for the future.

The day following Haig's failed efforts to achieve approval for his Flanders planning, Jellicoe presented a strategic overview of the war at sea to the members of the War Policy Committee. The blunt and pessimistic testimony of the First Sea Lord proved to be a bombshell. Jellicoe stated:

'That two points were in his mind, the first was that immense difficulties would be caused to the Navy if by the winter the Germans were not excluded from the Belgian coast. ... The position would become almost impossible if the Germans realized the use they could make of these ports. ... The second point he felt was that if we did not clear the Germans out of Zeebrugge before this winter we should have great difficulty in ever getting them out of it. The reason he gave was that he felt it to be improbable that we could go on with the war next year for lack of shipping. ... The Prime Minister said that ... [if Jellicoe's statement] was accurate then we should have far more important decisions to consider than our plans of operations for this year, namely, the best method of making tracks for peace.'

Jellicoe's opinion, though quite controversial, had the effect of tying Haig's Flanders planning to the strategic well being of the British war effort as a whole. Unwilling to resist the unity of military opinion represented by the Commander-in-Chief, the Chief of the Imperial General Staff and the First Sea Lord, a

General Sir William Robertson, who, as Chief of the Imperial General Staff, formed a powerful military alliance with Field Marshal Sir Douglas Haig in favour of continued operations on the Western Front. He resigned in February 1918, being replaced by Sir Henry Wilson.

only a month before the onset of operations, valuable time had been lost. Hedging its bets, though, the War Policy Committee only gave the offensive partial approval, and promised to reconsider its decision as the operation ran its course. After the war Lloyd George railed at the British military both for hoodwinking his Government into supporting the Third Battle of Ypres (or Passchendaele as it is commonly known) and then for badly botching the fighting itself. Much of the blame for the outcome of the battle, though, must fall to Lloyd George. Although he did not believe in Haig's scheme, Lloyd George did not stop the battle, fearing for his own political life if he stood so brazenly against unified military opinion. The Prime Minister also could have called a halt to the fighting at any time during its course, but such a course of action would have called for Lloyd George to put his own career on the line, something that he was, in the end, unwilling to do.

THE INITIAL ASSAULTS AT THE THIRD BATTLE OF YPRES

Eschewing the methodical Plumer, Haig made one of the most critical mistakes of his career and instead chose General Sir Hubert Gough to command his cherished and hard-won Flanders offensive. Gough had only limited familiarity with the terrain of Flanders, and had a reputation as a 'thruster'. The situation was so bad that several leading figures in the BEF warned Haig that, although Vimy Ridge and Messines had conclusively proven the efficacy of limited attacks, he would diligently have to guard against Gough's tendency to 'rush through' to decisive objectives. That Haig chose a man of Gough's reputation indicates that, while the Commander-in-Chief understood the importance of limited goals, he hoped for much more in light of recent optimistic reports concerning the impending collapse of German military morale.

majority of the members of the War Policy Committee shifted to a support of the continuation of Haig's campaign. Incensed at being outmanoeuvred by military leaders whom he had hoped to control, at a War Policy Meeting on 21 June Lloyd George lashed out at his tormentors and lobbied again for attacks through Italy aimed at knocking Austria out of the conflict. Further, the Prime Minister contended that the rough parity of forces on the Western Front and a potential lack of French military support might result in Haig's operation being a failure that would 'lower the morale of the people, weaken the army, and above all, undermine the confidence in the military advisers on which the government acted'.

After a few more days of bickering, on 25 June at its 11th meeting, the War Policy Committee gave Robertson and Haig approval to proceed with preparations for offensive actions near Ypres. With

Gough's military tendencies, when combined with Haig's great hopes, led to a command breakdown. At the Somme, Haig had meddled too much in the planning of his subordinates, transforming a rather limited attack into one that pressed for a breakthrough and fatally dispersed the preparatory artillery barrage in the process. During the planning for Third Ypres, Haig, if anything, remained too aloof from the planning. Although he had become a convert to the idea of sustained, limited advances (hoping that a series of such small victories would cause a German collapse), Haig was unable clearly to impart his complicated reasoning to Gough, who ignored cogent military advice in an ill fated attempt to achieve a breakthrough.

In late May, Gough produced a first draft of his attack scheme, which called for a general advance across a broad front to great depth. Haig and his staff rejected the plan as too risky and warned Gough to concentrate the bulk of his offensive operations against Observatory Ridge and Gheluvelt Plateau on the right flank of the advance. German defences on the high ground there were considerable; the ground dominated the battlefield and if unconquered would enable the Germans to devastate the main assault

General Jan Christian Smuts (left). A South African and veteran of the Boer War, Smuts was sent to Britain to sit on the Imperial War Cabinet. It was a testament to Smuts's abilities that he became a trusted member of the War Policy Committee under David Lloyd George.

further north with deadly enfilade fire. Haig also cautioned Gough that any attempts to have the infantry advance to depth would run afoul of the new German defensive system. Haig, through his head of operations General J.H. Davidson, advocated strictly limited offensives of only 1830m (2000 yards) in depth designed to destroy German reserves, and concluded; 'An advance which is essentially deliberate and sustained may not achieve such important results on the first day of operations, but will in the long run be much more likely to obtain a decision.'

Unhappy with the interference in his plans, produced by what he referred to as a 'pedantic and if you like methodical mind', Gough only claimed to take

German soldiers inspecting a captured British trench. In an effort to instil an attacking mentality in its troops, the leadership of the BEF directed that front-line trenches not be overly elaborate, which often resulted in the British trenches being rather more rudimentary than German trenches.

Haig's original strategic hopes for the Third Battle of Ypres. The first line (1) represents the initial breakthrough, whilst the further lines (2) and (3) reflect Haig's ambition of pushing through as far as Bruges and driving German forces away from the Belgian coast.

Haig's advice into account. In the second incarnation of his Flanders plan, Gough allotted only one more corps and no additional artillery to the important right flank positions of Observatory Ridge and the Gheluvelt Plateau, far too small a force to ensure their capture. Gough asserted to his subordinate commanders that the coming offensive would take the form of a 'series of organized attacks on a grand scale and on a broad frontage', which in the end had the effect of diluting the all-important artillery preparation over too large an area as at the Somme. Worse still, Gough contended that the coming attack would be decisive in nature and that the men of Fifth Army would press on quickly to their final objectives,

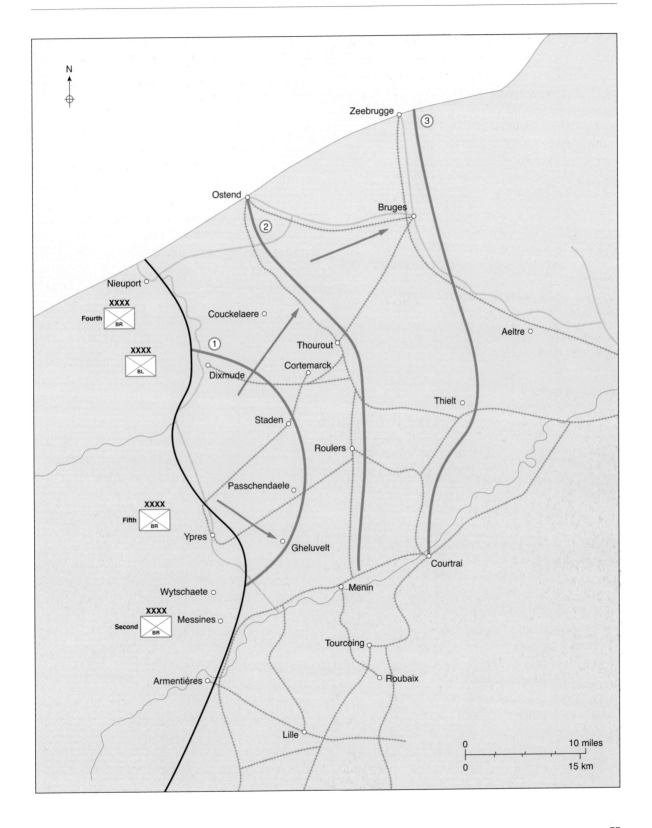

N

Zeebrugge
③

Ostend
②

Bruges

Nieuport

Couckelaere

Aeltre

XXXX
Fourth BR

XXXX
BL

①

Thourout

Dixmude

Cortemarck

Thielt

Staden

Roulers

Passchendaele

XXXX
Fifth BR

Ypres

Gheluvelt

Courtrai

Wytschaete

Menin

XXXX
Second BR

Messines

Tourcoing

Roubaix

Armentiéres

Lille

0		10 miles
0		15 km

The ruins of the Belgian cathedral city of Ypres. Germans overlooking British positions from high ground around the stricken city could call down artillery fire on troop movements, making the Ypres Salient one of the most deadly areas of the Western Front.

which would mean, 'that after some 36 hours of fighting we had reached a state of open warfare with our main forces moving forward under cover of advanced guards'. In the face of the German defensive scheme, a weakened barrage, coupled with efforts at distant goals, portended disaster.

Regardless of Haig's directions, Gough pressed on in planning the attack that he thought best. Later, during the compilation of the British official history, Gough admitted his actions:

'Put briefly, the main matter of difference was whether there should be a limited and defined objective or an undefined one. G.H.Q. favoured the former, I the latter. My principal reason was that I always had in mind the examples of many operations which had achieved much less than they might have done, owing to

excessive caution. … In all these operations victorious troops were halted at a pre-arranged line at the moment when the enemy was completely disorganized … this was the argument which I used, I claim with complete justification, with Douglas Haig.'

For nearly two months, from their positions atop the surrounding high ground, the Germans had been watching British preparations in and around Ypres. Their observations left them in little doubt regarding British intentions. By 12 June, Crown Prince Rupprecht of Bavaria, commanding the Northern Group of German Armies, pronounced a British attack in Flanders as 'certain', and, forewarned of the coming attack, the Germans had put the lull between Messines and Third Ypres to good use. Colonel von Lossberg, the German 'defensive battle expert', arrived on the scene on 13 June and began to supervise the construction of one of the strongest German defensive systems of the war. The forward zone, dotted with concrete pillboxes, was thinly manned to avoid heavy losses, and was designed to break up and slow the

British assault while giving ground. The battle zone consisted of more heavily manned strongpoints, designed to allow counterattack divisions to smash overextended attacking forces. In the third zone of defences lurked the heavy reserves, ready to move into the battle at a moment's notice. If needed the Germans could withdraw at any point in the battle, giving ground in return for time to create new zones of defence farther to the rear. By the end of July, the German Fourth Army confidently awaited Gough's assault.

On 16 July, the British preparatory bombardment opened, one of the heaviest of the entire war. The scale of the shelling impressed many, including D.H. Doe of the 51st Signal Company, who recorded in his diary:

'At 3.45 the great bombardment commenced in fullpower along the whole front. … I went out to watch it from the hill here + human eyes never saw a more terrible yet grand sight. The guns were flashing in thousands + one could see the big bursts of shrapnel etc.

… I could see the Germans frantic signals for artillery assistance – clusters of red rockets. They were going up in an absolutely frantic manner one after another. … My word what a bombardment.'

Before the soldiers of the Fifth Army went 'over the top', nearly 3000 artillery pieces, including 754 heavy guns, had fired four million shells into the German lines. However, the weight of shell was spread too thinly in a vain attempt to bombard German positions to depth. Additionally, Gough had failed to concentrate adequate levels of artillery fire against the heavily defended and tactically critical ridge system on the British right flank. Finally, the nature of the terrain and improved camouflage techniques had made it harder both to locate and to neutralize German

As World War I progressed, trench warfare came to be dominated by heavier and heavier pieces of artillery, which could pound enemy trench lines and communications, but were difficult to move forward. Here British artillerists struggle to move a heavy howitzer.

artillery. The barrage, though impressive, achieved only mixed results, leaving many attackers to face intact German barbed-wire entanglements and withering defensive fire.

The assault began at 3.50am on 31 July, under an overcast sky that prevented the Royal Flying Corps from undertaking effective spotting for the British artillery covering the assault, from right to left, of II, XIX, XVII and XIV corps of Fifth Army. Further to the British right, elements of Second Army aided in the offensive, while on the far left two divisions of the French First Army also moved forward. A creeping barrage assailed the German front-line defences for six minutes while the Allied infantry crossed no man's land, and then crept forward at a rate of 91m (100 yards) every four minutes.

In the centre and on the left, XIX, XVII, XIV corps and the French First Army made good progress, keeping in close contact with the creeping barrage and finding many of the German defences in the area destroyed by artillery fire. Amid the advance, the Guards Division demonstrated great ingenuity and easily dealt with the tactical obstacle formed by the muddy Yser Canal by floating across using specially designed buoyant mats. Along much of the front most units reached their second objectives on schedule, and some of the leading brigades even pushed on to their third objectives as they neared the German battle zone. Within the plan advocated by Haig, the attack would have halted at this point, with some units having moved forward roughly three kilometres (two miles), to consolidate in preparation to face the inevitable counterattacks that were part and parcel of the German defensive system. Instead, though, Gough's units, which were nearing exhaustion and losing cohesion, readied to move further forwards against fresh German units and into the teeth of the German defensive network. General

> 'The great brutal force of the initial blow has been parried. We survived the gruesome tension occasioned by the uncanny artillery fire, and we are able again to hold our heads high as the battle of living men is resumed.'
>
> Max Osborn, official German observer at Ypres

Tim Harrington, with Plumer and Second Army on the far right of the British lines, put the tactical dilemma well, stating, 'The further we penetrate his line, the stronger and more organised we find him … [while] the weaker and more disorganised we become.'

While the attack had gone well in the centre and left of the British lines, II Corps attacking the Gheluvelt Plateau achieved no such success. Realizing the importance of dominating the high ground, the Germans had studded the ridge with concrete strongpoints and had concentrated their defensive artillery barrage in the area as well. In addition, German defensive lines on the ridge ran through a series of narrow defiles and three wooded areas – Shrewsbury Forest, Sanctuary Wood and Chateau Wood – which the British artillery barrage had converted into nearly impregnable masses of tangled and fallen trees. Mired amid the wilderness of tree stumps, trunks, branches and shell holes, the leading battalions of II Corps struggled forward, but could only watch helplessly as the creeping barrage advanced too quickly and moved out of sight. Facing intact German defences without the advantage of a covering barrage, the efforts of II Corps were in vain, and resulted in a gain of only 457m (500 yards).

The failure of II Corps to seize Gheluvelt Plateau forced the advancing British and French forces on the centre and left of the lines into a narrow salient, overlooked and covered by deadly enfilade fire from the unconquered right flank, even as German forces massed for a counterattack. By afternoon, the Germans struck the centre of the British salient, and though desperate fighting resulted, British forces, who were more prepared to attack than defend, were pressed back. German counterattacks also negated many of the meagre gains made by II Corps on Gheluvelt Plateau.

As the German counterattack programme ran its course, and rain began to fall that transformed much of the tortured landscape into a sea of mud, British units consolidated their gains. In terms of land captured, the first day of Third Ypres, though better than the first day of the Somme, was a disappointment. At the end of the day, at a cost of roughly 30,000 casualties, British forces in the centre and British and French forces on the left held gains roughly 2743m (3000 yards) into the German defensive system – roughly halfway to Gough's overambitious goals. On the right flank, though, no gains had been made and the Gheluvelt Plateau remained in German hands. For such a meagre return, Fifth Army had lost 30 to 60 per cent of its fighting strength.

Gough had failed to heed the lessons of Vimy Ridge and Messines, and Haig, perhaps out of his own misguided optimism, had not held Gough to a strict adherence to the tactical idea of limited advance under cover of overwhelming firepower against the German defence-in-depth system. Instead of consolidating his forces after an advance of 1830 or even 2740m (2000 or 3000 yards) and then destroying German counterattacks, Gough had pressed on and placed the forces under his command at great risk. Essentially, Gough could have achieved the same advance at much

Heavy German artillery in action. It was fire from such artillery pieces that destroyed the city of Ypres, and made British positions in the salient so vulnerable that Haig called for an attack in part to seize the high ground surrounding the city.

As part of their ongoing military evolution, the Germans began to develop stormtroop tactics, designed to infiltrate and exploit weaknesses in enemy trench systems – tactics depicted here in a stormtroop advance.

less cost, while inflicting much greater damage on the Germans, had he adhered to the script of Messines.

Although Haig publicly professed to be pleased with the first day of the offensive, privately he could not have been happy with Gough's mishandling of his cherished Flanders campaign. Through a detailed tactical appreciation of the course of the day's events, Haig admonished Gough to place greater effort on the overthrow of the Gheluvelt Plateau. Most importantly, though, Haig informed his reluctant subordinate yet again of the strengths of the German defensive system, and of the need to only advance to a depth of 1830m (2000 yards) as to not dilute the covering artillery bombardment. Such tactics would leave British troops fresh and with ample artillery support to crush German counterattacks. Haig closed his instructions by stating, 'We must exhaust the enemy as much as possible, and ourselves as little as possible in the early stages of the fight.'

Although the orders were clear, and Haig was beginning to tire of Gough's handling of the offensive,

A First-Hand Account of the Third Battle of Ypres

Sergeant-Major J.S. Handley, who had already survived Second Ypres and the Somme, recorded his experiences in his diary:

'On the 31st July, we returned to Railway Wood to do our bit in the opening phase of the great battle to finish the war – as we thought. As we entered the trenches about midnight, it began to drizzle, increased to a fine wetting rain, when, next morning at a quarter to four, which was zero hour, we went "over the top". ... The tense ominous hours spent during the night waiting for zero hour, caused some men to pray, others to curse, and some to think and talk of home and loved ones. ... Awakened for the final "stand to", one is oppressed by the deathly silence that always precedes a battle. The calm before the storm. Even the enemy seemed to be saving his ammunition for the imminent cataclysm. We wait, tense, resigned, each and every one of us, to meet his end or whatever pain and anguish fate holds in

store for him. One gun breaks the heavy silence and in a split second comes ear-splitting thunder, as thousands of our massed guns fire simultaneously and continue firing, as we go forward to the attack. The whole battalion went forward in four waves or lines, with each company H.Q. in the centre of formation, but first we had to get through our own barbed wire. During the waiting period, parties, at intervals, went out, cut lanes through the wire and laid white tapes for the men to follow; then on getting out beyond our wire they would spread out into the waves. The first wave went forward on zero, immediately the guns fired the second wave went half a minute after, then over the parapet I climbed leading the company H.Q.; the other waves followed at half minute intervals. Following the white tape, I was horrified to find myself tangled up in our own wire. Knowing from experience, that the enemy would rain a deluge of blasting shells on our

Gough again went his own way. Haig was learning, arguably slowly, the tactics that best suited World War I; but his command system remained ridden with faults – faults that allowed Gough another opportunity to bungle the Flanders offensive. Gough went on to plan his second major effort, made up of two distinct phases, including a preliminary assault by II Corps on the Gheluvelt Plateau, three days after which the main advance would continue. Although rain slowed preparations, on 10 August, after a two-day artillery bombardment, II Corps launched its assault. However, Gough had once again erred: II Corps had received scant reinforcements and no additional artillery support. In essence, II Corps attacked alone, into the same German defences with the same amount of covering fire that on 31 July had failed so miserably to achieve any positive results. The outcome of the attack was predictable: the advancing forces were held up by German defensive strongpoints and lost contact with the creeping barrage, and at the end of the day the Gheluvelt Plateau remained firmly in German hands.

The failure on the right flank should have precluded the continuance of the main attack, but instead, on 16 August, Gough launched his second major offensive, known as the Battle of Langemarck. On the right flank II Corps played a familiar refrain, driving a wedge into the German forward zone of defences on the Gheluvelt Plateau before losing contact with the creeping barrage and being driven back. In the centre and on the left, British and French forces achieved more substantial gains only to be thrown back from their furthest penetrations by German counterattacks.

Haig and his staff officers at GHQ were livid both at Gough's continued wilful inability to follow the plan of limited advance and his inattention to the all-important right flank ridge system. Aware that he had incurred the wrath of his superiors, Gough attempted to share round the blame. At an army commander's conference, when confronted with the failure to seize the Gheluvelt Plateau, Gough questioned the bravery of his men. Convinced that the divisions on the right

---

front line within three minutes, at the most, I frantically tore myself through the obstructing wire, hurrying forward out of the most dangerous area. When I felt clear I looked about me, but in the darkness could see no one. There was no sign of the acting-captain … his servant, signallers, first aid men, stretcher-bearers and so forth. As far as I could make out I was alone, but I went forward, till, suddenly I fell, tripped up by the German wire. As I plunged into the mud several rifle shots flashed and cracked past my head, and incidentally, for weeks afterwards I was partially deaf in the left ear.'

As the first day of Third Ypres proceeded Handley had his first contact with the deadly Flanders mud:

'In my searchings I had come across a pack-mule sinking in the mud. His load had been removed and he had been left so far submerged when I saw him that only

the top of his back, neck and head were above the mud. I'll never forget the terror on his face with his eyes bulging out of their sockets. I just could not leave him in his agony, so, putting to his head a Smith and Wesson pistol I had found, I shot him.'

On 2 August, Handley's brigade left the line. On their return to the rear Handley recorded what was, for him, one of the most moving experiences of World War I:

'On marching back behind Ypres, Brigadier Duncan, that hard, stern soldier whom we feared, stood by the roadside taking the salute. "March to attention", rang out the order; "Eyes right"'and as we turned our heads we saw him standing erect, his right arm raised in the "salute" and – tears streaming down his face. It was indeed, a sorry brigade he saluted that day – the remnants of the battle – for barely a quarter of his men had returned.'

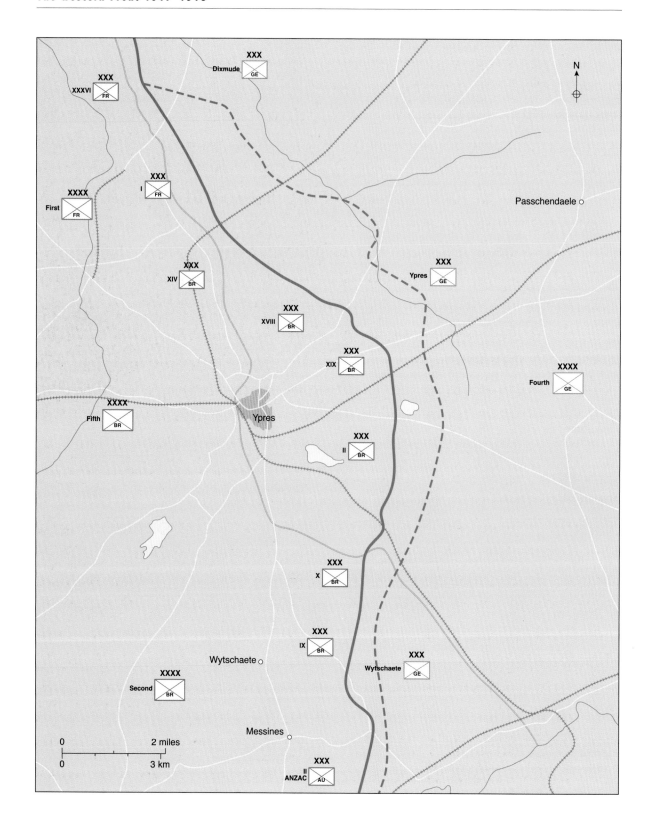

flank had failed to advance out of weakness of character, Gough suggested that he would find and deal with those responsible. It was the last move of a desperate man.

THE SECOND PHASE OF THE THIRD BATTLE OF YPRES

Perhaps worse, though, was the fact that Haig had realized what needed to be done in Flanders; he had come to understand the worth of step-by-step, methodical limited advances. However, instead of choosing Plumer, who thoroughly understood the nature of both limited advance and the German defensive system, Haig had chosen Gough in the hopes that he would better take advantage of any opportunities afforded by a great success. In what amounted to a meltdown of command, Gough had been unable to match his goals to the reality of the battlefield, and Haig proven unwilling to take the drastic action required to make good his command mistake until after the Battle of Langemarck. As the first stage of the campaign closed, though, Haig fully realized his error. In all, 22 divisions had been engaged in a series of battles that had cost 70,000 casualties, but had failed even to gain the objectives Gough had set out for the first day of the offensive. On 26 August, Haig belatedly shifted control of the Flanders campaign to Plumer, heralding the onset of a new and more productive phase of the Third Battle of Ypres.

Plumer, under close scrutiny from an increasingly vigilant Haig, devised a new plan, which involved a paramount effort to seize the Gheluvelt Plateau. In his planning, Plumer meant to avoid the problems that had beset the earlier efforts of Fifth Army by seizing

British stretcher-bearers navigating the maze of battlefield obstacles on their journey to the aid post. Such journeys were fraught with danger at the best of times, and became infinitely more difficult after the rains turned the battlefield into a sea of mud.

the high ground through four limited attacks, each of which proposed to advance only 1370m (1500 yards), well within the range of British artillery fire. Using this method Plumer hoped to deal harshly with German counterattacks. For his attack on the plateau, Plumer also concentrated a level of artillery fire that was three times stronger than that utilized previously by Gough. Besides concentrating fire, Plumer and his staff worked to redress some of the shortcomings demonstrated by the artillery in the August offensives. Artillerists worked on communications and liaison problems with the infantry, and instituted advanced techniques such as sound ranging in their counterbattery work. Finally, where the infantry under Gough had advanced in waves, Plumer organized more flexible methods of attack, like those utilized at

The gains made by the BEF on the opening day of the Third Battle of Ypres, gains that were much more limited than those called for in Haig's initial planning. The early weeks of the battle saw Fifth Army lead the way, before Haig shifted the balance of the attack towards Second Army.

British artillerymen at rest during a lull in the shelling. By 1917 artillery techniques were much more advanced than earlier in the war, allowing for accurate and lethal shelling to guard infantry advances from interference and break up any enemy counterattacks.

Messines, which included the use of skirmishing lines, specialist teams of bomb throwers and rifle grenadiers to deal with German strongpoints.

After completion of the trademark meticulous preparation that came to typify Plumer's battles, in clear weather on 20 September the infantry went 'over the top' at 5.40am, under the cover of a massive artillery barrage, into the Battle of the Menin Road. Advancing over the same ground of the Gheluvelt Plateau that had been twice captured and lost in August, British and Australian infantry quickly achieved their first objectives. After a short break to regroup, the infantry of the Second Army then moved out to seize their second and third objectives, only failing around an especially heavily defended area called Tower Hamlets. Further north, British and French forces did not have an artillery concentration equal to that of Second Army at Gheluvelt Plateau, but still enjoyed artillery fire twice as strong as that of the August offensives. Facing less formidable German defences, Allied forces in the centre and on the left flank achieved their ultimate goals with relative ease.

Plumer realized, though, that the true test of the battle was yet to come. Advance through the relatively thinly held German forward zone of defences had been swift, but now his forces had to hold against the inevitable counterattacks. Again, though, Plumer's preparation paid dividends. The German official history commented that counterattack forces, meant to join battle at 8.00am, could not get into action 'until late afternoon; for the tremendous British barrage fire caused serious loss of time and crippled the thrust power of the reserves'. In addition, every British assault division had held one brigade in reserve for use to defeat German counterattacks. Due to the tremendous difficulties imposed by Plumer's scheme, the German counterattacks did not get underway until 5pm, and then were met by a ferocious British barrage and well entrenched, fresh British and Australian infantry. The Germans persisted in their efforts for five days, but the British, Australians and French did not lose their gains as they had in August.

In the Battle of the Menin Road, at a cost of 20,000 casualties, the Second Army, Fifth Army and French forces had achieved and held virtually all of their gains, seized much of the high ground around Ypres and now in some places overlooked the Germans. Troops that had taken part in the advance quickly rotated out of the battle, and fresh forces that had been held in reserve took their place even while the artillery began to move forwards. Although gains had admittedly been minimal, the BEF had once again proven itself capable of besting German defence-in-depth tactics. The short gain, also, was but part of a plan to bite off a critical chunk of the German defensive network, and then hold it against counterattacks, before further

British cavalry at the ready near the front lines. Although it proved valuable on the Eastern Front and in the Middle East, cavalry was of little use on the crowded and lethal battlefields of the Western Front, dashing the hopes of the adherents of the breakthrough attack.

meticulous presentations enabled a repeating of the process. In short, Plumer was not involved in a battle, but rather a campaign in which battle victories led to further victories, which might result in a strategic gain. An enlisted man of the 55th Division commented favourably on Plumer's technique:

'*The advance up the slowly rising ridge to Passchendaele, once started, had to go on, but troops were not going over every day, as on the Somme. Periodical thrusts of greater compass had come to pass, and the creeping barrage. No longer could Jerry lie low in his dugouts, or in this case his pill-boxes, and know that the lifting of the barrage was an almost infallible signal of our attack. You followed the creeping shells now, and pounced on him still dazed and bewildered. The Somme had not been without its lessons.*'

At dawn on 26 September, after careful artillery preparations, British, Empire and French forces around Ypres repeated their 'bite-and-hold' success in the Battle of Polygon Wood. Along a shorter frontage that enabled an even greater concentration of artillery firepower, attacking forces advanced to achieve their

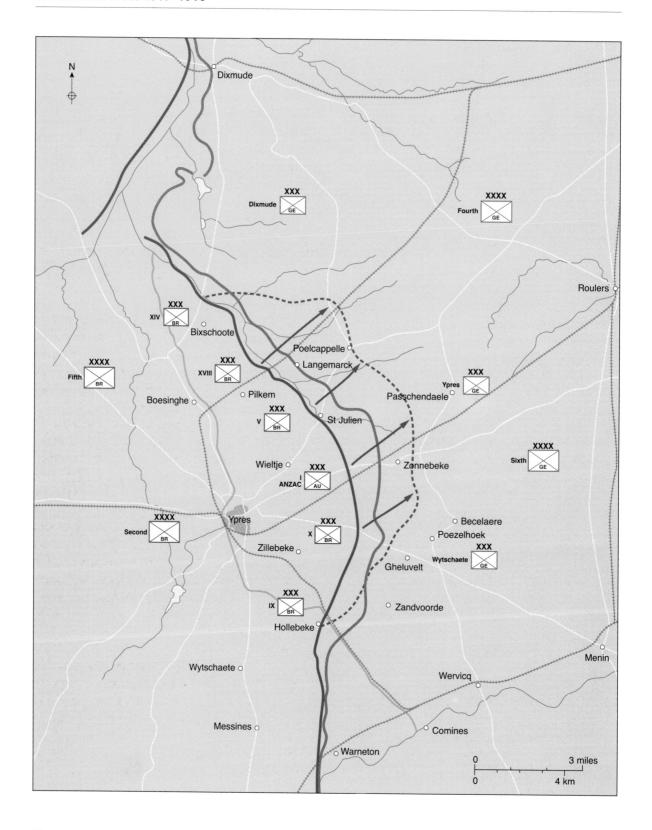

N

Dixmude

Dixmude XXX GE

Fourth XXXX GE

Roulers

XIV XXX BR

Bixschoote

Poelcappelle

Langemarck

Ypres XXX GE

Fifth XXXX BR

XVIII XXX BR

Boesinghe

Pilkem

V XXX BR

St Julien

Passchendaele

Sixth XXXX GE

Wieltje

I ANZAC XXX AU

Zonnebeke

Second XXXX BR

Ypres

Zillebeke

X XXX BR

Becelaere

Poezelhoek

Wytschaete XXX GE

Gheluvelt

IX XXX BR

Zandvoorde

Hollebeke

Wytschaete

Menin

Wervicq

Messines

Comines

Warneton

0   3 miles

0   4 km

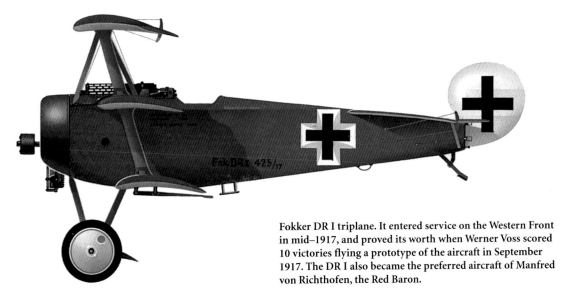

Fokker DR I triplane. It entered service on the Western Front in mid–1917, and proved its worth when Werner Voss scored 10 victories flying a prototype of the aircraft in September 1917. The DR I also became the preferred aircraft of Manfred von Richthofen, the Red Baron.

final goals, again with the exception of the stubbornly defended Tower Hamlets area. As before, German counterattack units had difficulty reaching the point of penetration in time, suffered heavy losses and failed to eject the attackers from their gains. With Allied forces having achieved virtually all of their objectives at a cost of only 15,000 casualties, Haig was understandably delighted, and was buoyed further by intelligence reports that indicated German strength in Flanders was crumbling.

Although he had hoped to wait until 6 October, fearing the onset of poor weather, Plumer agreed to a 4 October launch date for a renewed attack. After moving his artillery into position, and making certain that his fresh units had practised their assaults and knew their roles in the attack well, Plumer altered his basic planning, and he decided to attempt to gain surprise by eschewing the customary preparatory artillery barrage. Instead, especially heavy artillery fire began only at zero hour as the troops went 'over the top'.

As Plumer made ready to renew the battle, the Germans struggled to come to terms with Second

Army's methods. The continued fighting in Flanders had wounded the German military, while Plumer's tactics had negated much of the benefit of the German defence-in-depth system. Ludendorff later recorded that the costly battles in Flanders:

'… imposed a heavy strain on the Western troops. In spite of all the concrete protection they seemed more or less powerless under the enormous weight of the enemy's artillery. At some points they no longer displayed that firmness which I, in common with the local commanders, had hoped for.'

'The enemy contrived to adapt himself to our methods of employing counterattack divisions. There were no more attacks with unlimited objective, such as General Nivelle had made in the Aisne–Champagne battle. He [Plumer] was ready for our counterattacks, and prepared for them by exercising restraint in the exploitation of success.'

Increasingly concerned with the course of the Flanders fighting, and desperate to find a tactical solution to Plumer's techniques, Ludendorff rushed to the battlefront to discuss defensive options. After debating a number of ideas, Ludendorff and the local commanders decided to lessen their reliance on counterattack and chose instead to concentrate more manpower in their forward defensive zone to stem the British tide.

Once Plumer's Second Army became the main focus of the Allied attack the fighting became much more systematic, with a series of limited assaults aimed at securing specific objectives. This map shows the gains made between 16 August and 13 October 1917.

As the Germans were in the process of altering their defensive scheme, Allied forces struck at dawn on 4 October, launching the Battle of Broodseinde. Everywhere, coordination between the artillery and the infantry, along with the continued use of infantry techniques that more reflected a semi-mobile state of warfare, allowed British and French forces to gain the German front lines before the defenders had adequate time to react. Unwittingly the Germans had played into Plumer's hands, and Ludendorff later admitted that instead of halting the Allied advance, the concentration of German forces in the front lines merely resulted in a greater death toll and a higher number of prisoners in the face of the firepower and advanced infantry tactics of the BEF.

As in previous attacks, British, ANZAC and French forces achieved all of their admittedly limited goals, while artillery fire slaughtered the Germans who were packed into the front-line trenches. The heavy losses, including the capture of 5000 prisoners, prompted the

In the Battle of Broodseinde, the Germans made the mistake of concentrating their forces too far forward, resulting in the loss of 5000 prisoners to the British, including these men being marched to the rear by British guards.

German official history of the battle to refer to the fighting as 'the black day of October 4th', while a German regimental history described it as 'the worst day yet experienced in the war'. Ludendorff, who despaired for the future and saw Broodseinde as 'the culminating point of the crisis', worked to rush further reinforcements to the scene, even diverting some from as far away as Italy, and revamped the German defensive system yet again. Faced with heavy losses, 159,000 men by this stage in the battle, one faction within the German high command favoured a limited withdrawal to delay further British advance. Crown Prince Rupprecht, in command of the armies in the area, pronounced the situation to be so desperate that he advocated 'a comprehensive withdrawal' that would even cede the German-held ports of Ostend and Zeebrugge to British control.

As the Germans considered their options, Haig, impressed both with the relative ease of the advance and the seemingly demoralized state of many of the German prisoners, pressed Plumer quickly to follow up the victory in hopes that the next step in the process might seize the Passchendaele Ridge and force the Germans to give way. Ludendorff and the

Religion

Most soldiers on the Western Front were Christians, and to varying degrees turned to their religious faiths in time of war. On the home fronts, the Allies and Central Powers alike proclaimed that God was on their side and that their wars were righteous in nature. Religious figures in every nation did their best to place the war in terms of a religious crusade, perhaps best exemplified by the fiery sermons of evangelist Billy Sunday in the United States who compared German soldiers to a 'great pack of wolfish Huns whose fangs drip with blood and gore', and proclaimed the war to be a contest that pitted, 'Germany against America, hell against heaven'. Military forces provided chaplains to minister to the religious needs of their soldiers, and while the French only had one chaplain per 12,000 men, most nations had considerably more. Many fighting men indeed turned to religion for solace during wartime, and even believed certain wartime religious myths, including that angels guided British efforts in the Battle of Mons. Some other soldiers, though, were more hard-bitten. On one occasion, a chaplain asked a group of British veterans if they were

The famous evangelist Billy Sunday, who used his anti-German sermons to whip American crowds into a fervour of support for the war effort.

off to fight 'God's war'. The weary soldiers did not reply, prompting the chaplain to respond, 'Don't you believe in God's war?' One soldier looked at the chaplain and replied, 'Sir, hadn't you better keep your poor friend out of this bloody mess?'

Germans were becoming increasingly desperate, and perhaps Haig's overoptimistic hopes were not that far from the mark. The Australian official historian of the war later commented:

'For the first time in years, at noon on 4 October on the heights east of Ypres, British troops on the Western Front stood face to face with the possibility of decisive success … Let the student … ask himself "In view of the results of three step-by-step blows all successful, what will be the result of three more in the next fortnight?"'

BATTLES IN THE MUD – PASSCHENDAELE

While the Germans reeled and Haig urged Plumer forwards yet again, the conditions that made Plumer's successes possible in the first place began to evaporate. After the victory of 4 October, the rains returned to Flanders with a vengeance. Much of the area was very low lying and composed of reclaimed swampland, which relied on a complicated drainage system. The incessant shelling that had guarded the BEF's advances, though, had battered the landscape beyond repair. Shell-holes filled with water, and the countryside transformed into a sea of nearly bottomless, oozing mud. It is a common myth that Haig should have foreseen such weather and horrific battlefield conditions. However, Haig could not have known that autumn, which often heralded the onset of fine weather in Flanders, in 1917, was going to be one of the wettest on record. He wanted to keep the pressure on the reeling Germans, and hoped that the rain would stop. It did not.

In addition to the rains, Plumer's tactics had been complicated by their very success. Each battle required painstaking planning, and each leap forward required

Crowded into the confines of a sheltered area, Australian troops enjoy some of the last fine weather before the onset of rain in early October transformed the battlefields of Flanders into a sea of mud.

a difficult reshuffling of artillery. It was a complex dance of war. If Plumer waited too long to launch his next limited assault, the Germans would have more time to prepare. If he launched his next assault too quickly, the all-important artillery cover would not be adequate. Haig scheduled the next assault to take place on 9 October, which would have given Plumer enough time under normal circumstances. However, the rains and mud made moving artillery forward difficult in the extreme. Engineers had to create plank roads across the mud, which the Germans often shelled, while men and horses muscled the artillery forward one gun at a time. As it turns out, communications in the Ypres Salient had been showing strain even before 4 October; with the coming of the rains they had broken down.

The infantry also had a devilish time assembling in the waterlogged trenches to play their part in what would become known as the Battle of Poelcappelle. With agonizing slowness and great effort, soldiers made their way to their jumping-off points by

traversing slick, narrow duckboard paths atop the mud. One soldier recalled:

'It was an absolute nightmare. Often we would have to stop and wait for up to half an hour, because all the time the duckboards were being blown up and men being blown off the track or simply slipping off. … We were loaded like Christmas trees, so of course an explosion nearby or just the slightest thing would knock a man off balance and he would go off the track and right down into the muck.'

Many infantrymen did not reach their attack positions in time, while others found themselves exhausted by their exertions even before the attack began.

As the Allies moved forward on 9 October, it quickly became apparent that the artillery preparation had been spotty at best and had failed to silence either the German machine guns or artillery. With the failure of Plumer's trademark careful preparations, the infantry paid the price. A private in the Lancashire Regiment recorded:

'As dawn approached I could see the faint outline of a ridge about four or five hundred yards in front, and we then left the duckboards and moved to the white tape fastened to iron stakes. It was knee-deep in slush, and then I heard the sound of a heavy gun firing and immediately our barrage started; but we had not then arrived at the jumping-off point. Heavy German shells were already falling amongst us and shrapnel was flying all over the place. There were shouts and screams and men falling all around. The attack that should have started never got off the ground.'

The advancing infantry moved very slowly over swollen streams and waterlogged terrain, and quickly lost touch with the already ineffective covering barrage. German defenders, often behind intact barbed-wire entanglements and occupying concrete pillboxes, took a heavy toll on the advancing British and ANZAC forces. On most parts of the front, Second and Fifth Army failed to reach even their first objective, while on the right flank units that had lost touch with the barrage were forced back into their own trenches. Only in the north of the line, where the landscape had been less damaged by shellfire, did British and French forces make any significant advance from their startlines.

Unperturbed by the setback, both Haig and Plumer advocated a renewal of the offensive in three days' time. Preparations, though, still proved quite difficult, which again negated the advantage that the British had enjoyed in Plumer's previous successful assaults. Oddly enough, among the British senior command leadership, it was only a somewhat chastened Gough who counselled caution and a postponing of the attack to allow time for more

With its delicate drainage system shattered, the ground around Ypres became a wilderness of water-filled shell-holes, mud and duckboard tracks, across which men passed only with the greatest difficulty under constant enemy fire.

thorough artillery work. After consultation with his subordinates, though, Plumer decided to go ahead with the First Battle of Passchendaele.

Under a leaden sky and continuous rainfall, at dawn on 12 October, Allied forces advanced once again into the sea of mud. The artillery had not been able to move further forwards, and the mud had rendered many existing firing platforms unstable. Additionally, many high-explosive shells sank into the mud upon impact, lessening their effect. Exhausted after having spent the night either in transit or mired in their own muddy trenches, the infantry again quickly lost touch with the creeping barrage, and their advance floundered with high casualties before undamaged German defensive works. Plumer had hoped that his forces would proceed through a series of three limited objectives and seize the village of Passchendaele. Instead, only on the left flank did XIV Corps even achieve its first objectives for the day. At

other points of the line isolated infantry formations, fighting with great gallantry, moved into the German trench systems, only to be cut off and destroyed. Passchendaele had not fallen, the Germans had not broken, and the British offensive had once again bogged down. The air of futility that had surrounded Gough's attacks in August had returned.

Haig had rescued his failed offensive by replacing Gough with Plumer. After the heady days of September and early October, Haig had just reason for optimism. For this reason, he and Plumer can perhaps be forgiven their mistakes at Poelcappelle and First Passchendaele. The Germans by their own admission were reeling, the rain had to end soon and there seemed to be a real chance that a continued series of victories in quick succession could have strategic results. Weather and the

'I stood up and looked over the front of my hole. There was just a dreary waste of mud and water, no relic of civilization, only shell holes. … And everywhere were bodies, English and German, in all stages of decomposition.'

Lieutenant Edwin Campion Vaughan

realities of attempting to sustain an advance in World War I, though, had conspired to wreck Haig's planning. The offensive had reached its logical conclusion. Had the attacks ended at this point, Third Ypres might be remembered as a battle in which Haig had learned valuable lessons of command and in which the BEF had perfected the art of limited advance, only to have the elements deny what might have been an even

Two German soldiers converse at the bottom of a massive shell-hole, demonstrating the destructive force of firepower on the Western Front. Aerial photography of the battlefield of Third Ypres revealed over a million shell-holes in only two and a half square kilometres (one square mile).

greater victory. Instead, Haig chose to prolong the fighting, and Third Ypres would become known as Passchendaele for its final phase and will always be remembered only for mud and futility.

Haig, as it turned out, had come to the conclusion that the German lines in Flanders would hold, and instead chose to continue offensive operations there for other reasons. First he wanted to seize Passchendaele Ridge, both to give British forces a better defensive position and to allow them to move on to the high ground and exit the morass of mud in the valley below. Haig also had already begun to consider an offensive involving hundreds of tanks near Cambrai, and hoped that by keeping German attention squarely fixed on Flanders operations at Cambrai would achieve surprise. Most revealingly, perhaps, Haig wanted to seize Passchendaele to use it as a jumping-off point for further offensive operations in Flanders during 1918.

Planning a strictly limited advance, Plumer and Haig entrusted the assault on Passchendaele to the Canadian Corps, under the command of General

British troops pass the bloated bodies of dead horses and the wreckage of wagons at the apex of the Ypres Salient, known as 'Hellfire Corner', one of the most dangerous areas on the entire Western Front. The Germans targeted the crossroads to disrupt the flow of supplies and men to the front lines.

Arthur Currie, which moved in as fresh reinforcements to replace II ANZAC Corps. Although he was not happy with the task, Currie agreed that the seizure of Passchendaele was possible, given time for better preparations than those at Poelcappelle and First Passchendaele. Plumer and Haig assented to Currie's request for extra time to ready for the assault, and in turn the Canadian commander forecast that he would be able to take the ridge at a cost of 16,000 casualties. The Canadians, led by their chief engineer General W.B. Lindsay, worked feverishly to improve communications and logistic support in the area of attack and wrestled artillery pieces forward into firing position amid a break in the weather. The Canadians also built a plank road almost all of the way to the front line, enabling them to bring forward ammunition and supplies.

Mud

In the public imagination, the Third Battle of Ypres became known, in the main, for its final phase, in which British and Canadian soldiers struggled through a sea of endless mud toward their final goals. Experiencing the last days of the battle first-hand, Private A.V. Conn, recalled:

'"Mud": we slept in it, ate in it. It stretched for miles, a sea of stinking mud. The dead buried themselves in it. The wounded died in it. Men slithered around the lips of huge shell craters filled with mud & water. My first trip to this awful place was ... [at night]. For it was at night that men crept out of their holes at Passchendaele like rats. ... Each side of the [duckboard] track lie the debris of war. ... Dead mules. Their intestines spewed out like long coils of piping. Here an arm & a leg. It was a nightmare journey. ... Finally dawn broke, a hopeless dawn. Shell-holes and mud. Round about rifles with fixed bayonets stuck in the mud marking the places where men had died & been sucked down.'

Currie was thorough in his preparations, though even after two weeks of effort the Canadians were only able to utilize 60 per cent of their artillery, and planned to seize Passchendaele in four short, very limited assaults each of only 460m (500 yards) in depth. The steps, augmented by attacks by Fifth Army on the left flank, were to be separated by six days to prepare for the next forward move. Attacks were to be guarded by a creeping barrage of 640m (700 yards) in depth that advanced 90m (100 yards) every eight minutes.

The offensive, known as the Second Battle of Passchendaele, began at dawn on 26 October once again under the cover of an effective barrage. On the gently sloping ground of the Passchendaele Ridge, the Canadians achieved all of their goals, utilizing grenades to subdue the remaining German pillboxes in the area of advance. On the left flank, though, Gough's Fifth Army was not so lucky. Advancing

through the lowest territory in the region, some of the men of the 58th and the 63rd divisions sank in the mud up to their shoulders. Losing 2000 casualties, Gough's men achieved virtually no gains amid some of the worst conditions of the entire war.

Private A.V. Conn took part in, and was wounded during, this stage of the offensive. He recorded his experiences in his memoir:

'I just raised the bottle [of rum] to my lips when I felt a terrific blow on my right arm. I never heard the shell burst, but it was a 5.9 which had dropped very near our shell-hole. My mate who had taken my place [as lookout] fell back into the shell-hole; his head was shattered & cracked right open; he fell past us into the water in the bottom of the shell-hole. ... I stared stupidly at my arm; the jagged pieces of white bone were poking through a great gash in my forearm; my wrist was open & the blood was welling through & down my side; also there [was] a large wound on my right shoulder. ... They always said that you never heard the shell that was going to hit you.'

Conn then had to make his way to the dressing station:

'I am not very good at this kind of thing – real writers could do all this so much better. ... You know we lost a quarter of a million men in this sector; many thousands of them were unidentified. The dead buried themselves at Passchendaele, the mud sucked them down deeper & deeper. ... It was daylight when we started back & the things that were mercifully hidden by the darkness of night were now revealed to us in the light of day. All had their story to tell, – men who had struggled back only to give up & die when their strength failed them. Many had been pushed off the track to the sides to sink partly in the mud. There were mules & horses whose very intestines were spewing out of their swollen bloated bellies. The dead, their yellow teeth bared in ghastly grins, friend & foe alike were all clothed in the same filthy mud.'

After four days, amid yet another downpour, Canadian and British forces advanced again on 30 October and achieved similar results, the Canadians reaching their final objective and inching farther up the slope towards Passchendaele while the affiliated units of the Fifth Army on the left remained mired in

the morass and made no progress. As a result of the impassable conditions on the left flank, Haig and Plumer decided that the final push on the village of Passchendaele would fall to the Canadians alone.

On 6 November, the 1st Canadian Division, attacking from the southeast, and the 2nd Canadian Division, attacking from the south, converged on Passchendaele. Having thoroughly practised the varied elements of their short assault and operating under the cover of a withering artillery barrage, the Canadians struggled through the sucking mud and seized their final objectives and most of the village. On 10 November, the Canadians captured the remainder of Passchendaele and much of the rest of the ridge. At this point Haig called the offensive to a close.

The watery desolation that formed the battlefield at Passchendaele made forward movement almost impossible, while living conditions for the combatants became nearly unbearable. The battle has come to be seen as a byword for the suffering of the ordinary soldier on the Western Front.

The results of the final stage of the Third Battle of Ypres were decidedly mixed. Often obscured by the conditions of the battlefield is the fact that Currie and the Canadians had achieved their admittedly limited goals, actually suffering fewer than the projected 16,000 casualties in the process. Even in the worst of conditions, thorough artillery and infantry preparations had led to effective limited gains. However, the question remains: were the gains, no matter how effectively and bravely won, worth the

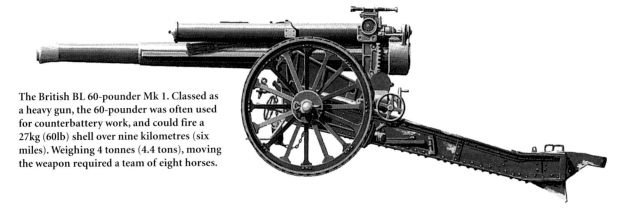

The British BL 60-pounder Mk 1. Classed as a heavy gun, the 60-pounder was often used for counterbattery work, and could fire a 27kg (60lb) shell over nine kilometres (six miles). Weighing 4 tonnes (4.4 tons), moving the weapon required a team of eight horses.

British forces traverse the tortured remains of the Menin Road, which, in Haig's initial plan, was to have been the road to victory in Flanders. The Menin Gate, at the entrance to Ypres, is now a major memorial to the missing.

terrible cost? The conditions of the advance brought the question into even sharper focus and were described by a British gunner:

'The conditions are awful, beyond description, nothing we've had yet has come up to it, the whole trouble is the weather which daily gets worse. One's admiration goes out to the infantry who attack and gain ground under these conditions. Had I a descriptive pen I could picture to you the squalor and wretchedness of it all and through it the wonder of the men who carry on. Figure to yourself desolate wilderness of water-filled shell craters, and crater after crater whose lips form narrow peninsulas along which one can at best pick but a slow and precarious way. Here a shattered tree trunk, there a wrecked "pillbox", sole remaining evidence that this was once a human and inhabited land. Dante would never have condemned lost souls to wander in so terrible a purgatory. Here a shattered wagon, there a gun mired to the muzzle in mud which grips like glue, even the birds and rats have forsaken so unnatural a spot. Mile after mile of the same unending dreariness, landmarks are
gone, of whole villages hardly a pile of bricks amongst the mud marks the site. You see it best under a leaden sky with a chill drizzle falling, each hour an eternity, each dragging step a nightmare. How weirdly it recalls some half-formed horror of childish nightmare.'

ASSESSMENTS OF THIRD YPRES

The Third Battle of Ypres, along with the Somme, has gone down in history as the very symbol of the futility of the British effort on the Western Front and has been the primary fuel of the argument that the BEF was an army of lions led by donkeys. On the surface the outcome of Third Ypres indeed closely mirrors that of the Somme: at a cost of 250,000 casualties the BEF had failed even to gain the final objectives that Gough had set for the first day of the campaign. However, coming to terms with the place of Third Ypres in history, even after the passage of 90 years, remains difficult. After the close of the conflict military personnel on both sides viewed the Flanders campaign as a hard-fought victory that was of central importance to the eventual winning of the war by the Allies. General Hermann von Kuhl, Chief of Staff to Crown Prince Rupprecht during the battle, remarked in his memoirs that Third Ypres had greatly depleted German reserves:

'On this point Field Marshal Haig has been quite right: if he did not actually break through the German front, the Flanders battle consumed the German strength to such a degree that the harm done could no longer be repaired. The sharp edge of the German sword had become jagged.'

Air Marshal Hugh Trenchard took his assessment of the battle even further during World War II:

'Tactically it was a failure, but strategically it was a success, and a brilliant success – in fact, it saved the world.

'There is not the slightest doubt, in my opinion, that France would have gone out of the war if Haig had not fought Passchendaele, like they did in 1940 in this war, and had France gone out of the war I feel, as all our manpower was in France, we should have been bound to collapse, or, at any rate, it would have lengthened the war for years.'

In truth, the verdict of Third Ypres lies somewhere between the two reactive extremes. It was not simply a battle of mud and futility. On the other hand it was also not the battle that saved the world. The campaign had done great service by not allowing the Germans to attack the beleaguered French. The Germans, who lost a total of 260,000 men in the battle, were much less better able to replace their losses than the Allies, which contributed to the ultimate German inability to achieve victory in their offensives of 1918 and to the

Canadian soldiers (and at least one sullen German prisoner) gather near an aid station after having survived the fighting at Passchendaele. The Canadians were highly rated for their fighting skills after their success at Vimy Ridge.

final German collapse by the end of that year. It was a battle, though, that also demonstrated the complexities of a BEF that was undergoing dramatic change from an amateur force to a fully professional military. The first stage of the battle demonstrated deep flaws in the command structure of the BEF. Under Plumer, British and Empire forces proved that they had learned much and improved since the Somme and were able to defeat the most powerful German defensive systems in bite-and-hold offensives.

The final stage of the battle, though the Canadians once again demonstrated their bravery, proved disastrous. Hoping for great results, Haig had rushed the offensive, negating many of the methodical preparations that had made victory possible, and pressed on through horrific conditions toward questionable goals for dubious reasons. Haig had made mistakes at the Somme, but his errors there

A British Great War cemetery. The Commonwealth War Graves Commission determined to inter the dead near to where they had fallen, and that there should be no distinction made on account of rank, race or creed.

The final advances during the Third Battle of Ypres. This map shows the final assaults of the campaign, culminating in the seizure of the village and ridge of Passchendaele itself by the Canadian Corps from 6 to 10 November. Haig called off the offensive once Passchendaele was secured.

could be forgiven since it was his first major battle as commander of the BEF. After Passchendaele, though, Haig would receive no such historical absolution. His failure to halt the battle after it had run its course, allowing the fighting to grind down and stall in the mud, would forever overshadow the hopeful aspects of change indicated by Plumer's limited gains during September and October. The BEF was evolving into a professional military capable of decisive victory in 1918. However, Haig's reputation would remain mired in the mud of Flanders. In 1935 an article in the *News Chronicle* said in relation to Haig's reputation, 'Why has not Haig been recognized as one of England's great generals? Why, as a national figure, did he count for less than Lord Roberts, whose wars were picnics by comparison? The answer may be given in one word – Passchendaele.'

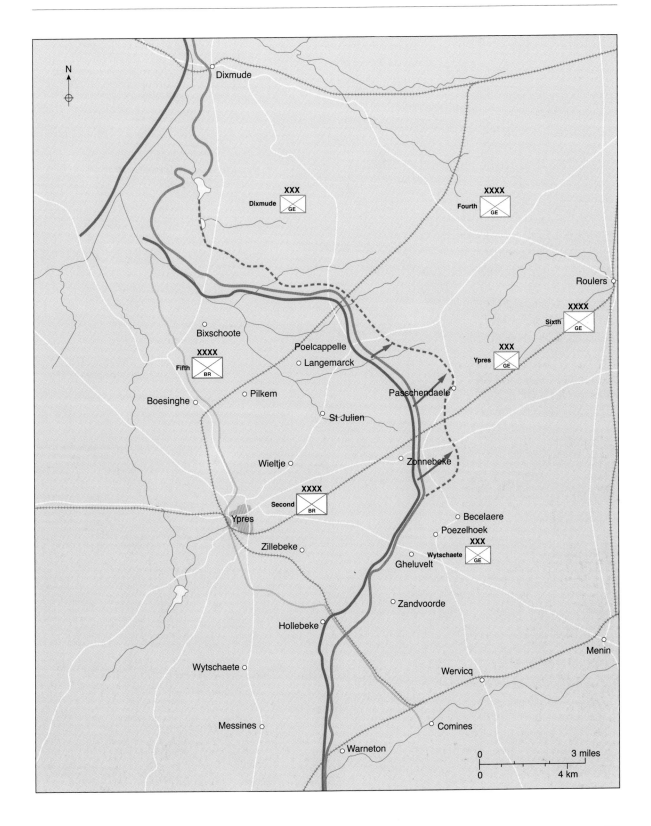

CHAPTER 4

Cambrai and the Americans

The Battle of Cambrai saw the first massed use of armour in warfare, while both British and German tactical advances evidenced at Cambrai heralded a sea change in modern conflict. Even as the combatant nations of Europe fought to yet another costly draw, though, the United States began to marshal its military might and stood ready to change the world.

The fitful progress of the Third Battle of Ypres further strained the already damaged relations between Haig and Lloyd George. The War Policy Committee had only approved Haig's offensive with great reluctance and against the wishes of the Prime Minister. Advances in tactics and attriting German military strength seemed only pyrrhic victories to the embattled Lloyd George, who in turn became less and less patient with Haig, Robertson and the command structure of the BEF. As the prospects for strategic victory in Flanders dwindled and casualties mounted, the War Policy Committee brought considerable criticism to bear on Robertson

British troops ready for battle. As 1917 drew to a close, new technologies and tactics altered the balance of the battlefield in World War I, once again bringing aggressive infantry tactics to the fore.

German Albatross DVa fighter plane. Produced in late 1917 as an answer to the Allied Sopwith Pup and SE 5, the Albatross DVa was widely used, but arguably still outclassed by the Allied fighters.

and Haig, focusing on the overly optimistic projections that had preceded the offensive, and Lloyd George again spoke in favour of shifting offensive action away from the Western Front. In a critical failure of political will, though, instead of ending the Flanders campaign, as was its right, the War Policy Committee contented itself with sniping at Haig's operation from the sideline. In the words of historians Robin Prior and Trevor Wilson:

'None of Lloyd George or Smuts or Curzon or Milner or Bonar Law seemed to be noticing that the Flanders campaign was his responsibility. It would continue not another day if they denied it authorization. … The most the nation's civilian rulers might do regarding it [Third Ypres] *was wring their hands and look about for additional military advisors to offer a "second opinion." … So as the rain fell in Flanders and thousands of Haig's soldiers prepared to struggle through mud to their doom, the Prime Minister who was proclaiming the futility of this undertaking failed to raise a finger to stop it.'*

PLANNING FOR CAMBRAI

There did, however, remain a military postscript to the Third Battle of Ypres. Proponents of the use of the tank had long advocated using armour en masse against German lines, instead of only in a piecemeal fashion as adjuncts to infantry. Although Haig was a chief proponent of the new weapons system, tanks had remained unreliable, few in number and of only marginal use in the great trench battles of 1917. As

the year continued and improved models of the tank appeared, though, Brigadier-General Hugh Elles, the Tank Corps commandant, and his senior staff officer Colonel J.F.C. Fuller, began, with renewed vigour, to press for an opportunity to use tanks in large numbers over suitable terrain. At the same time, General Julian Byng, in command of Third Army, developed a proposal for an offensive in the area of Cambrai, where German defences were particularly weak. Although he was intrigued by both ideas, Haig initially rejected them because the ongoing fighting around Ypres meant that reserve forces were in short supply. By mid-October, as the offensive in Flanders was winding down, though, the planning of the Tank Corps and Third Army had coalesced into a single proposal for a mixed tank and infantry assault on Cambrai. Although reserves were scarce, Haig realized that the conclusion to Third Ypres was at hand, and understood the need for a victory to mollify the politicians in London, and thus gave Byng's plan his blessing.

With little time to shift tanks from all over the British front to Cambrai, the Tank Corps worked feverishly to prepare for the start date of the attack. After practising tank–infantry cooperation, the tanks had to be entrained, transported to the new front and detrained, all in the greatest secrecy and only at night. From the railheads the tanks were driven, also at night, to assembly areas secreted away in the Havrincourt Wood on the front of IV Corps to await the attack.

While logisticians went about gathering the tanks, ammunition and supporting arms, the tacticians at Tank Corps headquarters had to solve a number of technical difficulties before the opening of the offensive. The most critical problem was the fact that the line to be assaulted included the first three trenches of the main Hindenburg Line, which were too wide for the tanks to cross. After trial and error, the Tank Corps decided that each tank should carry a massive, compressed bundle of sticks known as a 'fascine'. Triggering a mechanism inside the tank released the bundle of sticks, blocking the trench and creating a

bridge for the tank to cross. Central Workshops assembled 21,000 of the bundles, utilizing a thousand Chinese labour troops for the purpose. The fascines were then bound by chains and compressed by 18 specially designed tanks, which, according to a history of the Tank Corps, '... acted in pairs pulling in opposite directions at steel chains which had previously been wound around the bundles. ... So great was the

Although tanks, like this one pictured in training, were few in number and mechanically unreliable in their debut in the Battle of the Somme, Haig had seen their potential and remained a proponent of the new weapons system.

pressure thus exerted that months afterwards, an infantryman in search of firewood, who found one of these fascines and gaily filed through its binding chain, was killed by the sudden springing open of the bundle.'

The Tank Corps also worked to overcome the endemic supply and mechanical difficulties that had plagued all previous use of tanks in battle. For the offensive, a total of 98 supply tanks, some towing sleds heaped with petrol, oil and ammunition, supported the 378 fighting tanks, while only 54 tanks were held in reserve.

Although Cambrai is best known as the first major tactical use of the tank in battle, the attention lavished on the role of armour in the campaign has served to mask a more significant innovation in artillery technique. In previous battles, to get the range of their

targets gunners had to fire several rounds and then observe and adjust fire, resulting in the BEF sacrificing surprise in favour of punishing, cumbersome preparatory artillery barrages. However, on-the-job training, more accurate mapping, better use of meteorological data and efficient calibration of the guns themselves had resulted in an artillery technique known as 'silent registration'. Additionally, gunners had also become more familiar with the effects of barrel wear on the flight of shells, while the shells themselves were of more uniform quality.

Their caterpillar tracks notwithstanding, World War I tanks, like the one in this photograph, often had difficulty in crossing enemy trenches, resulting in the plan to use bundled sticks, known as fascines, to cross enemy trenches in the Battle of Cambrai.

The Tank

The tactical riddle posed by the trench deadlock led to a number of technological innovations designed to rekindle the power of the offensive, the most important of which was the British development of the tank. Early experiments with armoured tractors, propelled by caterpillar treads, though, were failures. With the support of Winston Churchill, however, in 1915 the Admiralty Landships Committee took over the task of designing a weapon capable of breaking through trenches, but got nowhere until Ernest Swinton joined the design team. Hoping to maintain secrecy, the builders of the new vehicle called it a water carrier, or tank. By 1916, tests of the first lozenge-shaped prototype went so well that the War Office ordered a hundred of what became known as the Mark I tank. The armoured vehicle contained a 105hp Daimler engine that produced a maximum speed of six kilometres per hour (3.7mph) and a range of 35km (22 miles), and carried a crew of four men. Half of the Mark Is, dubbed 'males', sported 6-pounder naval guns mounted in turrets on either side of the vehicle, while, the other Mark Is, dubbed 'females', carried four side-mounted Vickers machine guns. The success of the few Mark Is that saw action at the Somme prompted

The tank was not a war-winning weapon in World War I. It would require inter-war technological advances to bring the tank into its own.

Douglas Haig to order a thousand more such vehicles, which were to prove the success of the concept at the Battle of Cambrai. As the war progressed, tank design modernized, culminating in the more reliable and powerful British Mark V tank, which saw service in great numbers in the Battle of Amiens and the Hundred Days. Improvements notwithstanding, even in 1918 tanks remained too slow and unreliable to be a truly war-winning weapon.

Refinements in aerial photography also helped accurately to locate enemy defences, while techniques known as flash spotting and sound ranging fixed enemy gun positions.

For the first time, then, British guns could ensure accurate fire on German positions without sacrificing surprise to pre-registration. Confident in the newfound abilities of the British artillery, Byng chose to forego a preliminary bombardment. However, he also surprisingly decided not to employ a creeping barrage, which had become standard practice in the BEF. Instead, Byng planned for the tanks to crush the barbed wire and to keep the Germans cowering in their trenches rather than manning their defensive positions. To carry out their vital role, replacing both

a preparatory and a creeping barrage, the tanks would advance in the van of the offensive, something that they had not done since the Somme over a year before.

THE BATTLE OF CAMBRAI

At dawn on 20 November, the five infantry divisions and the tanks of the Third Army's III and IV corps moved forward, supported by 1003 artillery pieces and the Royal Flying Corps acting in a ground-attack role. Due to Byng's careful preparations, the offensive caught the two defending German divisions and their supporting 150 artillery pieces totally by surprise, a far cry from the opening days at the Somme and Third Ypres. The tanks led the assault and quickly gained the German front lines; unheralded by a preliminary

barrage and emerging from under the cover of a thick mist and a smoke screen, the tanks suddenly burst upon the German defenders, sowing fear and chaos. One British soldier recalled the stunning effects of the tanks, 'The German outposts … were overrun in an instant. The triple belts of wire were crossed as if they had been beds of nettles. …The defenders of the front trench … saw the leading tanks almost upon them … [and] were running panic stricken, casting away arms and equipment.'

The attack quickly rumbled through the first and second defensive networks of the vaunted Hindenburg Line, and, in most places along the 10km (six-mile) front, Third Army seized all of its intended objectives, advancing up to eight kilometres (five miles), something that had not been achieved in four months of fighting at Third Ypres. The results,

Although many Germans were initially terrified by the sight of tanks, the German high command soon developed anti-tank weaponry and tactics that took a heavy toll on the slow moving machines, including these tanks that have been captured by German forces.

though, were far from perfect. On the left flank, near Flesquières village, the 51st (Highland) Division failed to achieve a meaningful advance against a stubborn German defence, which included the use of anti-tank guns. As a result of the check, Third Army was unable to seize the dominating high ground of Bourlon Wood. Making matters worse, the tanks suffered heavy losses on the first day of the offensive. Several were lost to German fire and mechanical malfunctions, but in many instances crews were simply incapacitated by the sheer physical effort of operating the tanks due to high interior temperatures and carbon monoxide poisoning. Lacking a method of communication, by the end of the day even the 297 operational tanks that remained had lost all semblance of tactical unit cohesion.

To this point the Battle of Cambrai was another example of British tactical proficiency, utilizing startlingly new techniques to achieve nearly unheard of gains, including the capture of more than 4000 prisoners at slight cost. While Haig and Byng had realized that a limited advance at Cambrai would reap an attritional advantage, they had also hoped for greater things, and, as a result, the cavalry was on hand

British gains during the first stage of the Battle of Cambrai, gains so great that church bells in England pealed for the first time since the beginning of the war. Subsequent German counterattacks retook much of the captured ground.

in an attempt to exploit any wider success. Hampered by the approach of darkness, the cavalry did move forward, but, after achieving initial gains, failed to pierce the final lines of German resistance. Haig's plan had arguably succeeded, for the Third Army had achieved an almost complete breakthrough of the vaunted Hindenburg Line. However, both tanks and the cavalry had failed as weapons of exploitation and, even though the BEF had attained tactical mastery, the defensive remained dominant, and it proved impossible to maintain the momentum of battle and rupture the German lines.

If there had ever been a chance to achieve a greater success, it had passed with the close of the first day of the Battle of Cambrai. With no other available reserves, weakened as the BEF was from Third Ypres, there

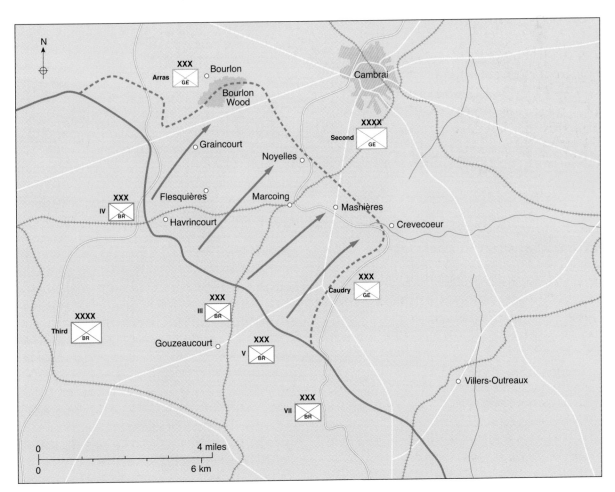

Some of the 4000 German prisoners taken during the quick British advance at Cambrai. The combination of the new artillery tactics and the shock value of the armoured assault led to the German line collapsing in a number of places.

remained little Haig could do to further his initial victory. The preconditions that had enabled Third Army to achieve its stunning success had evaporated: surprise was gone, the tanks, fewer and fewer in number, had lost their unit cohesion, artillery fire as usual dwindled in its effectiveness as the gunners laboriously wrestled their pieces forwards, and the

> 'With the help of their tanks, the enemy broke through our series of obstacles and positions which had been entirely undamaged. … At the end of the year, therefore, a breach in our line appeared to be a certainty.'
>
> Paul von Hindenburg, 19 November 1917

units engaged in the battle were under strength and tired, while the Germans rushed both infantry and artillery reserves to the area. The check of the initial advance around Flesquières, though, had resulted in the British gains being limited to a pronounced salient. In an effort to straighten the lines of Third Army and

make the salient less vulnerable, Haig and Byng pressed the attack for a further seven days, in an attempt to capture Bourlon Ridge.

By 27 November, IV Corps of Third Army succeeded in taking most of the ridge in a series of limited, attritional struggles, and the offensive ground to a halt while the surviving tanks exited the area to regroup. Although the fighting around Bourlon Ridge had been difficult, Third Army had achieved a major tactical success and began to settle into its new defensive lines for the winter. The Battle of Cambrai, such a quick advance when compared to Third Ypres, had seemingly salvaged Haig's reputation. In Britain there had been great celebration of the victory, with the ringing of church bells for the first time since the onset of the war. However, the celebration was premature, for Ludendorff, though he had been caused great anxiety by the initial British gains, believed that the newly formed British salient at Cambrai was the perfect place to test new German operational techniques and gathered reinforcements for a massive counterattack.

It was now the turn of the British Third Army to be surprised, as the tired men of III and IV corps faced an attack by 25 fresh German divisions. Only IV Corps in the northern part of the salient noticed the German preparations and made ready, while forces in the remainder of the salient retained an offensive posture. In some ways the British had advanced too far too fast, and were now to pay the price. The failure first to notice and then to prepare for the onslaught must fall in part to Byng, but mainly resides with Haig, who later took full responsibility for the resulting setback. On 30 November, the Germans struck, utilizing methods of attack similar to those employed by the

BEF, which would be perfected and become familiar in their Spring Offensives of 1918, including a short, precise artillery barrage, infiltration tactics (dubbed stormtroop tactics) and low-flying aircraft in a ground-attack role. In the north, where IV Corps had anticipated the attack, the Germans faced intense defensive artillery fire and made scant gains. In the south, though, the attackers caught III and VII corps off guard and pushed the British back beyond their start point of the Cambrai offensive. Tanks of the 2nd Tank Brigade, which had been withdrawn from the salient but were not too far distant from the battlefield, returned to the fighting and helped check the German advance.

Ludendorff and the Germans now faced the tactical reality that bedevilled all Allied efforts to advance on the Western Front, for the British rushed reinforcements to the scene even as the Germans outstripped their artillery support and the attack lost its forward momentum. By 7 December, the Battle of Cambrai drew to a close, with both sides having gained a roughly equal amount of territory each at a cost of 50,000 casualties. Although the inconclusive battle was small when compared to the Somme or Third Ypres, it was their equal in importance. The innovative tactics of both the BEF and the Germans – modern, all-arms tactics – presaged a revolution in modern warfare and the resurgence of the offensive.

Haig's great victory had turned, at best, into a costly draw, which nearly brought his career crashing down

As demonstrated in this photograph, German prisoners were often enlisted to aid British medics and stretcher-bearers in the clearing of wounded from the battlefield. In this case a winch has been used to haul a stretcher out of a dugout.

in a situation that closely resembled that of Nivelle in the wake of the failed attack on the Chemin des Dames. Still smarting over the meagre tangible results of Third Ypres, Lloyd George had at first been silenced by Haig's success at Cambrai. The German counterattack, though, convinced the Prime Minister of the futility of attempting to seek a military solution on the Western Front, and Lloyd George decided once again to find some way to wrest strategic control of the war from Haig and Robertson.

Complicating matters further, seismic events in the other theatres of World War I suddenly convinced

Haig, perhaps the ultimate optimist, that the initiative in the conflict had shifted. Even while the British and French had to send forces to the Italian Front in the wake of the Italian setback at Caporetto, the collapse of Russia enabled the Germans to begin to shift the preponderance of their military strength to the

Western Front. In a volte-face that stunned Lloyd George, Haig and Robertson, far from preaching imminent victory, urged the government to send all available troops to the Western Front to redress a forecast increasing imbalance in manpower. The shift in strategic fortunes galvanized Lloyd George to action, and a letter from Robertson served to warn Haig of the coming storm:

'His [Lloyd George's] *great argument is that you have for long said that the Germans are well on the down-grade in morale and numbers and that you advised attacking them though some 30 Divisions should come from Russia; and yet only a few Divisions have come, and you are hard put to it to hold your own! He claims that five Divisions* [that the government had directed sent] *to Italy and absence of necessary drafts are not sufficient to account for the Cambrai events, but that the latter are due to Charteris's error of judgment as to the numbers and efficiency of German troops.'*

As 1917 drew to a close, the military situation for the Allies was grim. With his forces battered, Haig faced a challenge to his military authority and the French were engaged in rebuilding their military strength, all while German forces gathered for a climactic offensive on the Western Front. Only the arrival of the Americans could once again redress the strategic balance.

THE UNITED STATES ENTERS THE WAR

When war swept across the European continent in 1914, the United States remained neutral, dominated by isolationism and content to let the old world sort out its own problems. As the war progressed and worsened, though, American President Woodrow Wilson became more and more interested in mediating an end to the conflict, while powerful economic and military forces nudged the United States towards support of the Allies. While the British imposition of a naval blockade on Germany was met

The Cunard liner *Lusitania*, which was torpedoed on 7 May 1915 by *U20* off the coast of southern Ireland , with the loss of 1198 lives, including 128 Americans. The attack caused the suspension of the U-boat campaign against merchant shipping until spring 1916.

by the United States with strong protest and remained a source of consternation throughout the war, the effects of the blockade tied American business ever closer to the economic fates of Britain and France. Cut off from trade with Germany, American exports to the Allied powers rose from 825 million dollars in 1917 to over three billion dollars in 1916, and by 1917, the Allied nations had borrowed over two billion dollars from American financial firms.

Unhappy with America's Allied-friendly form of neutrality, and smarting from British propaganda aimed at the United States that luridly portrayed German atrocities in occupied Belgium, the German Government decided to blockade Britain in turn through use of the submarine. Where the British blockade of Germany relied on surface ships that could intercept and seize suspect merchant vessels, German U-boats, which relied on stealth, enforced their blockade by sinking merchant vessels. On 7 May 1915, *U20* torpedoed the Cunard liner *Lusitania* with the loss of 1198 lives, including 128 Americans. Fearing that continued sinkings could cause a rupture

General John 'Black Jack' Pershing (centre) with Douglas Haig to his right and their respective staffs. Pershing was insistent on keeping the AEF a separate entity, and relations with his French and British allies were often fraught.

with the United States, the Germans eschewed further attacks on merchant shipping until spring 1916, when *U29* torpedoed the French passenger steamer *Sussex*, injuring several Americans. Bowing to public pressure, Wilson threatened to cut off diplomatic relations with Germany, which resulted in another cessation in the submarine war.

Although he still hoped to avoid open conflict with Germany, and ran as the peace candidate in the closely fought presidential election of 1916, Wilson did begin to take steps to prepare the United States for war. He signed into law the National Defense Act, which forecast increasing the strength of the US Army from 90,000 men to a force of over 200,000 and established a Council of National Defense to coordinate industry and resource allocation in the event of war. Wilson's desire to play the role of peacemaker and hopes of remaining neutral, though, were dealt a grievous blow with the German announcement in February 1917 of the resumption of unrestricted submarine warfare. The situation became critical with the interception of the Zimmerman Telegram, which proposed a German military alliance with Mexico in the event of war with the United States.

Amid a climate of public revulsion against Germany in the wake of the Zimmerman Telegram, on 12 March the *Algonquin* became the first American merchant ship lost to the German U-boat offensive, and three more torpedoings quickly followed. By 20 March, Wilson's cabinet agreed unanimously that the country had to enter the war on the side of the Allies and, on 2 April, Wilson went before Congress to request a declaration of war on Germany. In his speech, Wilson expressed a moralistic tone that would

both make him one of the most important leaders of the world and set him in opposition to his future Allies. Wilson proclaimed that American participation in the war would help make the world 'safe for democracy' and went on to promise that:

'… we shall fight for the things which we have always carried nearest to our hearts – for democracy, for the right of those who submit to authority to have a voice in their own Government, for the rights and liberties of small nations, for a universal dominion of right by such a concert of free peoples as shall bring peace and safety to all nations and make the world itself at last free.'

Although Congress debated the proposal for three days and neutralists spoke against American entry, there remained no hope for peace. On 6 April 1917, Congress approved Wilson's request and the United States was at war.

Race in the US

As America prepared for war, US industry required an influx of manpower, and black Americans answered the call. In what the *Chicago Defender* called the Great Northern Drive, between 350,000 and 500,000 blacks moved to the industrial cities of the north not only to escape segregation but also to take jobs where they could earn four times more than they had working as sharecroppers in the south. Not all northern cities, though, were accepting of the new migrants. When more than 10,000 black workers arrived in East St Louis, Illinois, angry whites accused them of stealing their jobs and of making the crime rate rise. On 1 July 1917 the tension boiled over as a mob of angry whites roamed the streets, clubbing down the blacks that were unlucky enough to cross their path, including women and children. The mob even seized a crippled black man and burned him alive. They then shot a black child and threw his body into a burning building. National Guardsmen, called out to halt the unrest, did little to stop the riots, which lasted for four days during which time more than 100 blacks died and more than half of the black population fled the city. As

Although American black soldiers fought for liberty and their nation, they found their segregated social standing little changed upon their return.

racial unrest throughout the nation grew, an African-American university professor, Kelly Miler, wrote to President Wilson about the role of black Americans in the war: 'The Negro, Mr. President, in this emergency will stand by you and the nation. Will you and the nation stand by the Negro?' Wilson never replied.

The Springfield rifle was the standard front-line weapon used by the US Army throughout World War I. It was actually a modified Mauser, which was first adopted in 1903 and remained in service until the Korean War. Its box magazine held five .30in rounds.

Initially it seemed that the Germans had been right not to fear the United States. The National Defense Act had yet to achieve its goals and, on 1 April, the US regular army consisted of only 5791 officers and 121,797 enlisted men. There were also 66,594 National Guardsmen under federal service, and 101,174 under state control. Broken in the main into smaller formations, there were as yet no coherent divisions in the US Army, which suffered from a severe and chronic shortage of weaponry and had no units of any kind that were ready for service in Europe. The army remained, in the earlier words of Secretary of War Henry Stimson, 'a profoundly peaceful army'. Facing

the gargantuan task of creating an armed force of millions almost from scratch, in May Wilson turned to General John 'Black Jack' Pershing to command the nascent American Expeditionary Force. Pershing had seen service in the campaign in Cuba in 1898, and, as America had lurched toward war, was one of the few officers in the US Army to command forces in battle, having led the chase for Mexican bandit Pancho Villa in 1916.

Seeking to provide Pershing with the necessary raw materials for war, Wilson signed the Selective Service Act into law on 18 May. Learning from problems that had occurred in America's only previous experience with conscription during the Civil War, the federal government left the draft in the hands of local civilian boards tasked with raising quotas of men from among 'their friends and neighbors'. On 5 June, all men between 21 and 31 filled out draft registration cards

The Zimmerman Telegram

The German Government and high command were acutely aware that the declaration of unrestricted submarine warfare in 1917 would bring the United States into World War I, and the German Foreign Secretary, Arthur Zimmerman, was determined to be ready for such an eventuality. On 19 January 1917, Zimmerman sent a telegram to Count von Bernstorff, the German ambassador in Washington DC, outlining a possible German–Mexican military alliance in which Mexico would attack and reconquer Texas, New Mexico and Arizona in the event of war with America. British intelligence, however, intercepted the telegram and, with a certain amount of glee, turned it over to

President Wilson, who sought confirmation of the authenticity of the telegram and its alliance offer. Unbelievably, Zimmerman himself confirmed that the contents of the telegram were genuine, which Wilson had reprinted in several newspapers. Already stunned by the German submarine campaign, the American public saw the Zimmerman Telegram as tantamount to a declaration of war – and demanded an American response. With strong isolationist tendencies and a large German minority, entering World War I on the side of the Allies was at best a difficult prospect in the United States, but one made into a near certainty by the Zimmerman Telegram.

that included all relevant personal information, plus any reasons why they should not be drafted. Then each candidate received a small green card bearing a number. On 20 July, Secretary of War Newton Baker donned a blindfold and reached into a jar full of tiny capsules, each of which contained a registration number. Surrounded by members of the press, Newton withdrew the first capsule with the number 258. The drawing went on until late the following morning to determine the selection of draft order to be transmitted to the local boards.

Although the war was fought for the domination of a distant continent, Americans answered the call to conflict in unprecedented numbers, eventually raising a military force of over three million and tipping the balance of the war. Many suffered chronic seasickness on the journey to France.

Across the nation, stars and celebrities turned out to speak at rallies and urged all citizens to play their part in the war. In New York City, famed evangelist Billy Sunday made impassioned pleas for God to 'strike down in his tracks' any man who did not register for the draft. 'If hell could be turned upside down,' he screamed, 'you would find stamped on its bottom, "Made in Germany!"' Sunday, though, need not have worried, for Americans, like their European brethren before them, rushed to the colours in a patriotic fervour. Even so, as a late comer to the war, the United States' level of manpower commitment to the war never compared to that of its European allies. By the end of the war, 24,234,021 American men had registered for the draft, and a total of 3,099,000 served in the military, or roughly three per cent of the population. In contrast during the war France called up 7,800,000 men, or one-fifth of the total population, while in Britain 5,704,416, or 10 per cent of the population, served.

With millions willing to serve, though, the United States had to create an infrastructure capable of housing, training, arming and commanding its massive new military. Shortages of everything from clothing to weaponry were severe; in 1917 the US military only possessed 400 light field guns, 150 heavy

artillery pieces and 1500 machine guns. The government quickly constructed 16 training camps, often staffed with instructors borrowed from the French or British military. Due to a critical shortage of trained officers, the military also created a variety of additional training programmes. Perhaps the most difficult challenge, though, was the conversion of American industry away from its chaotic and often cutthroat peacetime policies to controlled wartime production. In an effort to take control of the situation, the Council of National Defense created the War Industries Board, which eventually took control of all aspects of industrial production.

Although America was the mightiest industrial nation on the planet, it had come to the war too late fully to realize its massive potential power. While the United States provided mountains of raw materials, including iron and copper, the millions of American soldiers who served in Europe in the main utilized weaponry produced in Britain and France. Most Americans reached Europe aboard British or French

To the war-weary French, the arrival of American forces, no matter how ill trained, was a tonic, and resulted in spontaneous celebrations as American units marched through towns on the way to their training bases. British civilians also experienced a similar boost in morale.

ships, and were transported to the front in French trains or on French or British trucks. As an example of America's dependency in the area of military hardware, of the 3499 artillery pieces used in battle by the AEF, only 130 were American made. While US forces expended an estimated 8,116,000 artillery rounds in battle, only 8400 were American made.

AMALGAMATION AND THE AMERICAN EXPEDITIONARY FORCE

In 1917, though, the gathering of America's military might had only just begun, and projections of the numbers of troops that the United States would eventually send to France were cold comfort to the

'They looked larger than ordinary men; their tall, straight figures were in vivid contrast to the under-sized armies of pale recruits to which we had grown accustomed. … They seemed, as it were, Tommies in heaven.'

Vera Brittain on American soldiers, from *Testament of Youth*

battered Allies. The crisis was fast approaching as German troops poured westwards from conquered Russia. Pétain spoke for many when, upon meeting Pershing for the first time, he remarked concerning American entry into the conflict simply, 'I hope it is not too late.' Many British and French leaders agreed with Pétain's assessment, for even the most optimistic projections forecast that the AEF would not be able to play a meaningful role in the war until mid to late 1918, while more gloomy prognostications focused on 1919 or even 1920. The Germans, though, were going

to attack at the earliest opportunity in 1918, potentially achieving victory while the AEF was in its training camps or in troopships at sea.

Facing the prospect of their imminent destruction, the heavily taxed British and French understandably made it their top priority to ensure that American troops reached the Western Front as quickly as possible. Upon the American declaration of war, both Britain and France sent high-level political and military delegations to the United States. Fearing that it would take too long to raise, train and equip an independent AEF, both Allies proposed that the US send to Europe 500,000 to one million untrained men, who would then receive training and join already established British or French units. The European Allies hoped that through such an arrangement, dubbed amalgamation, American soldiers could have a more immediate impact on the outcome of the war. When the remainder of the AEF was finally ready for battle it could then reabsorb the amalgamated

As in the case of this US infantry unit, most American formations arrived in France with only rudimentary training and had to spend considerable time under the tutelage of a British or French training cadre.

Anti-German Reaction

After the American entry into World War I, the Committee on Public Information wasted little time in producing propaganda posters and literature designed to heighten public feeling against both German militarism and the 'Hun'.

As part of the patriotic war effort, then, Americans tried to rid their nation of nearly everything German. Americans no longer ate frankfurters or kept dachshunds as pets, instead they ate Liberty Sausages and cared for Liberty Dogs. All over the nation, schools stopped teaching German, and by 1918, almost half of the states had laws restricting the use of the German language or banning it altogether. Americans also questioned the loyalty of the eight million German-Americans in their midst, often accusing those of German ancestry with defeatism or of espionage. Mobs often took the law into their own hands, forcing their German-American neighbours to kiss the American flag or curse the German Kaiser to prove their allegiance. In the most extreme reported case, Robert Prager, a German-American who had been rejected for military service due to bad eyesight, was abducted by a mob and accused of spying. The mob, driven by drunkenness, wrapped Prager in the American flag and forced him to sing patriotic songs. Tiring of their sport, the members of the mob finally tied a rope around Prager's neck and hanged him from the nearest tree. Prager's last wish was to be buried in the flag of his adopted nation.

soldiers, who would in turn form the battle-hardened core of an otherwise untested military. The British even went one step further and requested permission to recruit soldiers in the United States for service in the British military.

On the advice of his cabinet, Wilson flatly rejected the amalgamation schemes. Military men, including Pershing, believed that American troops should not be placed under foreign commanders, while Wilson hoped that an independent AEF would give the United States a much stronger bargaining position at a post-war peace conference. Major-General Tasker Bliss summarized American fears in a letter to Secretary of War Newton Baker:

'When the war is over it may be a literal fact that the American flag will not have appeared anywhere on the line because our organizations will simply be part of battalions and regiments of the Entente Allies. We might have a million men there and no American army and no American commander. Speaking frankly, I have received the impression from the English and French officers that such is their deliberate desire. I do not believe our people will stand for it.'

Wilson, who favoured a less recriminatory 'peace without victory', looked on the war aims of Britain and France with distaste. Believing that both the Allies and Germany had been blinded by years of war, Wilson held the United States diplomatically aloof from the goals of the belligerents, even referring to

The Browning automatic rifle. Designed in response to the need for an American assault rifle on the Western Front, the Browning could fire 550 rounds per minute. The Browning only entered service on the Western Front in late 1918, too late to have a meaningful impact on the fighting.

Britain, France, Italy and Japan only as 'associated powers' in an attempt to solidify both America's freedom of action and power in any peace settlement. In line with his thinking, Wilson gave Pershing his final instructions before sending him off to France:

'*In military operations against the Imperial German Government you are directed to co-operate with the forces of the other countries employed against the enemy; but in so doing the underlying idea must be kept in view that the forces of the United States are separate and distinct components of the combined forces, the identity of which must be preserved. This fundamental rule is subject to such minor exceptions as particular circumstances or your judgment may approve. The action is confided in you and you will exercise full discretion in determining the manner of co-operation.*'

Denied their request for immediate aid, the French and British delegations asked that the Americans at least send a division, no matter how poorly trained, to

With the Allies' knowledge that the Germans were readying for an all-out attempt to achieve victory on the Western Front in 1918, training US personnel was a race against time in an effort to have American forces reach the front lines before it was too late.

France to show the flag and raise Allied morale. Assenting to the request, Pershing directed the dispatch of the American 1st Division. Supposedly a regular division, the 1st actually had been gutted of many of its most skilled soldiers to serve as instructors for other units, and had its ranks replenished by the addition of raw recruits. Henry Russell Miller, who served in the 1st Division, recalled, 'Physically it was less impressive than any other outfit I have ever seen. In intelligence it was probably a little below the American average, in education certainly. ... Its manners were atrocious, its mode of speech appalling, its appetite enormous, its notions of why we were at war rudimentary.'

Partly trained and wearing ill fitting new uniforms, the 1st Division landed in France at the port of St Nazaire on 26 June 1917 to a joyous greeting and disembarked singing:

Good-bye Maw! Good-bye Pa!
Good-bye mule with yer old hee-haw. …
I'll bring you a Turk an' a Kaiser too,
And that's about all one feller can do. …

On 4 July, the 1st Division paraded through the streets of Paris. Besieged by a joyous crowd, Pershing wrote, 'With wreaths around their necks and bouquets in their hats and rifles, the column looked like a moving flower garden.' Amid the turmoil a few of the French observers noticed that their saviours seemed to be military amateurs, with one bystander remarking, 'If this is what we may expect from America, the war is lost.' As if in agreement with the judgement, on 10 July the 1st Division entered a training area near Condrecourt-le-Château, and would not see battle for nearly a year.

In the wake of the 1st Division's arrival in France, millions of American soldiers completed their initial training in the United States and then made their own way across the Atlantic. For many of the Doughboys, few of whom had ever been aboard a ship, the journey was agonizing. Sergeant Ira Redlinger recalled that on

board his troopship, during a particularly stormy crossing, that he and his compatriots got, 'six meals a day – three down and three up'. Although conditions on the troopships were often appalling, it was much worse on ships carrying horses and mules. One sergeant recalled that his ship, carrying 1600 such animals, encountered bad weather:

'The mountainous waves rolled us around like a ball. The horses in housings on the top deck were thrown all over the deck. … The screaming and yelling of the animals was pitiful. … There were 250 dead animals lying around. We tossed them over the side. … When we arrived at Saint-Nazaire [and] *started to unload our animals it was just a little more than some could take. They went down the gangplank onto the dock, let out a heehaw, and dropped dead.'*

While American units entered France with agonizing slowness, the rush of military events prompted a renewed call for amalgamation from Britain and France. As Haig had predicted after Cambrai, the balance of forces on the Western Front

When the German hammer blows fell in 1918, US units were not yet in the line in any great numbers. However, before the tipping point was reached, fresh and fit American units reached the front, much to the chagrin of understrength and spent German formations.

Even while their units were training, American forces often sent their military bands to show the flag in an effort to raise sagging Allied morale. For the majority, it was their first experience of Europe.

started to shift as the Germans rushed troops westwards in ever growing numbers, while Britain and France both suffered from severe manpower shortages and their American saviours languished in training camps awaiting the formation of an independent AEF. In December 1917, both Lloyd George and Pétain suggested placing intact American formations, a policy termed 'brigading', within British and French divisions so that American manpower could be rushed into the front lines. Given the desperate nature of the situation, Secretary of War Baker gave the idea his grudging support. Even prominent figures within the US military, including General Tasker Bliss, contended that American units should enter the line under British or French control to help stem the expected German assault.

Pershing, though, remained adamant that American troops would only enter battle together in an independent command with its own section of the front lines. Although the renewed struggle over amalgamation became very confused, and involved bickering in the very highest level of Allied command in the newly formed Supreme War Council, by February 1918 Pershing agreed to the 'six division plan', which called for six American divisions to locate with and be

War Work in the United States

As in most nations involved in World War I, the United States had to make use of new sources of labour to offset the loss of men to the armed forces. In America, the new sources of labour included both African-Americans and women. One African-American woman, who had previously been a domestic servant, said of her experience working in a railyard during the war:

'All the colored women like this work and want to keep it. We are making more money at this than any work we can get, and we do not have to work as hard as housework, which requires us to be on duty from six o'clock in the morning until nine or ten at night, which

is mighty little time off and at very poor wages. ... What the colored women need is an opportunity to make money. As it is, they have to take what employment they can get, live in old tumbled down houses or resort to street walking, and I think a woman ought to think more of her blood than to do that. What occupation is open to us where we can make really good wages? We are not employed as clerks, we cannot all be school teachers, and so we cannot see any use in working our parents to death to get educated. Of course we should like easier work if it were opened to us. With three dollars a day, we can buy bonds ... we can dress decently, and not be tempted to find our living on the streets.'

trained by the British. Even though the furore over the issue of amalgamation had calmed, when the German attack fell on Allied lines in March, American units had not yet taken their places in the front lines.

One reason that Pershing had resisted amalgamation until it was almost too late is that the American commander believed that the British and French had been fighting the war incorrectly and that American training and tactical dogma were superior. Although there were arguments within the US military, Pershing decided that the French and British relied too heavily on overwhelming artillery firepower and techniques of trench warfare. American drill regulations contended that regarding trench warfare, 'any officer … could get in a hole in the ground and take care of the situation at hand'. Instead, Pershing insisted that the American training regimen concentrate on open warfare, arguing that, 'victory could not be won by the costly process of attrition, but must be won by driving the enemy out into the open and engaging him in a war of movement'. The British and French, through a brutal process of trial and error, had learned the difficult lesson that attacks on the Western Front required painstaking preparation and even then had only a limited life span. Rejecting much of the strategic experience of their Allies as flawed, the Americans relied on a policy of attempting to achieve a clean breakthrough of the German lines, which doomed American soldiers to suffer through their own Battle of the Somme.

Although the United States was only in World War I for a short time, its unfettered economic power, which included the use of female factory workers, presaged America's position as the 'arsenal of democracy' in World War II.

CHAPTER 5

The Spring Offensives

Having won the war in the east, Hindenburg and Ludendorff gambled everything on a final chance for victory in the west. Utilizing novel tactics, the Germans won a series of victories, but a lack of strategic coordination and a staunch Allied defence doomed the plan to failure. Instead of winning the war, Ludendorff had exhausted the German Army.

The strategic situation for Germany in early 1918 looked more promising than it had since the outbreak of the war. Russia, riven by revolution and civil war, was out of the conflict, as was Romania. Italy had been soundly defeated at Caporetto, while both Britain and France were mired in manpower difficulties and plainly on the defensive. The United States, which in the words of one member of the German general staff could 'yet be able to turn the page of history', was slow in bringing its power to bear. With the initiative again on their side, German forces gathered from around Europe to launch a bid for victory on the Western Front.

German troops dash forwards during the Spring Offensives of 1918, a desperate gamble by the German high command to win World War I before the arrival of substantial American forces tipped the balance of the conflict.

While Germany demonstrated a high level of tactical planning and prowess during the Spring Offensives, the strategic goal of the offensives remained fatally muddled, leading to ad hoc alterations of the plan to fit circumstances on the ground and no clear set of final goals.

The window of strategic opportunity for Germany was, though, quite narrow, for the strain of a lengthy multi-front war of attrition had already begun to show on the home front. In the summer of 1917, the authorities had quashed a budding mutiny among German sailors at Wilhelmshaven, while in the winter of the same year, politics in Germany neared a breakdown with the socialist parties, who advocated peace without annexation, squaring off against parties of the right, who demanded a punitive peace. Political and social unrest came to a head in January, when a wave of strikes swept across the nation in which hundreds of thousands of workers demanded peace and more food. Although the wave of strikes subsided, the turmoil remained just below the surface, and differences were only momentarily put aside in the expectation of final and cathartic victory in the west. German politician Kurt Riezler commented, 'All depends on the offensive – should it succeed completely, then we will have the military dictatorship

that the public will cheerily put up with – should it not succeed [then there will come] a severe moral crisis which probably none of the present government leaders has the talent to master peacefully.'

Both Hindenburg and Ludendorff not only understood the vulnerable condition of the German home front but also were aware of the more closely guarded secret of the frailty of the German military. In late 1917, war-related industries had been thoroughly combed to make up for manpower losses in the west and reserves were being called up at a rate of 58,000 trained and 21,000 untrained men per month. Even such complete measures, though, only covered the projected needs of the army in the west until January 1918. With the nation reaching the end of its manpower tether, many German commanders originally advocated standing on the defensive in 1918, a strategy that eventually would cede control of the war to the Americans. The final collapse of Russia had changed the situation, though, and allowed Ludendorff the option in his words 'to deliver an annihilating blow to the British before American aid can become effective'.

Both militarily and socially, then, the German offensive of spring 1918 was a last roll of the dice. The great gamble, which first involved a logistical miracle of moving vast numbers of men and material from Russia to the Western Front, had to achieve victory before American forces arrived in such numbers as irrevocably to tip the balance of war against Germany. The German Army, though skilled and resilient, would never be able to match the Americans in numbers, and the German home front would not be able to stand further years of war. It was victory or defeat, all or nothing. In his planning, though, Ludendorff consigned the offensive to eventual defeat and sealed

Germany's doom in a fit of greed. The German general staff initially planned to shift 45 divisions from the Eastern Front to France and Flanders. Germany, though, had taken so much land from Russia in the Treaty of Brest-Litovsk, land that Russian revolutionary forces might try to retake, that Ludendorff only approved the removal of 33 divisions from the east. As German forces launched their climactic offensive in France, left behind in Russia were a total of 40 infantry and three cavalry divisions, a force that could have tipped the balance in the close-run and desperate battles of 1918.

Having made the decision to gamble on victory in the west, the only thing that remained was to decide on a place for the attack. Prince Rupprecht, supported by Hindenburg, suggested an attack near Ypres, while other commanders advocated their own pet projects, including a renewal of operations at Verdun. On 11 November 1917, Ludendorff called a staff conference to weigh the various options for the coming year, at which, after considerable discussion, he decided to attack the BEF, believing that they were more determined to fight than the French. If he could defeat the British – better yet drive them into the sea – Ludendorff believed that French morale would collapse. The question then became where to strike. Ludendorff preferred to attack in Flanders where German forces were within reach of the critical

Kaiser Wilhelm II of Germany, on an inspection tour. Having lost a large measure of control over his nation to the military during the war, the Kaiser was optimistic that the Spring Offensives would set things to right.

Channel ports. However, the tortured state of the ground and the continued bad weather in the region dissuaded him. Instead, Ludendorff chose to attack near the old Somme battlefield – at the vulnerable juncture between the British and French armies. The immensity of the decision was not lost on Colonel von Thayer of the general staff who commented, 'Here in the west we stand before the future as a dark curtain. The coming events will bring tremendous and for many horrible things.'

The experiences of Verdun, the Somme and Passchendaele would seem to indicate that Ludendorff's hope that a climactic battle could drive the British into defeat was foolhardy at best. However,

German experiences in their own victorious offensives on the Eastern Front, as well as lessons learned by suffering through the Allied attacks in the west, indicated that technological advancements had redressed the balance of warfare and once again allowed hope for attacking forces to achieve a breakthrough.

TECHNOLOGICAL AND TACTICAL CHANGE

In the great battles of the first phase of the conflict, infantry had been nearly helpless in the face of intact barbed wire and entrenched enemy forces. However, by 1918 the foot soldier was once again a force with which to be reckoned. Carrying an array of portable firepower that included light machine guns, grenades and mortars, in 1918 infantrymen could deal with an enemy strongpoint or machine-gun nest on their own, rather than have their forward momentum stop while

Senior German officers watch machine-gun training. The German high command hoped that the combination of training with new weaponry and advanced infiltration tactics would tip the tactical balance of the war in its favour.

awaiting artillery assistance. By the close of the conflict, the infantry also carried more exotic weaponry, such as flame-throwers and Bangalore torpedoes, which aided in overthrowing enemy trench systems. Newly powerful, and once again capable of manoeuvre in battle, the infantry, after three years of relative impotence, finally was ready to reassume a major role on the battlefield.

During the great trench battles of 1915–17, attacking forces had come to rely almost exclusively on the flawed power of artillery in their efforts to achieve victory. Lacking either effective infantry or a weapon of exploitation, attackers had asked the artillery to carry the entire weight of battle. In such fatally tactically imbalanced battles, the artillery first had to flatten the enemy's first line of defence, the deadly entanglements of barbed wire. Next the artillery had to destroy the entirety of the enemy's intricate trench system and silence his deadly machine guns, all while providing cover for advancing infantry. Last but certainly not least, the artillery had to destroy the enemy artillery that stood ready to rain death upon attacking infantry in no man's land. The reliance on artillery had been too heavy, and the tasks assigned it were too varied and difficult, contributing to the continuing dominance of the defensive during World War I.

In the battles of 1918, though, the artillery was called upon to do much less, thus restoring the balance of warfare. Given the renewed strength of the infantry, the artillery no longer had to destroy everything in the path of the foot soldiers and defeat the enemy single-handed; now it only had to keep the defenders' heads down until the newly powerful infantry arrived at his trenches. Without the need for prolonged preparatory artillery barrages, surprise was also once again a factor in strategic and tactical thinking. Finally, improved technology and communications made the artillery much more lethal in its remaining tasks, including counterbattery fire. For the first time since the heady days of 1914, infantry and artillery could work seamlessly together, aided even by close cooperation with air forces, in a fluid battlefield situation instead of relying on brute force and overly choreographed fire plans. The war had changed and entered a new phase

The Western Front, even during its rare moments of calm, remained a deadly place, as evidenced by this German soldier wearing rudimentary body armour as protection against shrapnel. Known as *Sappenpanzer* (trench armour), over half a million suits of this body armour were produced.

in which it seemed that technology had once again tipped the balance of warfare in favour of the attacker.

The Germans are often credited with being the first to experiment with updated tactics that made use of the strength of the war's new technological developments. In reality, though, all sides were busy developing more modern methods of attack throughout the conflict, with the British effort at Cambrai utilizing predicted fire and massed formations of tanks, and Russian tactics in the Brusilov Offensive, standing out as examples of Allied innovation. It was, however, in the German Spring

German soldiers training for the Spring Offensives near Sedan. With so much riding on the outcome of the Spring Offensives, the German high command left little to chance, ensuring the training of German stormtroop units to a fever pitch of readiness.

Offensives of 1918 that the new offensive tactics both gained fame and were used together in a truly systematic way.

Like the Allies, the Germans had been experimenting with tactics since their *Pionier* (combat engineer) units first had utilized grenades to destroy enemy fortifications. In early 1915 the first *Sturmabteilung* (storm detachment) had been formed, which utilized firepower and manoeuvre to deal with enemy strongpoints, rather than weight of artillery. While playing only a small role in the battles of 1916, stormtroop tactics gained wider relevancy in 1917. In the Battle of Riga on the Eastern Front, the German Eighth Army, under the command of General Oskar von Hutier, in combination with the advanced *Feurwaltz* (creeping barrage) tactics developed by

artillery innovator Lieutenant-Colonel Georg Bruchmuller, won a stunning victory. Similar tactical innovations were on display at the successful attack at Caporetto in Italy and the counterattack at Cambrai. As is so often the case in warfare, the important tactical innovations had originated at lower levels of command as talented individuals came to grips with the realities of their war. By November 1917, as planning for the Spring Offensives got underway, Ludendorff assigned Captain Hermann Geyer to study the tactical ferment that had been taking place on all fronts in the German military. In January 1918 Geyer presented Ludendorff with a paper entitled *Der Angriff im Stellungskrieg* (*The Attack in Position Warfare*), which guided German planning for the remainder of the war.

The new tactics called for German infantry units not to attack across the front en masse, but instead to strike in small, mobile formations that first sought out weak points in the enemy line. Having located vulnerable positions, the infantry was directed to infiltrate Allied lines, avoiding centres of resistance, and to penetrate 'quickly and deeply' into the enemy's rear. Infantry units were not to be concerned about whether other units on their flanks advanced in concert or to halt for any reason; the attackers had to press on to depth regardless of the situation. Fresh reserves, held near the front, would then leapfrog through the advanced units to maintain the tempo of the advance. The artillery would lay down quick and accurate barrages, designed only to keep the enemy pinned in place. The key to success was the tactical suppleness and uninterrupted forwards movement of the infantry, which was instructed that the, 'surprised adversary should not be allowed to regain consciousness'. Such tactics, it was hoped, would shock and dislocate the enemy defensive system. It was a far cry from the waves of advancing infantry often utilized in the great battles of 1916. Using their newfound firepower, infantry would probe and advance quickly, avoiding the strongest points and leaving them for mopping up at a later, more convenient time. The Germans were, in effect, planning to use blitzkrieg without tanks.

Geyer realized, though, that the German Army had suffered greatly in recent years, and estimated that only roughly 30 per cent of all soldiers, those between 25 and 35 years of age, were suitable for the rigours of a mobile battle. As a result, Ludendorff divided the units for the coming offensive into three categories: 44 'mobile' divisions received the most training and the best weapons and were to be used in the van, 30 'attack' divisions received similar equipment and were slated for use as first-line replacement units, while more than a hundred 'trench' divisions were stripped of their best officers, men and equipment and were intended for only defensive purposes.

Ludendorff, though, was certain that training and tactical proficiency would more than outweigh any potential weakness of numbers, and contended later in his memoirs:

'It was necessary to create anew a thorough understanding of the extent of front to be allotted in attack and to emphasize the principle that men must do the work not with their bodies alone, but with their weapons. The fighting-line must be kept thin, but must constantly be fed from behind. As in the defence, it was necessary in the attack to adopt loose formations and work out infantry group tactics clearly. We must not copy the enemy's mass tactics, which offer advantages only in the case of untrained troops.'

PLANNING THE GERMAN SPRING OFFENSIVES

To gain the proposed level of tactical mastery required to undertake the Spring Offensives, the German Army trained at a fever pitch throughout the winter of 1917–18. Ludendorff ordered each of his armies to establish schools to teach the elements of Geyer's new doctrine to the officers and men of the mobile and attack divisions. The courses, which lasted four weeks each, stressed rigid discipline and physical exercise, but were mainly concerned with combined-arms operations. Geyer's planning and stormtroop theory stressed that the various arms of the German military – infantry, intelligence, communications, air assets and artillery – all had to work seamlessly both to seize and then maintain the initiative in battle.

The German planning for the coming offensive seemingly left nothing to chance. Machine-gun crews learned that

A German stormtrooper, wearing armour protection, at the time of Operation Michael. This soldier is armed with classic trench-fighting tools, a Mauser Model 14 pistol and two hand grenades, as well as a sharpened entrenching tool.

133

the fine dust in the area of the advance could cause their barrels to malfunction and received special cleaning instructions to keep their weapons in working order. A small army of 4000 cartographers laboured to map British defences down to the last machine-gun nest. Communications specialists trained both dogs and pigeons to transport messages from the advancing troops. Amid the care for detail, though, one pivotal factor was lacking. Ludendorff, by his own design, did not engage in any operational or strategic planning. He was concentrating his energy, and that of the German military, on the tactics of how to achieve a breakthrough. Inexplicably there was no planning for what the goals of the German Army

should be after a breakthrough occurred, or regarding a fail-safe plan for a scenario in which a breakthrough failed to occur. Ludendorff cut short those commanders who questioned the lack of an operational or strategic goal, stating, 'I object to the word "operation". We will punch a hole into [their line]. For the rest we shall see. We also did it this way in Russia!'

In substituting tactical mastery for strategic thought, Ludendorff had committed a fatal error. His overall plan, though it made use of revolutionary techniques, had no overall goal. To undertake the final offensive, dubbed Operation Michael in honour of the patron saint of Germany, Ludendorff gathered his most successful and innovative commanders. The plan called for the Seventeenth Army, under the architect of the victory at Caporetto, General Otto von Below, to attack towards Bapaume. The Second Army, under

German soldiers at Bapaume. After so many years of fighting on the defensive on the Western Front, the morale of the German infantrymen soared when Germany once more went on the offensive in 1918.

German troops carry their machine guns forwards into new positions during the Spring Offensives. Increased infantry firepower was critical to the successful implementation of Germany's new infiltration tactics.

north and destroy the vulnerable British position in Flanders, or in the south against the French Army Group North. The follow-on attacks would thus rupture the entire Allied line, and lead to ultimate victory.

The overall balance of strength on the Western Front seemed to bode well for the Germans, who had gathered 192 divisions against only 178 Allied divisions. However, the number, which included many seriously understrength divisions, represented a peak for the Germans, while the Allies could count on a swelling of their ranks as more and more Americans reached France. As regards the machinery of war, the Germans were also at a growing disadvantage: the Germans had 3670 aircraft against 4500 Allied, 14,000 artillery pieces against 18,500 Allied and 10 tanks against 800 Allied. More

General Georg von der Marwitz who had led the German counterattack at Cambrai, was to strike southwest toward Albert, while the Eighteenth Army, under the victor of Riga, General von Hutier, attacked from St Quentin. On the right and left flanks of the advance respectively, the German Sixth and Seventh armies stood in readiness to launch subsidiary operations, dubbed Mars and Archangel, to build on the expected successes of Michael.

If all went well, the German Eighteenth, Second and Seventeenth armies would rupture the front of the British Fifth and Third armies, severing the vital connection between the British and French forces on the Western Front. In the process, Ludendorff hoped that his attacking armies would first pin and destroy substantial British forces in the Cambrai Salient and then follow the Somme River northwest and drive the British towards the sea. The brunt of the offensive would fall to Below's Seventeenth Army, which as a result received the lion's share of supplies and reserves. Depending on where success was the greatest, additional German attacks would then fall in the

A captured British artillery piece in 1918. After suffering privations due in large measure to the blockade, advancing German troops were shocked to discover how lavishly supplied the BEF was in terms of both food and munitions.

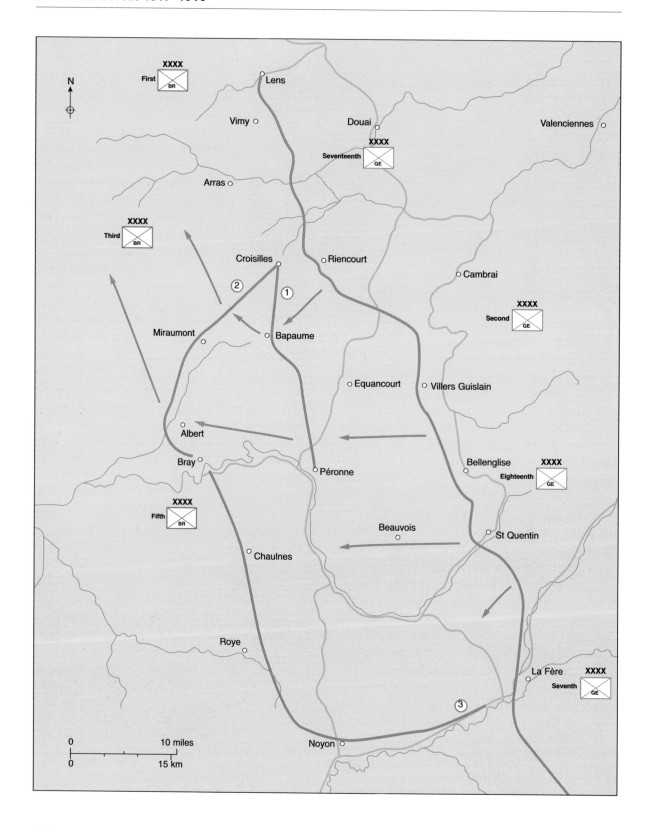

N

XXXX
First
BR

Lens

Vimy

Douai

Valenciennes

XXXX
Seventeenth
GE

Arras

XXXX
Third
BR

Croisilles

Riencourt

Cambrai

② ①

Miraumont

Bapaume

XXXX
Second
GE

Equancourt

Villers Guislain

Albert

Bray

Péronne

Bellenglise

XXXX
Eighteenth
GE

XXXX
Fifth
BR

Beauvois

St Quentin

Chaulnes

Roye

La Fère

XXXX
Seventh
GE

③

Noyon

0   10 miles
0   15 km

The Spring Offensives

Ludendorff's three-stage plan for Operation Michael, which called for the Eighteenth, Second and Seventeenth armies to rupture the British lines through an assault on the British Fifth Army (1 and 3), before turning north through Third Army and then driving the BEF into the sea (2).

disturbing, though, was the fact that so few of the German divisions, only 77 in total, were trained in the new style of warfare. These mobile and attack divisions, the shock forces of the German army, were irreplaceable and as such had to achieve victory quickly. Their superior tactics had to offset all of the other Allied advantages. Germany could not afford a battle that dragged on or became attritional in nature, lest the stormtroops themselves and the German hope for final victory be destroyed.

ALLIED DEBATE AND DEFENSIVE PLANS

While the Germans prepared for their assault, the Allies had to ready themselves for a defensive battle, having lost the initiative in the west for the first time since the onset of trench warfare. Although the situation on the Allied home fronts was not as bad as that of Germany, political tension in both France and Britain during the winter of 1917–18 rose to a fever pitch. Their military efforts and nearly four years of war had seemingly availed nothing, for despite the investment of blood and treasure Germany seemed ascendant as all awaited the onset of the coming onslaught. Blame for the sorry situation was abundant: the military leadership had mishandled the great battles of the war, politicians had meddled in strategy too often, the Allies did not act together effectively as one and the Americans had not agreed to amalgamation. Recriminations abounded, testing the very fabric of the alliance at a crucial time.

Although their relationship was often strained and involved tumultuous debates

over strategy, Pétain as commander-in-chief and Foch as chief of staff had together worked miracles in revitalizing the French military after the mutinies of 1917. Utilizing a mix of discipline and reform, Pétain had stabilized the situation to the extent that in June and July 1917, the Fourth, Sixth and Tenth armies, which were among the most affected by the mutinies, were able to launch limited offensives intended to draw German reserves away from the British operations at Messines and Ypres. Although further French offensives in support of Third Ypres both came later than promised and fell short of Haig's expectations, for the remainder of 1917 Pétain's armies fought well and regained their confidence. Adhering to the concept of the limited advance, and covered by overwhelming firepower, the French in August 1917 launched a successful attack at Verdun. Most importantly, though constant delays in its onset frustrated Haig, in October 1917, the Sixth Army achieved a cathartic victory by seizing the heights of the Chemin des Dames in a model limited offensive, suffering only one tenth of the casualties that Nivelle's forces had lost in their failed attempts to conquer the same objective only five months previously.

Although improvements within the French military were heartening for the Allies, nothing could offset the grim strategic reality that the balance of forces on the Western Front had shifted in favour of Germany. The prospect of facing a renewed German assault in the west was so

A captain of the Royal Flying Corps in France. While reconnaissance and counter-reconnaissance remained a primary role of air forces in 1918, utilizing aircraft in a ground-attack role gained prominence as the year progressed.

137

dire that it finally drove the reluctant British and French toward a more unified command. As early as August 1917, Painlevé had suggested to Lloyd George that Foch be named chief of an Allied general staff, but the British Prime Minister had refused. However, in the wake of Passchendaele, Lloyd George once again decided to seize control over the strategic leadership of the conflict and moved to shift British power away from France and Flanders to other, hopefully more profitable, theatres of war. Realizing that the alliance formed by Haig and Robertson remained powerful, and that any overt move to oust them would endanger his government, Lloyd George chose indirect methods of achieving his goals.

In response to the devastating Italian defeat at Caporetto, in November 1917 the Allies met at the Rapallo Conference, where Lloyd George proposed the formation of a Supreme War Council to coordinate Allied efforts and guide a united strategy. Although the new advisory body, which met at Versailles, had little real power, it was the first, halting step toward a unified command. For his part, though, Lloyd George saw the Supreme War Council as a way to wrest control of the war from Haig and Robertson. By appointing his military ally, General Sir Henry Wilson, to Versailles, Lloyd George effectively had two sets of military opinion from which to choose. He, thus, hoped never again to pit his amateur strategy against a monolithic military bloc.

The shift in command, however, did little to calm the political turmoil in France, and only a week after Rapallo, the French Government fell. The situation was so dire that the British ambassador had even reported that a civil war in France was possible. As Pétain had done for the army, France needed a strong leader to heal its gaping political wounds. For the difficult position, President Poincaré chose Georges

Scottish prisoners taken at Bapaume during Operation Michael. With its troops concentrated too far forwards, owing to a failure to construct an adequate defence in depth, Gough's Fifth Army lost a disproportionate number of the 90,000 prisoners taken during the initial German attack.

Field Marshal Sir Henry Wilson, who was a close military confidant of David Lloyd George, rose to prominence as Chief of the Imperial General Staff in February 1918, replacing Sir William Robertson. Wilson was later shot and killed by the IRA in London in 1922.

Clemenceau, known as 'the Tiger'. Fiery and imbued with an indomitable will, Clemenceau proved an inspired choice who immediately clamped down on dissent, declaring, 'Neither personal considerations, nor political passions will turn us from our duty. … No more pacifist campaigns, no more German intrigues. Neither treason, nor half treason. War. Nothing but war.' The new French leader soon discovered that he had a kindred spirit in General Ferdinand Foch, who was a hard-charging optimist, as opposed to Pétain, who was becoming increasingly pessimistic about the outcome of the war.

In Britain, a growing manpower crisis added another level of intrigue to the ongoing civil–military struggle for control of the war. With his reserves depleted, and facing an unprecedented German build up, Haig requested 600,000 new men to keep the British armies overseas up to their recommended establishments. Lloyd George was livid, for compliance with the request would have crippled the very British industrial efforts that made the war possible. In December 1917, the Prime Minister had made his

> 'We must strike at the earliest moment before the Americans can throw strong forces into the scale. We must beat the British.'
>
> Erich Ludendorff on the Spring Offensives

frustration with Haig clear in a letter to Lord Esher: 'Now he [Haig] wrote of fresh offensives, and asked for men. He would get neither. He had eaten his cake, in spite of warnings. Pétain had economized his.' Seizing upon control over manpower as another weapon to use in his conflict with Haig, Lloyd George approved only 100,000 new men for the military, placing the armed

forces behind both shipping and agriculture in importance. The Prime Minister was playing a dangerous game, hoping to curb Haig's ability to prosecute offensive warfare by denying the military needed manpower in a time of impending crisis.

Matters came to a head at the 30 January meeting of the Supreme War Council, which focused its attention both on easing the manpower situation and forming an Allied general reserve. Although both Haig and Pétain contended that they did not have any available forces to spare for the formation of a reserve, the idea was accepted in principle with the details to be decided at a later date. In the charged political atmosphere, though, what concerned Haig, Robertson and Pétain most was the decision to place control of the general reserve under the Supreme War Council, an arrangement that strengthened the hands of both Foch and Lloyd George. In frustration over his loss of power, Robertson resigned as Chief of the Imperial General Staff, and was replaced in that position by Wilson. Lloyd George would never again have to face

General Sir Hubert Gough. One of the most controversial British military figures of World War I, Gough presided over the failed first attacks in the Third Battle of Ypres and the failed defence in depth against Operation Michael. Gough's failure led to his replacement by Sir Henry Rawlinson.

George nor Clemenceau chose to press the issue, leaving Foch as its lone champion, and the idea of raising a general reserve was shelved until sufficient numbers of American troops had arrived in France to make a reserve practicable.

Although the Allies had taken a step toward true coalition warfare, the move had been more about political battles for control over the war than about Allied unity. The failure meant that the alliance remained not only fragmented but also at odds as it awaited the German attack. Wilson remarked regarding the situation that the failure to unify the Allied command meant that Haig, 'would have to live on Pétain's charity, [in case of an attack on the British lines] and he would find that very cold charity'.

While political dramas played out in London and Paris, Allied forces made ready to face the German attack. Haig correctly judged that the main weight of the German offensive would be directed against the BEF, but, misled by his own fears and German deception, he misjudged the axis of the German advance. Haig was most concerned by the prospect of a German attack in the neighbourhood of Ypres, where Allied forces had little strategic depth and any substantial retreat would place them in danger of catastrophic defeat. Haig realized that another vulnerable point was at the juncture of the British and French armies, but he reasoned that Gough's Fifth Army, which defended the area, could, at need, give ground while awaiting the reserves that Pétain had promised before any German advance in the region threatened the nearest target of strategic value, the distant communications hub of Amiens. Weighing his tactical options, Haig distributed his available forces from north to south: Second Army with 14 divisions defended 37km (23 miles) of front, First Army with 16 divisions defended 53km (33 miles) of front, Third Army with 14 divisions defended 45km (28 miles) of front. The dispositions, though based on sound

the united opinion of Haig and Robertson in strategic debates. One of the great personal alliances in British military history had come to an end.

Ironically, since Lloyd George and Wilson had achieved their main aim of removing Robertson from power, their support for the Supreme War Council and the issue of a general reserve waned. At the same time Haig continued to fret about manpower issues, writing in his diary on 10 March:

'The manpower situation is most unsatisfactory … with heavy fighting in prospect, and very few men coming in, the prospects are bad. We are told that we can only expect 18,000 drafts in April! We are all right under normal conditions for men for the next three months, but I fear for the autumn! And still more do I fear for the situation after the enemy has started the attack.'

Pétain, too, was worried that he did not have enough men to cover his own front, let alone contribute to the formation of a reserve. Instead of a formalized Allied reserve, both Pétain and Haig preferred to abide by an informal pledge to send their own reserves to the other's aid in time of need. In the face of united Allied military opinion neither Lloyd

reasoning, left Gough's Fifth Army with only 12 divisions to defend 68km (42 miles) of front. Haig's decision had left the Fifth Army at a great disadvantage, and the official historian later remarked, 'Never before had the British line been held with so few men and so few guns to the mile; and the reserves were wholly insufficient.'

Making matters worse, for years the BEF had practised offensive warfare, and was as a result a comparative novice at defensive battle. As it became clear in the winter of 1917–18 that the initiative had slipped to the Germans, the BEF slowly shifted its lines from an offensive posture to a defensive one. Based on the experiences of Third Ypres, Haig opted to install a system of defence in depth, which required massive amounts of labour in the creation of forward redoubt

systems and battle zones within the British lines. The conversion of the trench systems into true defensive networks was painfully slow, in part due to a critical manpower shortage for labour battalions. Ominously, the situation was particularly bad on the front of Fifth Army, which had only recently taken over the area from French forces and found the defences there in a state of disrepair.

The BEF also had to alter its tactical defensive doctrine away from the practice of positioning large numbers of men in forward positions. The new defensive system called for using light forces,

As World War I dragged on, the armies of the Western Front consumed ever greater quantities of supplies, including these unfortunate local chickens on their way to a soldiers' mess. Soldiers caught stealing could face stiff penalties, however.

augmented by heavy firepower, in the forward positions and giving ground while drawing attacking forces into the battle zone where they would be destroyed. At a conference of his army commanders Haig explained:

'Depth in defensive organization is of the first importance. … The economy of forces in the front line system is most important in order that as many men as possible may be available in reserve. The front line should generally be held as an outpost line covering the main line of resistance a few hundred yards in the rear.'

In many areas, especially that of the Fifth Army, neither the construction of defences nor the doctrinal shift was complete before the German attack. In

German soldiers steal some rest time while one of their number stands guard during the frenetic advance of the Spring Offensives. The unrelenting pace of the advance wore out the leading troops and ensured that momentum was lost, allowing the Allies valuable time to reinforce their lines.

addition to being severely outnumbered, Gough failed to understand the new defensive scheme, and played into the Germans' hands by stationing too many of his men forwards. In a scene that was reminiscent of the command breakdown of Third Ypres, Haig warned Gough against lavish use of manpower and cautioned that Fifth Army would have to rely more on firepower and a sound defensive system. Haig even argued that it might be necessary to engage in a fighting withdrawal

Hello Girls

Instead of relying on Signal Corps' members to man and operate the prodigious number of telephone switchboards needed to facilitate the communications needs of the AEF while in France, Pershing decided to import French-speaking American women as operators. Of the 7000 women who applied for the positions, 223 were chosen and received special training in their tasks at AT&T headquarters in Evanston, Illinois. Having to purchase their own uniforms, the operators earned a very respectable pay of 60 dollars per month. The women received first-class accommodation aboard troopships bound for France, but were forbidden to fraternize with the troops. Nellie Snow, formerly chief telephone operator for the New England Telephone Company, protested the ban, and the policy was abandoned. One of the operators wrote home:

'There were some seven or eight thousand troops on board … so you may imagine that the girls had a gay time … we soon became acquainted with a number of officers who made the days pass pleasantly. All were obliged to wear life belts during the day, and it was an amusing sight to see couples trying to dance in them.'

Once in France the operators served an invaluable function, and, because of their merry style of greeting,

American women, known as 'hello girls', performed a vital communications role for the US military on the Western Front.

earned the name 'hello girls'. After the war, though, the hello girls were surprised to learn that they had merely been employees of the military, and were not veterans and thus were unable to receive benefits. Not until 1979, after a lengthy campaign by former hello girl Louise Le Breton Maxwell, did the army belatedly admit its mistake, giving the few surviving hello girls honourable discharges and military benefits.

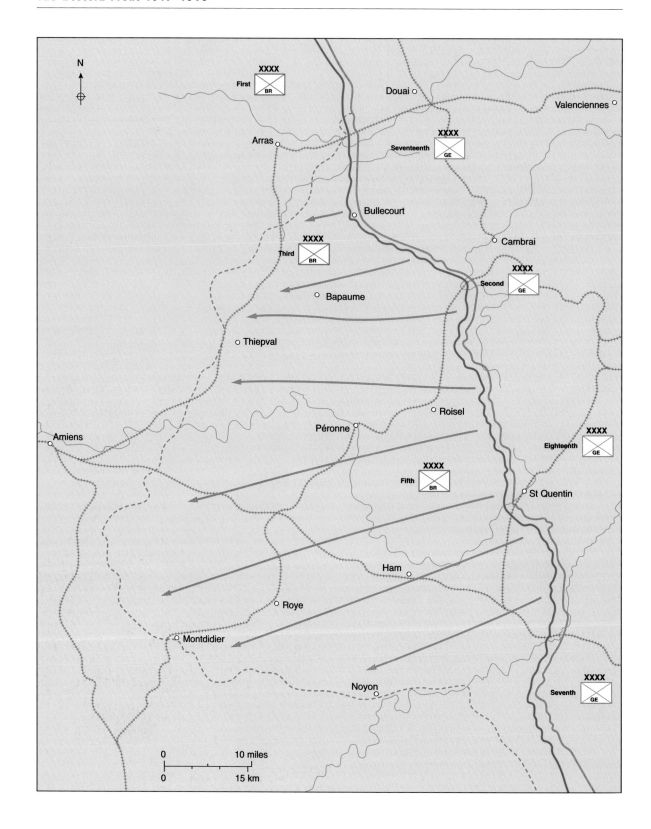

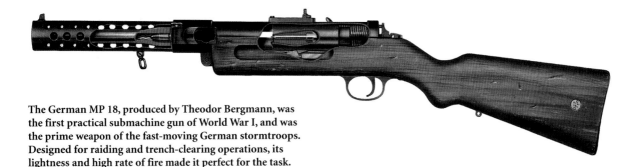

The German MP 18, produced by Theodor Bergmann, was the first practical submachine gun of World War I, and was the prime weapon of the fast-moving German stormtroops. Designed for raiding and trench-clearing operations, its lightness and high rate of fire made it perfect for the task.

to the area of Péronne on the Somme while awaiting the promised French reserves to stall the German attack. The situation was bleak as Fifth Army, outmanned, occupying substandard defences, under a commander who did not fully understand his task and under a commander-in-chief who expected an attack elsewhere, made ready to face a new style of warfare. Even so, as the German offensive neared, Haig confided to his wife, 'I must say I feel quite confident, and so do my troops. Personally, I feel in the words of 2nd Chronicles, XX Chap., that it is "God's battle" and I am not dismayed by the numbers of the enemy.'

THE GERMANS STRIKE

At 4.40am on 21 March, 43 German divisions moved to the attack, as 10,000 German guns and mortars opened fire on the fronts of the British Fifth and Third armies, announcing the beginning of Operation Michael. One German artillery officer remembered satisfaction at turning the tables on the Allies:

'Within seconds of the bombardment opening, we could see sparks and columns of fire in the enemy trenches and their rear area. A terrific roar, an immense noise greeted the young morning. The unbearable

LEFT The course of Operation Michael from 21 March to 4 April 1918. Changing his plan on the fly, Ludendorff, instead of pushing the BEF into the sea, opted for an ill fated attempt by Eighteenth Army to drive a wedge between the British and French armies.

RIGHT German infantrymen on the assault between Arras and La Fère in March 1918. The men of the 'mobile' and 'attack' divisions of the German Army proved adept at exploiting the fluidity of the 1918 battlefield, but their numbers were extremely limited.

tension eased. We were ourselves again and knew that it had come off all right. In the past the French and the tommies had bombarded us for seven days without pause; we would do it now in five hours. We laughed and looked happily at each other. Words were useless; the hell of the inferno outside saw to that. There was only lightning and noise.'

To the British soldiers on the receiving end of the fire, it seemed like the world was ending. Private E. Atkinson recalled:

'Artillery was the great leveller. Nobody could stand more than three hours of sustained shelling before they start falling sleepy and numb. You're hammered after

A mixed unit of French soldiers and a British Vickers machine-gun team preparing for defensive action near the Somme River. The shock of Operation Michael forced closer military relations between the often fractious French and British militaries.

three hours and you're there for the picking when he comes over. It's a bit like being under an anaesthetic; you can't put a lot of resistance up. The first to be affected were the young ones who'd just come out. They would go to one of the older ones – older in service that is – and maybe even cuddle up to him and start crying. An old soldier could be a great comfort to a young one. On the other fronts that I had been on, there had been so much of our artillery that, whenever Jerry opened up like that, our artillery retaliated and gradually quietened him down but there was no retaliation this time. He had a free do at us. I think we were sacrificed.

'Then a shell must have burst in our trench, but I don't remember it. I woke up with just my head free, the rest of me was buried in sandbags and muck. I was completely stunned. I don't know how long it was before this fellow from the Durhams pulled me out. My helmet and gas-mask had disappeared. I saw my corporal – his head was blown off – and the rest of the section must have been buried. I think it was being up on the fire-step as lookout that had saved me, but I found out later that I had been wounded by a bit of shell that had cut right through the muscle in my shoulder.'

The *Feurwaltz*, directed on the front of the Eighteenth Army by its originator Lieutenant-Colonel Georg Bruchmuller, kept the British in their defences until the German stormtroops, advancing through a thick mist, were upon them. Utilizing their new tactics, the Germans quickly penetrated the British forward zone almost everywhere, and made their way into the battle zone, leaving behind pockets of disoriented defenders for follow-on units to mop up. For most the men of Gough's Fifth Army, German mobility and flanking tactics were a mystifying new experience. One British soldier of the 51st (Highland) Division recalled:

'There were no dugouts in our front line; it was very thinly held to prevent casualties. We had to huddle up under the parapet during the shelling; there was no other shelter. When the bombardment lifted, we were not attacked frontally. We were considerably shaken by the shelling. It was a moment of fear. "What's coming next out of the mist?" We fired our rifles blindly into the mist then heard firing from our left and from the rear. We realized that we were being outflanked. The men started to drift back until we were left with only two men, myself and a sergeant.

'The next thing I knew was that two Germans were coming up the trench on our left; they were about ten yards away. The sergeant had been at the rum for some time. I cleared off; I wasn't going to get caught. The last thing I saw of the sergeant he was shaking his fist at the Germans and using strong language. I saw him taken prisoner.'

In the north, facing the relatively strong defences of Byng's Third Army, the German Seventeenth and Second armies, which were slated to play the major role in Operation Michael, fell well behind schedule and became entangled in bitter fighting in the British battle zone. To the south, though, Hutier's Eighteenth Army broke through the battle zone of Fifth Army, causing Gough to order III Corps to retreat behind the Crozat Canal. By evening the situation for Fifth Army had become critical, with the defences in the south having been surrendered and having lost 500 guns and 38,000 casualties. However, the situation on the other side of the battlefront was also grim. The Germans had fallen well short of expectations, in most areas only advancing only halfway to their assigned goals. In the fighting more than 78,000 Germans had been

German troops rush forward through destroyed Allied positions, searching for weak points in the Allied defensive lines. German troops sought to penetrate to depth and maintain the momentum of their advance, leaving bypassed strongpoint to be cleared by follow-on units.

wounded and killed, the highest single day total for the entire war – losses almost entirely suffered by irreplaceable stormtroop units.

On 22 March, Operation Michael continued, and in the north, Byng's Third Army held in its defences, while to the south Fifth Army reeled under the German onslaught. XVIII and XIX corps fell back to match the earlier retreat of III Corps, which completely unhinged the Fifth Army's defensive network and threatened Third Army's flank. Against the crumbling defences, Hutier's Eighteenth Army in places advanced over 19km (12 miles) in two days of fighting and tore a 80km (50-mile) gap through the Allied lines. In total the BEF had lost 200,000

German troops advance during Operation Michael. Long hours of training and careful coordination of efforts in the months preceeding Operation Michael, combined with the reorganization of the German divisional system, ensured that the initial asssaults of the campaign went smoothly.

casualties, 90,000 prisoners and 1300 artillery pieces. The victory, though, came at considerable cost for the Germans, with the Eighteenth Army alone losing 56,000 casualties.

Ecstatic, Kaiser Wilhem II ordered schools in Germany closed to mark the occasion and presented Hindenburg with the highest medal that Germany had to offer, the Iron Cross with golden rays, last awarded to Prince Blücher for actions against Napoleon. As Hutier and his staff toasted their good fortune with champagne provided by the royal family, the Kaiser dreamed of his glorious future as he celebrated with his closest confidants. He informed his entourage that, 'if any English delegation came to sue for peace it must kneel before the German standard for it was a question here of a victory of the monarchy over democracy'.

Ludendorff, though, remained concerned that the Seventeenth Army, the lynchpin of his planning, had achieved relatively little against Byng's forces. As a

result, as Hutier's men crossed the Crozat Canal on 23 March, Ludendorff made the decision to change his master plan on the fly. Instead of the Seventeenth and Second armies pushing the British into the sea, Ludendorff altered the axis of his advance to the front of the Eighteenth Army, which he now intended to drive a wedge between the British and French armies. In effect the Germans had taken a concentrated effort against the British and diluted it into a series of more limited offensives against both the British and increasingly the French. In dispersing the effort of the German military, rather than concentrating it, Ludendorff had made a fatal mistake.

While the German advance against Fifth Army continued and Ludendorff altered his planning, the French Government prepared to evacuate to Bordeaux, and dissension struck the Allied ranks. With his front in jeopardy, even after moving what British reinforcements that could be spared to the scene, Haig

> ## Operation Michael as Experienced by Hermann Gasser, 110th Grenadier Regiment
>
> *'We moved steadily, encouraged by the feeble opposition. Small parties of enemy soldiers – from three to seven men – surrendered. They gave us cigarettes for which we gave them a friendly pat on the shoulder and sent them off to the rear.*
>
> *'Then we came under heavy fire from a strongpoint in the ruins of the château in Selency. The fog had lifted by then. Our creeping barrage had missed this, and we had fallen behind the barrage. We attacked one post here without success, and then I found a way round to get at it from the rear. We tried six times in all, and at last we captured it and the English defenders. There was a captain and one other officer and 14 men. The captain was wounded and I took him to our dressing station, where our doctor, an affable gentleman with the rank of major, dressed his wound. They had quite a talk. The captain said, "We English always say that there's not enough room in the world for both us and the Germans and, now, here I am sharing a hole only a metre wide with a wounded German grenadier!"'*

called on Pétain to concentrate 20 French divisions in the area of Amiens. Fearing that the German attack was but a ruse to lure French reserves away from the defence of Paris, Pétain declined. Shocked, Haig recorded in his diary, 'I at once asked Pétain if he meant to abandon my right flank. He nodded assent and added "it is the only thing possible, if the enemy compelled the Allies to fall back still further"'.

The Allies were at a dangerous impasse. It seemed to many within the French military that the British, who in their view had fallen back too quickly, were going to disengage from the French Army to defend the Channel ports. The British, on the other hand, believed that the French were leaving the BEF to its fate and had chosen to defend Paris rather than fight a unified Allied campaign. The BEF and the French were in grave danger of fighting two separate wars.

Amid the deteriorating situation, the Supreme War Council met in emergency session on 26 March, at the city hall of Doullens. Clemenceau planned to use the meeting to push for a unified Allied command, and initially favoured Pétain for the position. However, when Pétain arrived at the meeting he was despondent and told Clemenceau, 'The Germans will defeat the

Capturing Allied Supplies

As German troops moved forward in Operation Michael, they came upon mountains of Allied supplies, commodities that they had not seen for years. Ernst Jünger recalled upon capturing a British military kitchen:

'There was a whole boxful of fresh eggs. We sucked a large number on the spot, as we had long since forgotten their very name. Against the walls were stacks of tinned meat, cases of priceless thick jam, bottles of coffee-essence as well, and quantities of tomatoes and onions; in short, all that a gourmet could desire. This sight I often remembered later when we spent weeks together in the trenches on a rigid allowance of bread, washy soup, and thin jam. For four long years, in torn coats and worse fed than a Chinese coolie, the German soldier was hurried from one battlefield to the next to show his iron fist yet again to a foe many times his superior in numbers, well equipped, and well fed. There could be no surer sign of the might of the idea that drove us on. It is much to face death and to die in the moment of enthusiasm. To hunger and starve for one's cause is more.'

Although Jünger took the obvious supply disparity between German and Allied soldiers almost as a badge of honour, many of his compatriots saw the bursting British kitchens as a sign that if the attacks of spring 1918 failed Germany could not hope to hold out much longer against such well supplied foes.

English in open country, after which they will defeat us.' Foch, though, stood firm, and when Pétain suggested the evacuation of Paris Foch yelled, 'Paris has nothing to do with it! Paris is a long way off! It is where we now stand that the enemy will be stopped!' Clemenceau then asked Foch for his thoughts on the situation. Foch responded:

'Oh, my plan is not complicated. I would fight without a break. I would fight in front of Amiens. I would fight in Amiens. I would fight behind Amiens. I would fight all the time, and, by force of hitting, I would finish by shaking up the Boche; he's neither cleverer nor stronger than we are. In any case, for the moment it is as in 1914 on the Marne; we must dig in and die where we stand if need be; to withdraw a foot would be an act of treason.'

Foch's optimism invigorated those present, and, surprisingly to many, Haig proved to be one of the greatest supporters of the idea of placing Foch into a position of supreme command. Having won the day, the Supreme War Council authorized Foch to 'coordinate the action of the Allied armies'. After the

> 'One Lewis gunner was left behind in the long tangle of empty trenches. … Every minute widened the distance between him and his comrades, and, if he were to be wounded, he had neither help nor pity to expect.'
>
> The Munsters in the Retreat from St Quentin, 27 March 1918

agreement had been reached, Clemenceau remarked to Foch that he now had the command that he had wanted, to which Foch replied, 'It is a fine present you've made me; you give me a lost battle and tell me to win it.' Although the situation remained critical, Foch was pleased to find that one of his first visitors after his appointment was Pershing, who volunteered to put his fears of amalgamation to one side for the common cause, stating, 'The American people would

A destroyed British tank being examined by German soldiers, although it appears to have been stripped of anything of worth already. Although of great value in attacks, Allied armour had very little use in defending against the fast-paced German Spring Offensives.

consider it a great honor for our troops to be engaged in the present battle. … Infantry, artillery, aviation, all that we have is yours; use them as you wish.'

While the Allies sorted out their command situation, the German advance edged closer to the critical rail junction of Amiens. Although too much blame was attached to his command failings and too little claim given to new German methods, Haig replaced Gough with Rawlinson and the British defence stiffened, even as Foch worked to rush Allied reinforcements to the threatened area. However, it was, in many ways, the tactical reality of battle in World War I that forced Operation Michael to grind to a halt. As in previous Allied advances, the German forward movement had negated the tactical advantages that had made the advance possible. German forces had taken heavy losses, were tiring, had outrun their critical artillery support and most importantly had also outpaced their own supply system. Thus, as defenders gathered in ever-greater numbers, it became clear that the Germans had not actually ruptured the Allied lines, but only bent them.

After the British Third Army decisively defeated the second phase of the German offensive, Operation Mars, on 28 March, the forward movement of Operation Michael stalled outside Villers-Bretonneux, well short of Amiens. The Germans had succeeded in achieving a tactical wonder, and in places had advanced nearly 64km (40 miles) and captured 90,000 prisoners of war, while inflicting 178,000 casualties on the British and 70,000 on the French. However, the gains had come at the prohibitive cost of 239,000 German killed, wounded and missing. Victory had not

ABOVE German troops rush through the area of a gas attack. Although gas had become much more lethal by 1918, effective defensive measures meant that gas was more of a nuisance weapon, designed mainly to sow confusion among defending forces.

RIGHT Operation Georgette, the German offensive against the British Second Army in Flanders. Although they managed to drive the Second Army back from their front-line positions, the Germans failed to break through to the critical Allied rail junction at Hazebrouck.

been achieved, the British had not been pushed into the sea and the French had not collapsed. For all of their effort, Ludendorff's men had only created a vulnerable bulge into the Allied lines, and had captured no goal of strategic significance. Making matters worse, losses were most heavy among the stormtroops that had occupied the van of the advance. Virtually all of the mobile and attack divisions, those trained in the tactics that had made Operation Michael such a notable tactical success, were now exhausted, with many down to a strength of only 2000 men.

After the close of the conflict, several of the younger members of the German general staff ascribed the failure of Operation Michael and the other German spring offensives of 1918 to the command limitations of Ludendorff himself. Operation Michael had begun as a planned effort to roll up the British flank toward the sea, but Ludendorff had altered his planning in an attempt to build on gains where they were the easiest, on the front of the British Fifth Army, rather than

where those gains would net the greatest strategic result. In consequence, the German drive only made gains where the Allies could afford to give ground, and finally settled on Amiens as a goal almost by default. Major Wilhelm von Leeb, who later became a field marshal under the Third Reich, recorded his thoughts and commented, 'OHL [the German general staff] has changed direction. It has made its decisions according to the size of territorial gain, rather than according to operational goals. … We had absolutely no operational goal. That was the trouble.'

ATTACK IN FLANDERS

Certain that the Germans would soon resume their offensives, and fearing that their aim would shift to the vulnerable Channel ports, Haig asked Foch to transfer French reserves northwards. Ever optimistic, though, Foch demurred and began planning for a limited Franco-British offensive south of the Somme. Haig, however, had proved prescient, for on 9 April the

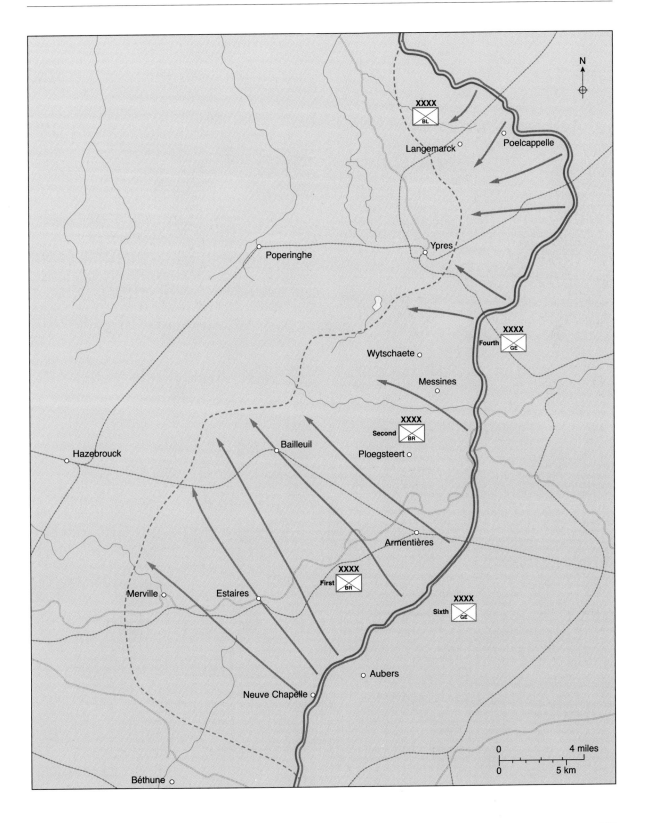

N

XXXX
BL

Langemarck ○   ○ Poelcappelle

○ Poperinghe   Ypres ○

Fourth
XXXX
GE

Wytschaete ○

Messines ○

Second
XXXX
BR

○ Hazebrouck   Bailleul ○   Ploegsteert ○

Armentières ○

First
XXXX
BR

Merville ○   Estaires ○

Sixth
XXXX
GE

○ Aubers

Neuve Chapelle ○

0			4 miles
0			5 km

Béthune ○

German Fourth and Sixth armies struck British lines in Flanders, opening Operation Georgette, which had as its goal the severance of the critical Allied rail junction at Hazebrouck. Demonstrating the cost of the attrition suffered during Michael, the 55 German divisions that took part in the offensive included only attack and inferior trench divisions, instead of the elite mobile divisions that on 21 March had achieved such

success. Although the offensive was weaker than that of Operation Michael, it struck a part of the lines of the British First Army occupied by two poorly trained and understrength Portuguese divisions. Shocked by the ferocity of the assault, the Portuguese divisions gave way and fell back nearly six kilometres (four miles) in a single day, threatening the Allied lines in the region with collapse.

Fearing the worst, Haig again appealed to Foch for reserves, but the commander-in-chief, believing the German attack to be a diversion, initially refused to intervene directly in the battle. Frustrated, Haig rushed what reserves he could to the scene, and placed

German soldiers around and atop their massive A7V tank. Sporting as many as six machine guns, as well as a main gun, the A7V could carry up to 18 men. Although produced in too few numbers to have an effect on the war, the A7V first saw combat at St Quentin in March 1918.

German Crown Prince Wilhelm at St Quentin in May 1918. Confident of victory, the German royal family prematurely toasted the coming end of the war with champagne. Wilhelm commanded the Army Group Crown Prince, which controlled the Seventh, First and Third armies.

the defensive battle in Flanders under the control of one of his most effective commanders, General Plumer. With German forces nearing Hazebrouck, the capture of which would dislocate all British defensive planning, Haig on 11 April issued the following order of the day:

'*Many of us are now tired. To those I would say that victory will belong to the side which holds out the longest. … There is no course open to us but to fight it out. Every position must be held to the last man: there must be no retirement. With our backs to the wall and believing in the justice of our cause each one of us must fight on to the end. The safety of our homes and the freedom of mankind alike depend upon the conduct of each one of us at this critical moment.*'

Haig fumed that the BEF faced the threat alone, while the French stood by awaiting a presumed German offensive further to the south and on 14 April reiterated his need for reinforcements to Foch stating, 'If the necessary measures are not taken, the British army will be sacrificed and sacrificed in vain.' Even without significant French aid, though, the British defence soon began to stiffen, but not until Plumer had made the difficult decision to abandon much of the ground gained during the previous year's fighting

The mighty German Paris Gun, which began shelling Paris on 23 March 1918. Six of the powerful weapons eventually fired 367 shells on the French capital, resulting in 880 casualties. It was destroyed by the Germans before the war's end.

its greatest gains in the first few days of fighting. Soon, though, the resilience of the BEF, combined with the tactical realities of World War I, forced the German advance to stall. Although the German Fourth and Sixth armies had advanced in some places nearly 19km (12 miles), they had failed to achieve any of their strategic goals and had only created another salient into Allied lines that would prove difficult to defend, all at the cost of 100,000 additional casualties. Ludendorff had failed to grasp the fact that offensives in World War I, no matter their technical wizardry, had a limited life span. Tactical proficiency alone was not the answer to winning World War I.

After the conclusion of Georgette, there existed considerable tension in the Allied camp, with the British questioning the late French entry into the Flanders fighting. Many within the BEF felt that the British had borne the heaviest burden of fighting off the two massive German offensives, while the French had done but little. In fact, the French were still bearing the greatest burden of all, occupying 580km (360 miles) of the Allied front lines, against only 135km (84 miles) for the British and 35km (22 miles) for the Belgians. In part to soothe Haig's ruffled feathers, and as a component of a general reshuffling of Allied lines to move more strength to the north of the Oise River, Foch arranged for the transfer of four exhausted British divisions to a quiet sector of the French front. The quiet sector, though, was along the Chemin des Dames, which placed the British divisions directly in the path of the next great German offensive.

THE GERMANS STRIKE TOWARD PARIS

Having failed in his first two attempts to win victory, Ludendorff concocted a new plan for a two-stage offensive beginning with a diversionary attack on the Chemin des Dames aimed towards both Reims and Paris, which he hoped would force the Allies to shift reserves away from Flanders. Then, with Allied forces in the north fatally weakened, the main German

at Passchendaele in favour of a withdrawal to more defensible lines closer to Ypres. After the Germans struck Belgian forces on 17 April north of Hazebrouck, Foch belatedly realized that Georgette was in fact the next German effort at victory on the Western Front, and he quickly formed the Detachment of the North and inserted it into the fray.

With Allied reserves shifting the strategic balance in the north, on 29 April, after a minor tactical victory in seizing Mount Kemmel from French forces, Ludendorff brought Georgette to a halt. As usual, the offensive had begun with optimism and had achieved

Paris Gun

In 1916 the Germans began efforts to develop a 'super artillery piece' capable of shelling Paris. Choosing to modify a 15in naval gun for the task, the Germans developed a weapon with a barrel that was 40m (43 yards) in length and weighed 128 tonnes (142 tons). The massive gun, which could only be transported by train, fired a projectile to a distance of 129km (80 miles), which, during flight, reached into the upper stratosphere, some 39km (24 miles) high, and then fell silently to the ground. On 23 March 1918 the Germans unleashed their new weapon, six of which eventually entered service, on the unsuspecting inhabitants of Paris. Through 9 August 1918, the terror weapons fired 367 shells at Paris, resulting in 880 casualties, including 250 killed. However, the shelling was so sporadic that it failed to damage French morale, and thus did not aid materially in the German war effort. Late in World War II, though, Adolf Hitler would copy the purpose of the Paris Gun, when he too decided to place emphasis on revenge weapons aimed at crushing Allied morale.

offensive would fall in Flanders, driving the British into the sea. Facing the German attack on the Chemin des Dames were six Allied divisions (three French and three British) of the French Sixth Army, under the command of General Denis Duchêne, which held a 50km-long (31-mile) front. Earlier in the year, Pétain had given his commanders express advice that German advances had to be met with a defence in depth, advising them that, 'We do not have enough infantry divisions to accept a defensive battle on the first position. It is necessary then to manoeuvre and make the terrain work for us.' Duchêne, though, chose to ignore Pétain's guidance and placed most of his defenders forward atop the Chemin des Dames, well within the range of German artillery fire, in positions especially vulnerable to stormtroop tactics.

At 1.00am on 27 May, the heaviest single German artillery barrage of the war, involving 4000 guns firing more than two million shells in under five hours, struck Duchêne's Sixth Army. Of the 36 German divisions massed for the assault, of which 27 were veterans of Operation Michael, three struck the French 21st Division, five the French 22nd Division and four the British 50th Division. Outmanned and slaughtered in their forward positions, the Allied divisions gave way, and the Germans surged forwards. Although Duchêne attempted to retrieve the situation by throwing reserves into the fray, he did so rather indiscriminately and by the end of the day the victorious Germans had seized bridges across the Aisne

The Paris Gun was a marvel of modern engineering, boasting a barrel 40m (43 yards) in length, which could fire a projectile to a distance of 129km (80 miles).

River and had halted just outside Fismes on the Vesle River. For the next four days the Germans moved forward an additional 35km (22 miles), reaching the Marne River only 90km (56 miles) from Paris. Operation Blücher had already achieved much more than Ludendorff had intended, and he now faced his last major strategic decision of the war. Should he adhere to his original plan and strike the British in Flanders, or continue the advance toward Paris? Even though the Allied defence was already stiffening, and the prerequisites for tactical success were fading as exhausted German forces moved more than 145km (90 miles) from their logistical railheads, Ludendorff

French cavalry on patrol passing a British artillery unit. In the semi-fluid warfare of 1918, cavalry reconnaissance patrols once again had renewed value. In fact all sides continued to use cavalry throughout the battles of 1918.

again chose tactics over strategy, gambling all on an effort to take Paris.

Ludendorff seemingly had ample reason for optimism. Pétain informed Foch on 1 June, 'Since May 27 the battle has absorbed thirty-seven divisions, including five British. Seventeen of these divisions are completely exhausted; of these two or three may not be able to be reconstituted. Sixteen have been engaged for two, three or four days.' The situation was so bleak that the French general staff even began planning for withdrawing completely from northern France in an effort to consolidate defending units around the capital. Foch, though, remained firm in his belief in victory, and unleashed a flood of reserves, including the Fifth and Tenth armies, directing that the incoming reinforcements form a coherent line of defence near Château Thierry.

Cantigny

As Operation Blücher got underway on 27 May, American forces launched their first offensive action at Cantigny, near Montdidier in the Somme region, an operation undertaken in many ways to test the offensive abilities of the newly arrived American forces. The 28th Infantry Regiment of the American 1st Division led the assault on Cantigny, which served as a forward observation point for General von Hutier's Eighteenth Army. On 28 May, supported by the fire of 368 French heavy guns and French flame-thrower teams, American troops quickly seized their objective and captured 200 German prisoners. With continued French artillery support, the Americans withstood seven German counterattacks in the next few days, but held on to their gains at the cost of 1603 casualties, including 199 killed. Boleslaw Suchocki of the 28th Infantry Regiment recalled that after crossing the German barbed wire:

'I noticed that the boys were falling down fast. A shell burst about ten yards in front of me and the dirt from the explosion knocked me flat on my back. I got up again but could not see further than one hundred feet. … The German artillery was in action all the time. … I stopped at a strongpoint and asked the boy in the trench

The arrival of American forces on the battlefront, including these soldiers rushing into the attack, helped to revive flagging Allied morale.

if there was room for me to get in. [He responded] *"Don't ask for room, but get in before you get your* [!#%&] *shot off!"'*

Although the offensive at Cantigny was only a minor operation, it, coupled with later American actions at Château Thierry and Belleau Wood, indicated that the AEF was ready to play an ever-greater role in World War I, which portended disaster for Germany.

As part of Pershing's agreement to allow the use of American forces in battle, US troops saw their first meaningful combat of the war as part of the effort to defend against Operation Blücher, with the 1st Division launching a minor offensive near Cantigny, while the 3rd Division took part in defensive fighting at Château Thierry during the first week of June and the 2nd Division fought a confused engagement at Belleau Wood. In each case the American units acquitted themselves well, which, as the German drive stalled during the first week of June, signalled the ultimate failure of the German effort to achieve victory. Paris had not fallen, the British had not been driven into the sea and valuable German resources were being wasted in tactical masterpieces that only

created salients into the Allied lines, while 250,000 fresh American troops arrived on the battlefronts of France every month. The appearance of the Americans was a tonic for the morale of the battered French Army and the BEF. A French officer commented on the meaning of the first American battles:

'The spectacle of this magnificent youth from across the sea, these youngsters of twenty years with smooth faces, radiating strength and health in their new uniforms, had an immense effect. They offered a striking contrast with our regiments in soiled uniforms, worn by the years of war, with our emaciated soldiers and their sombre eyes who were nothing more than bundles of nerves held together by an heroic, sacrificial will. The

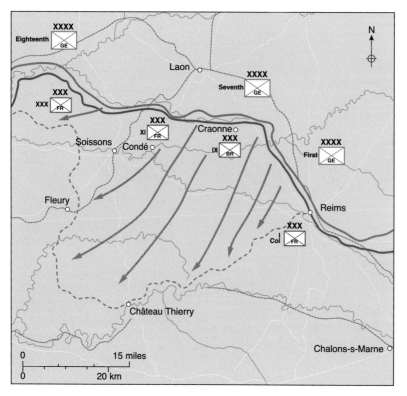

German gains during Operation Blücher, the offensive across the Chemin des Dames Ridge and the Aisne River. French defensive mistakes allowed German troops to get as far as the Marne River, within 90km (56 miles) of Paris.

forwards, which helped to make the German advance possible.

Allied forces, though, had not been surprised and had learned how to counter German tactics, and within two days, reserve divisions entered the battle and stopped the German advance in its tracks. Marking a fulcrum point of the war, on 11 June a force of five divisions, two of which were American, launched the first major Allied counterattack of the spring. The Allied divisions, under the command of General Charles Mangin, made only sporadic gains, but shocked the Germans who, after having held the initiative for so long, were suddenly thrown onto the defensive. Having lost 40,000 casualties for minimal gains, on 13 June Ludendorff cancelled Operation Gneisenau.

general impression was that of a magical transfusion of blood taking place.'

Still confident that superior German tactics would provide ultimate victory, on 9 June, Ludendorff launched his fourth attack of the spring, Operation Gneisenau, north of the Oise River between Noyon and Montdidier. The attack, which if successful would join the salients created by Operations Michael and Blucher and put the German Army in a better position to threaten Paris, pitted Hutier's Eighteenth Army against the French Third Army. Warned of the coming attack by accurate intelligence, the French had pre-positioned in the area 12 infantry and three cavalry reserve divisions, and even began their counterbarrage before the German guns opened their own preparatory fire. The French barrage notwithstanding, at 4.00am the German infantry went over the top into the attack, and advanced nearly eight kilometres (five miles) on a 24km (15-mile) frontage. Having learned little from Duchêne's mistake at the Chemin des Dames, Third Army had located its defenders

PLANNING AN ALLIED COUNTEROFFENSIVE

Exhausted and bloodied, having lost 209,000 men in June alone, the German Army had once again reached the gates of Paris. However, the situation had become critical. Because of their tactical successes, the weakened and increasingly dispirited Germans had to occupy an additional 120 kilometres of undulating and vulnerable front lines. The Prussian War Ministry warned Ludendorff that the stormtroop formations had been destroyed, while General Hutier reported mounting indiscipline even within the ranks of his elite Eighteenth Army. On the German home front the Berlin police warned the government that increasing numbers of civilians were demanding 'peace at any price'. In the Allied camp, even the notoriously pessimistic Pétain noted that increasing German weakness coupled with the arrival of the Americans had shifted the balance of the war stating, 'If we can hold until the end of June, our situation will be excellent. In July we can resume the offensive. After that, victory is ours.'

Believing that attack remained the key to victory, and unable to admit the failure of his ambitious scheme to win the war, Ludendorff prepared to drive his weary troops into battle yet again, on both the eastern and western sides of Reims. By the second week of July, though, French intelligence had discerned the location of the coming offensive, which allowed Foch to gather reserves, while Pétain's forces made ready their defences. Having become fully conversant with German methods, the French held their front lines very thinly, while main forces waited out of artillery range to blunt the German assault. Most important, though, Foch and Pétain, aided by the fiery Mangin who had been elevated to the command of the French Tenth Army, decided that Ludendorff's offensive was a perfect opportunity to launch a massive counter-offensive designed to destroy the Aisne–Marne Salient.

After considerable discussion in early July, Foch and Pétain agreed that French forces would first blunt the German offensive. Then the French Tenth and Sixth armies would strike the western face of the Aisne–Marne Salient at Soissons, while subsidiary counterattacks took place on the eastern face of the salient near Reims and along the Marne River to the south. So sure were Foch and Pétain in their planning that they committed virtually the entire Allied reserve to the coming battle, even convincing a reluctant Haig to send his reserves south to take part in the fighting. By the time of the battle, the French had a reserve force of 38

A German stormtrooper in 1918. Although the Spring Offensives had achieved remarkable tactical goals, by June the stormtroop formations that made the gains possible had been destroyed for little of strategic value.

infantry (including four British and five American) divisions and six cavalry divisions in the Marne area. Only one division remained in reserve in the entire region between the Argonne and Switzerland, while only one British division was held in reserve on the front covering Paris itself. At the crucial point of the war, Foch and Pétain had taken decisive action and had literally bet everything on the outcome of the coming battle. It was also a testament to Foch's ability as supreme commander that in what became known as the Second Battle of the Marne, for the first time in the war French, British and American forces joined in the same battle, making it a truly Allied affair.

Attacking on the morning of 15 July, the German First and Third armies made only fitful progress against the well prepared French Fourth Army east of Reims, which led Ludendorff quickly to suspend offensive action in that sector. Southwest of Reims, though, the German Seventh Army made better progress against the French Fifth Army and crossed the Marne River near Dormans. Only the French 39th Division and the US 3rd Division held their place on the Marne near Château Thierry. Shaken by the German advance, on 15 July, Pétain ordered reserves to be taken from the units slated to take part in the counterattack to aid in the defence of the Marne. Foch, though, rescinded the order and promised Pétain reserves from other parts of the front.

Foch proved correct, and after only minimal further gains along the Marne, on 17 July the German attack stalled. Although all seemed ready for the massive Allied counterstrike, Foch still had to contend with distractions. On the eve of the counterattack, Pétain called for units to be taken from the Tenth Army to solidify the defences of Paris. The very next day Haig, who feared a renewal of the German offensive in Flanders, demanded the return of the British units scheduled to take part in the Marne counterattack. Foch refused both requests. While both Pétain and Haig lost their nerve at the critical moment, Foch refused to allow the subversion of his strategic vision. The supreme commander had taken a great risk in overruling the advice of the commanders of the French and British armies, and, thus, to Foch falls the credit for the subsequent victory in the Second Battle of the Marne.

Allied forces gathered quickly to undertake their historic counterattack, with the American 2nd Division marching for 50 hours in a 72-hour period just to reach its jumping-off point near Buzancy. Mangin's French Tenth Army, which was to play the most important role in the counterattack, stood as testament to the Allied nature of the battle. Of the 22 infantry and two cavalry divisions that made up Mangin's force, two were American (the 1st and 2nd divisions), two were British (the 15th and 34th divisions), the French 58th Division was from

Morocco (which in fact also contained numerous Senegalese soldiers), and many of the troops had been transported to the front by trucks driven by Vietnamese labourers.

The powerful force gathered by the Allies had ambitious goals. The Tenth Army, supported by 1545 artillery pieces and over 300 tanks, was slated to attack toward the vital German communications network south of Soissons, severance of which would imperil the entire German position in the salient. The French plan also called for the Sixth Army, which contained eight front-line divisions including the American 4th and 26th divisions, to advance on Mangin's right flank, supported by 588 artillery pieces and 147 tanks. In the south, tasked with pinning the Germans in place and eradicating the Marne bridgehead, the Ninth Army consisted of six French and two American divisions (the 3rd and 28th) plus 644 artillery pieces and 90 tanks. Finally, on the eastern face of the salient, the Fifth Army was tasked with sealing off the German retreat. To achieve that end the Fifth Army contained

Sacrificial Units

Realizing that the Germans were going to attack in July near Reims, Foch and Pétain decided to absorb the blow before launching their counterattack, which became the Second Battle of the Marne. Reliant on a defence in depth, the French planned only to hold the front lines thinly. Peopled by volunteers, it was the task of the units in what became known as the 'sacrificial trenches' to sell their lives dearly, delay the German advance and make victory possible through subsequent counterattacks. When French Premier Georges Clemenceau visited the 'sacrificial trenches' of the French Fourth Army just days before the battle he was impressed by the quality of men who chose to give their all for France. Their eyes, he wrote, 'burned with an invincible resolution' as they prepared for the battle. 'He who has not lived through such moments,' Clemenceau noted, 'does not know what life can give.' As the German attack began, the soldiers in the

sacrificial trenches responded by throwing hand grenades and firing machine guns. When the avenues of German approach became evident, they fired rockets, which enabled Allied units in rear areas effectively to place their reinforcements and direct field artillery. Slowing the German advance as much as possible also caused the attackers to lose touch with their all-important creeping barrage.

Once it became obvious that they could no longer hold out, the soldiers in the sacrificial trenches destroyed their heavy weapons to prevent them falling into the hands of the enemy and withdrew to fight alongside their comrades in carefully prepared positions in the second line. Although their loss rates were understandably high, the soldiers of the sacrificial trenches succeeded in their task, for, though the Germans sent seven waves of attacks at the Allied second line, none broke through.

eight French infantry divisions, four French cavalry divisions, two Italian divisions, two Colonial (Moroccan and Senegalese) divisions and two British divisions, the 51st and the 62nd, supported by 902 artillery pieces and 45 tanks.

Allied forces gathered in the greatest secrecy, marching at night and encamping in forests while camouflaging the movements of the tanks. For their part, the Germans remained in an offensive posture, readying for further attacks in the area around Château Thierry. As a result the greatest weight of German forces were in the southern portion of the salient, and no real thought had been given to the defence of the salient's vulnerable flanks or to the critical communications network south of Soissons. Accordingly, only eight exhausted German divisions, which had not yet bothered to construct a defensive trench network, stood between Mangin's Tenth Army and its goal. The scene had been set for one of the most important Allied victories of World War I.

THE SECOND BATTLE OF THE MARNE

Without a preliminary barrage, the Germans had no warning whatsoever when, at 4.35am on 18 July, Allied forces moved to the attack supported by a creeping barrage fired by 2100 artillery pieces. Across the front, Allied forces advanced quickly against German defenders who were oftentimes obviously undernourished and demoralized. The greatest gains, though, took place on the fronts of the French Tenth and Sixth armies, where the honour of the deepest penetration of German lines fell to the US 1st Division, which advanced nearly eight kilometres (five miles) and interdicted the communication route between Soissons and Château Thierry, threatening to unhinge the entire German position in the Aisne–Marne Salient. The terrible defeat, in which Allied forces captured 20,000 prisoners of war, 518 artillery pieces and 3000 machine guns, shook many on the German general staff, with some even calling for a general withdrawal to the Hindenburg Line. Ludendorff initially remained optimistic and only withdrew German forces from the Marne bridgehead and ordered the defenders to stand firm in the remainder of the salient.

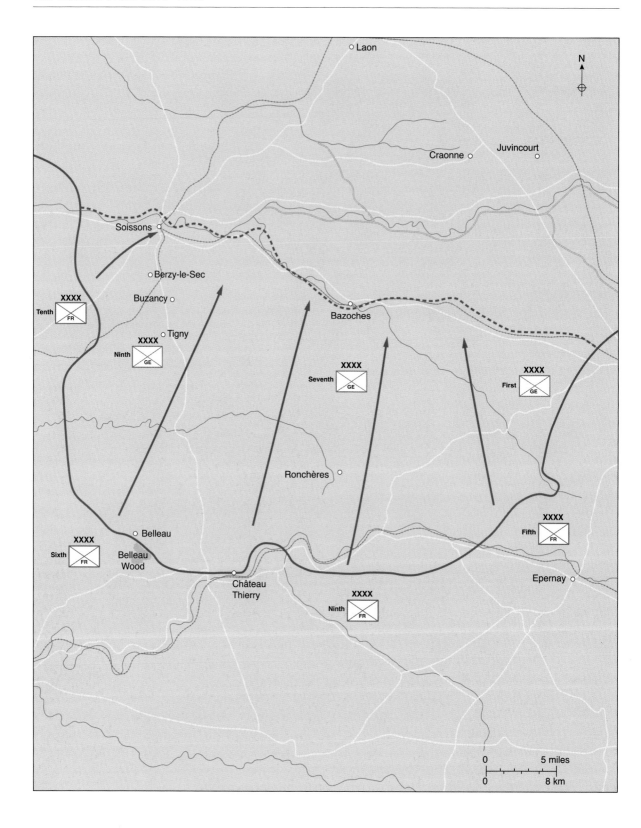

Allied gains during the Second Battle of the Marne, a coalition battle that marked the turning point of World War I in 1918. It also marked the first time that American troops had been commited to battle in large numbers, though serving under French command.

As was typical in World War I, after great gains in the opening phase of the battle, fighting in the Aisne–Marne Salient settled down to more of an attritional struggle once surprise was gone, tanks had broken down and Allied forces moved beyond the effective range of their artillery support. In ferocious fighting, though, the Allies pushed the defenders into an ever-shrinking area, while German logistic support faltered. As the tactical situation worsened, Crown Prince Wilhelm, in overall command of the forces in the area, concluded that efforts to hold the salient would be too costly and suggested a withdrawal. While he initially favoured an attack in the area of Soissons

to lessen the pressure on German forces, by 24 July Ludendorff agreed to abandon the Aisne–Marne Salient. Under constant pressure from continued Allied attacks, tenacious and dedicated rearguards covered a fighting withdrawal as by 3 August the majority of German forces had withdrawn to strong defensive positions behind the Aisne and Vesle rivers, where the Allied advance came to a halt.

The Second Battle of the Marne, which had begun as a German advance, had ended with one of the greatest Allied victories of the war. Pushed back from the gates of Paris, the Germans had lost 170,000 casualties and 30,000 prisoners during the battle, and had lost the initiative in the war. For all of the

German soldiers retreating from the Marne Salient. Falling back from the gates of Paris, the Germans would be forced into a stubborn retreat for the remainder of the conflict on the Western Front.

technical proficiency of the German Army, Ludendorff and Hindenburg had never come to terms with the realities of offensives in World War I. No matter how many great gains were made on the first few days of offensives, defenders could still rush reserves to the lines more quickly than exhausted attackers could move forward. Like Haig at Passchendaele, Ludendorff had been blinded by the possibilities that seemed to exist in the first heady days of his offensives. In each case he had succumbed to the chimerical belief that

British officers inspect men of the Motorcycle Machine Gun Corps, a special branch of the Machine Gun Corps. With their speed and manoeuvrability, military motorcycles were of ideal use in a war that was once again becoming mobile.

another push would certainly force the teetering Allied lines to break, and had poured reserves into offensives that had already run their course rather than devising a true operational scheme on the Western Front. In 1923 Ludendorff attempted to defend his actions by stating, 'I always had only the one great goal of victory before my eyes. The means to accomplish this were dictated by the prevailing situation. ... For the offensive I always asked, where do I best break through, where is the enemy's weakest point?'

Although Ludendorff was loathe to admit his defeat, and even harboured hopes of renewed offensives on the Western Front, most other observers realized that the turning point of the war had passed. Ludendorff's

Spring Offensives had run their course, and the balance of war would only tip ever further against a depleted and demoralized Germany as more and more American power was brought to bear. In recognition of the great victory Clemenceau promoted Foch to marshal of France, and signified the importance of the Second Battle of the Marne in his presidential decree:

'Paris disengaged, Soissons and Château Thierry reconquered by force, more than 200 villages freed … the high hopes proclaimed by the enemy before his attack shattered, the glorious allied armies advanced with a single victorious will from the edge of the Marne to the banks of the Aisne: those are the results of a manoeuvre admirably conceived by the high command and superbly executed by incomparable leaders.'

After the Second Battle of the Marne, Hutier admitted that the men of his army were tired and dispirited. Petrol for trucks was running low, ammunition for the artillery was in short supply, reserves coming to the front were greeted with jeers

British and French soldiers firing a machine gun in the open. Unlike the static fighting from late 1914 to 1917, the battles of 1918 often involved units advancing across open terrain in semi-mobile warfare. For many soldiers, the return to mobile fighting came as a surprise after so long in the trenches.

and shouts as 'strike breakers'. Some battalions in his army had fallen in strength from 900 to only 100 men. The German Army would fight on and would fight well, but no longer had any real hope for victory on the Western Front. Regarding the jarring shift from high hopes at the outset of Ludendorff's final failed attack to defeat at the Marne, German Chancellor Georg von Hertling recalled:

'At the beginning of July 1918, I was convinced, I confess it, that before the first of September our adversaries would send us peace proposals. … We expected grave events in Paris for the end of July. That was on the 15th. On the 18th even the most optimistic among us knew that all was lost. The history of the world was played out in three days.'

CHAPTER 6

The Hundred Days

Under the supreme command of Marshal Ferdinand Foch, the Allies unleashed waves of attacks that even pushed the Germans from the mighty defences of the Hindenburg Line. As the Allies proved their tactical mastery of the battlefield, and Americans entered the lines in ever-greater numbers, even Ludendorff came to the realization that the war had been lost.

E ven before the Second Battle of the Marne had fatally shifted the balance of the war against the Germans, several leading Allied commanders had sensed that the tipping point was near and had begun planning to retake the initiative in the war. Within the BEF, on 5 July, General Rawlinson, in command of Fourth Army, proposed to Haig an attack near Amiens, after a successful assault by Australian forces near Hamel had proved both the resurgent nature of the BEF and the relative weakness of German defences. Intrigued by the idea, Haig gave Rawlinson the go ahead to continue his planning.

Supported by tanks and lethal artillery barrages, British infantry units proved capable of utilizing infiltration tactics to redefine the nature of combat on the Western Front as the balance of power shifted once more towards the Allied side in 1918.

While Haig and Rawlinson laid the groundwork for their offensive, Foch thought in even more grandiose terms and by mid-July was hatching a plan to launch a series of blows against German defences all along the Western Front, aimed initially at retaking Dunkirk and Calais in the north, and reducing both the Amiens and St Mihiel salients farther south. In a 24 July meeting, Foch laid his proposals before Haig, who agreed that the time had come to pass to the offensive. The two commanders, though, still had to convince their reluctant governments, which had been made skittish by past military predictions of impending victory that had ended only in futile battles of attrition.

In London, Lloyd George was particularly ambivalent concerning the chances of any offensives on the Western Front and hoped to hold Haig in check while awaiting the arrival of more American forces before launching any counterattack. Ironically, though, Foch's position as supreme commander, which the Prime Minister had thought would limit Haig's strategic independence, actually served to shield the commander-in-chief of the BEF from Lloyd George's wrath. Foch, however, also had to face questions from Clemenceau, for even the Tiger felt that French forces were too exhausted to undertake a meaningful offensive. To convince reluctant politicians, Foch utilized his considerable powers of persuasion and his ebullient optimism, proclaiming that the momentum had changed and said, 'We're holding them. We're hitting them in the flank. We're kicking and punching them. We're killing off the enemy. Our dead … my son … my son-in-law … are avenged.' When he faced Clemenceau's rebuttal that Allied forces were dropping with fatigue, Foch replied, 'The Germans are dropping with still more fatigue.'

Trench Conditions

Even as the war came to a close, battlefield conditions were quite trying for the fighting men of all of the belligerent nations. Living in the open, as battle raged, men had only fleeting access to food and water, and had precious little time to bury the dead or care for their own hygiene needs. Wearing the same uniforms for weeks on end, amid the open sewers that made up their defensive positions, soldiers often became covered in lice. Private W.A. Quinton of the BEF recalled:

'We did not notice the lice so much when standing, perished with cold, on lookout. But when we got in our tiny dugouts, and our bodies began to get warm, then out would come the lice from their hiding places in our clothing, forming up in columns of fours, would start route marching over our flesh. Yes! They were our bosom companions, and although we have joked about them, there have been times when, utterly worn out, both physically and mentally, yet unable to sleep because of the lice, I have known men to actually cry and curse the lice, and He who made them.'

Life in the wilderness of the trenches during World War I was fraught with danger, even in times of relative calm.

Although Foch later wrote that his statements caused many political and military leaders alike to take him 'for a madman', his arguments won the day. Regardless of their exhaustion the Allies were going to attack.

PLANS FOR AN ALLIED OFFENSIVE

The opening assault within Foch's broader offensive scheme was that of Rawlinson's Fourth Army, in conjunction with the French First Army under the command of General Eugène Debeney, in the area of Amiens. Judging that the Germans around Amiens had done but little to construct defensive works and were under strength, Rawlinson and Haig realized that speed was of the essence and took only three weeks to plan and prepare the coming offensive. The smoothness of the planning process in and of itself demonstrated both the progress that the BEF had made in the years since the Somme and the maturation of Haig as a commander. Rawlinson's draft scheme called for an attack by 11 divisions on a 17,375m (19,000-yard) front from Morlancourt to Demuin, which aimed at penetrating the German lines to a depth of 5490m (6000 yards), a mammoth goal considering the relative lack of forward movement in earlier British offensives.

Both technological and tactical innovations within the BEF in the years since the Somme made seeking such gains realistic in 1918. Infantry units now packed a considerable punch, with each British battalion including 30 Lewis guns (portable machine guns), eight light trench mortars and 16 rifle-grenadiers, enabling it effectively to deal with enemy strongpoints without having to wait for cumbersome artillery support. Aided by a force of over 500 tanks, the infantry units of the Fourth Army, instead of moving forward in waves, planned to utilize speed and infiltration tactics to advance to depth in an attack reminiscent of Cambrai. Rawlinson and Haig had also gathered a force of 1236 field guns and 677 heavy guns

General Sir Herbert Plumer and French Premier Georges Clemenceau discuss the course of the Allied counterattack. Although the civilian leaders on the Allied side were nervous about the prospects of attacks in the summer of 1918, the Allied military commanders were keen to forge ahead.

to support the offensive, against only 530 German guns in the area. As at Cambrai, the British artillery utilized silent registration and chose to forgo a preliminary bombardment in order to maintain surprise. Of the greatest importance, intelligence, including flash spotting and aerial reconnaissance, had pinpointed the exact locations of no fewer than 504 of the German guns, which would enable counterbattery fire effectively to silence the German artillery on the day of the attack. Finally, in the Amiens sector the Allies had gathered a force of 1900 aircraft, against only 365 German machines, and planned to utilize their resultant command of the air in a ground-attack role

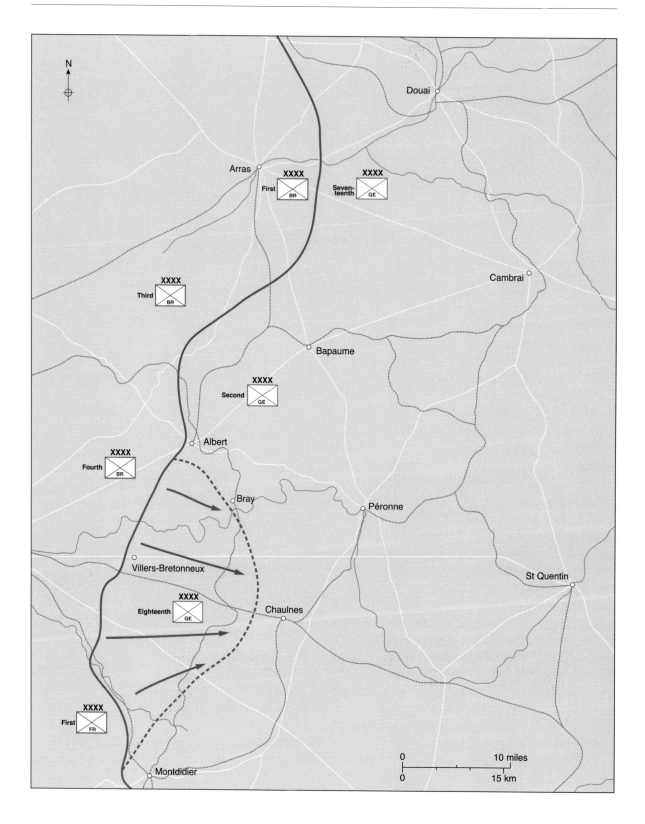

N

Douai

Arras

XXXX
First
BR

XXXX
Seven-
teenth
GE

Cambrai

XXXX
Third
BR

Bapaume

XXXX
Second
GE

Albert

XXXX
Fourth
BR

Bray

Péronne

Villers-Bretonneux

St Quentin

XXXX
Eighteenth
GE

Chaulnes

XXXX
First
FR

Montdidier

0   10 miles

0   15 km

The Battle of Amiens, launched on 8 August 1918, saw the British Fourth Army under Sir Henry Rawlinson reduce the Amiens Salient, it was the offensive action that touched off the 'Hundred Days'. In common with many late war British offensives, it was spearheaded by Dominion troops.

to augment the advance. Through years of learning, the BEF by 1918 had become an integrated weapons system, one that used the most modern tactics within a rubric of all-arms coordination that in some ways more foreshadowed the tactics of World War II rather than hearkened back to the Somme. Lieutenant-General John Monash, the commander of the Australian Corps, put the new British military system into words: 'A modern battle plan is like nothing so much as a score for a musical composition, where the various arms and units are the instruments, and the tasks they perform are their respective musical phrases. Each individual unit must make its entry precisely at the proper moment, and play its phrase in harmony.'

Haig and Rawlinson went to great lengths to ensure the secrecy of the coming offensive, including gathering forces at night and massing tanks in wooded areas as aircraft buzzed the German front lines to cover the telltale noise of the tanks' engines. Much effort also went into deception, especially as regards the movements of the Canadian Corps. Under the command of First Army, the Canadians represented

the most powerful and cohesive corps within the BEF, were well rested since they had not seen much action during the German Spring Offensives, and were regarded by the Germans as the shock troops of the BEF. Understandably, Rawlinson and Haig wanted the Canadians to play a major role in the fighting at Amiens, but realized that quickly shifting the corps from the front of First Army to Rawlinson's Fourth Army would be a red flag to German intelligence. In order to confuse the Germans, the British ordered two Canadian battalions to move to the front of Second Army, in the vicinity of Mount Kemmel, and to simulate the presence of the entire corps through the use of false radio traffic. The security measures undertaken by Haig and Rawlinson were a complete success, enabling Fourth Army to amass a strength of more than 400,000 men against only 37,000 German defenders, who, having become complacent during their string of successful attacks, had not taken the time to construct effective defensive networks.

AMIENS

The first that the Germans knew about the attack was when, at 4.20am on 8 August, from left to right the British III Corps, the Australian Corps and the Canadian Corps advanced under cover of a thunderous barrage and emerged from a heavy mist,

The Sopwith Camel, the most famous British fighter of the war, produced in response to the German Albatros D-types. The Camel's manoeuvrability and agility made it a match for nearly every German aircraft.

an assault augmented shortly thereafter by an advance of French First Army on the right flank. Shocked by the ferocity of the attack, without supporting artillery fire and constantly harassed by strafing aircraft, the German defenders quickly gave way. The strongpoints and machine-gun nests that did hold out against the initial attack soon found themselves surrounded by the quick-moving infantry or facing destruction by the accompanying tanks. The resulting victory was spectacular, with Fourth Army, except on its extreme flanks, reaching all of its major goals, advancing up to

British tankers examine a captured German weapon meant to fire armour-piercing rounds. The large numbers of tanks available to the Allies ensured that they would play a major role in the campaigns of 1918. However, the Germans had also developed a number of countermeasures.

13km (eight miles), capturing 400 enemy guns, inflicting 15,000 casualties and capturing 12,000 prisoners, all at a cost of only 9000 casualties. On the right flank Debeney's French First Army fell somewhat short of its final objectives, failing to capture the village of Fresnoy, but it still advanced nearly eight kilometres (five miles), while capturing 3000 prisoners. Haig was understandably heartened by the victory, due in great part to the brave accomplishment of Dominion forces, and recorded in his diary that, 'the situation had developed more favourably for us than I, optimist though I am, had dared even to hope!'

With Haig and Rawlinson expecting even greater results, possibly including cavalry action, the attack continued the next day. Although the renewed offensive achieved an advance of a further five

On the first day of the Battle of Amiens, BEF formations captured in excess of 12,000 German prisoners. This was one of the first occasions on which German troops gave themselves up in large numbers, something that worried Ludendorff more than the loss of territory.

kilometres (three miles), the entropy began to set in that so typified even successful attacks during World War I. Exhausted units began to lose cohesion in the advance and outran their vital artillery support, tanks broke down in droves and communications suffered terribly. The attack slowed further on 10 August, with only the French, with Debeney unleashing two fresh corps into the attack, making substantial gains, in some areas advancing nearly six kilometres (four miles). As the attackers weakened, in contrast the Germans rushed reinforcements, both men and guns, to the battle area. Without a weapon of exploitation, the gains of the first day of the offensive, made possible by detailed planning and overwhelming firepower, were no longer possible as the initiative in

the battle shifted back to the defender. In similar situations during the German Spring Offensives, Ludendorff had sacrificed his strategic aim to pursue the chimera of tactical breakthrough, pursuing his offensives long after they had lost the prerequisites for forward momentum. Such, though, was not to be the case with Haig and Foch.

After only four days of fighting Haig called an end to the Battle of Amiens, a halt initially designed only to allow Rawlinson's Fourth Army and Debeney's First

German troops retreating during the Battle of Amiens. Ludendorff referred to the opening day of the attack, 8 August 1918, as 'the black day of the German Army'. The Germans suffered the loss of 48,000 men in the battle, 29,873 of whom became prisoners of war.

Army a chance to regroup. However, the commander of the Canadian Corps, General Arthur Currie, whose soldiers had done so much to make the victory possible, informed Rawlinson and Haig that he believed the continuation of the offensive to be a 'desperate enterprise', given the shifting balance of forces. After listening to his subordinate, Haig called off a further attack in the area in favour of shifting the weight of a continued BEF offensive onto the fronts of the First and Third armies. At a meeting on 14 August, though, Foch pressed Haig to continue advancing at Amiens, a demand to which Haig responded angrily, recording in his diary, 'I spoke to Foch quite straightly and let him understand that *I was responsible to my Government and fellow citizens for the handling of the British forces*.' Foch found Haig's reasoning, supported by Rawlinson, Currie and Debeney, to be sound and agreed that the Battle of Amiens had run its course. The supreme commander, like Haig, had already come to the independent conclusion that what was required on the Western Front was not a single offensive prosecuted beyond the tactical point of reason. Instead, both Foch and Haig advocated a series of interrelated offensives, aimed at applying constant pressure on the Germans while keeping them off balance: short, sharp offensives that benefited from thorough preparation and forced the Germans constantly to shift their dwindling reserves from place to place, all the while never knowing from where the next attack would come. Unlike Ludendorff, the Allied command team of Foch and Haig, who commanded military formations that were as tactically adept as the Germans, had discovered how to prosecute battles at the operational level of war.

The Battle of Amiens, coming fast on the heels of the reverse suffered in the Second Battle of the Marne, came as a severe psychological blow to Ludendorff, who, in his memoirs, wrote: 'August 8 was the black day of the German Army in the history of the war.

Gas

World War I saw the widespread use of poison gas, ranging from phosgene, which attacked the lungs, to mustard gas, which caused severe burning both to the skin and to the respiratory system. Although both sides developed countermeasures against such attacks, the gruesome deaths suffered by gas victims made the weapon among the most feared of the entire war. Private W.A. Quinton of the BEF recalled reaching a front-line trench in which he discovered the remnants of a company that had suffered a gas attack:

'Black in the face, their tunics and shirt fronts torn open at the necks in their last desperate fight for breath, many of them lay quite still while others were still wriggling and kicking in the agonies of the most awful death I have ever seen. Some were wounded in the bargain, and their gaping wounds lay open, blood still oozing from them. One poor devil was tearing at his throat with his hands. I doubt if he knew, or felt, that he had only one hand, and that the other was just a stump

Soldiers left unprotected during a gas attack faced the grim prospect of a lingering death, as their lungs slowly rotted away.

where the hand should have been. This stump he worked around his throat as if the hand were still there, and the blood from it was streaming over his bluish black face and neck.'

This was the worst experience I had to go through. … August 8 made things clear for both army Commands, both for the German Army and for that of the enemy.'

WIDENING THE ASSAULT

Unnerved by the reverses, Ludendorff was certain that Germany had lost the war. Blaming the impending defeat on 'agitators' and a breakdown of civilian morale rather than on his own misguided military efforts, Ludendorff offered his resignation, which the Kaiser refused. After the Battle of Amiens had ended, Ludendorff regained a measure of composure, but still, along with Hindenburg at a conference on 14 August, informed the Kaiser that the German Army had, 'reached the limits of our endurance'. Regardless of the perilous circumstances, though, the German command team chose to have the German Army make a stand in France in the faint hope that a bloody attritional battle centred on the Hindenburg Line would force the Allies into a negotiated peace. Having

weathered a crisis of confidence, Ludendorff had chosen to fight on until the end.

Determined to press their advantage, Foch and Haig orchestrated a series of offensives over the next weeks that denied the reeling Germans any respite. To the south the French armies assailed German lines, and on 20 August General Mangin's Tenth Army drove the Germans back nearly 13km (eight miles) in the area between the Oise River and Soissons. At the same time, Haig's forces spread the attack to the north, with the British Third Army, under General Julian Byng, attacking near the old Somme battlefield. Without the element of surprise or the numerical superiority that had characterized British success at Amiens, Byng moved into the Battle of Albert rather cautiously, earning Haig's ire, and scheduled a pause in the offensive after only one day to consolidate very limited gains. Mistaking the pause in operations as a defensive victory, General von Below ordered his German Seventeenth Army to counterattack on 22 August.

With their forces weakened and facing stiff British resistance, the Germans suffered heavy casualties, which only served to ease the resumption of Byng's offensive. Supported by 98 tanks, Byng's forces renewed their advance on 23 August, and reached their final objectives across most of the front, unhinging the German defensive position. Although less spectacular than the gains made in the Battle of Amiens, in the Battle of Albert Byng's forces captured 10,000 Germans, and helped to convince Haig that the German Army was crumbling. Heartened by the prospect, Haig's natural sense of optimism returned, and he instructed his army commanders:

German troops rest during the retreat, but remain in readiness to face a gas attack. Although there were increasing numbers of motor vehicles being used to supply the armies on the Western Front, all sides relied on horse transport, with as many as 3000 horses per infantry division.

'Methods which we have followed, hitherto, in our battles with limited objectives when the enemy was strong, are no longer suited to his present condition.

'The enemy has not the means to deliver counter-attacks on an extended scale, nor has he the numbers to hold a position against the very extended advance which is now being directed upon him.

'To turn the present situation to account the most resolute offensive is everywhere desirable. Risks which a month ago would have been criminal to incur, ought to be incurred as a duty.'

On 26 August, the BEF extended its attack frontage north by opening an offensive on the front of General Henry Horne's First Army, which, spearheaded by Currie's Canadian Corps, advanced nearly five kilometres (three miles). A few days later, further to the south, Third and Fourth armies attacked, which resulted in Australian forces seizing

the critical German defensive positions of Mont St Quentin and Péronne. At the same time, the French First and Third armies pushed forward nearly 13km (eight miles) and seized Noyon. Although they had been forced to give up a great deal of territory, the retreating Germans finally took shelter in the powerful belt of defences known as the Drocourt–Queant Switch Line, a subsidiary of the vaunted Hindenburg Line, where they hoped to hold through the winter and impose a morale-sapping war of attrition on their foes.

Now engaged in a series of semi-mobile battles rather than the all-too-familiar trench warfare, Horne's First Army paused before the imposing German defences of the Drocourt–Queant Switch Line to prepare for a difficult battle. Utilizing an innovative tactical plan developed by General Currie, and aided by deception as well as attacks on other fronts, the First Army, again spearheaded by the Canadians, assaulted the position on 2 September. Canadian and British soldiers advanced on a narrow front, covered by the withering fire of 762 guns, which fired 18,597 tonnes (20,500 tons) of ammunition – more than had been fired in the entire Battle of Amiens. The attack was an unqualified success, rupturing the Drocourt–Queant Switch Line on a frontage of 6400m (7000 yards), and taking 8000 prisoners. Allied forces had proven that they could break even the most powerful German defensive positions, while near constant attacks kept the enemy wrong footed.

The capture of Péronne and the breaking of the Drocourt–Queant Switch Line shattered the German plans for the remainder of the year and led Ludendorff to sanction a withdrawal to the main Hindenburg Line. As the Germans pulled back to what many considered a nearly impregnable defensive network, it became

> 'This advance gives a sense of the enormous movement behind the British lines, and there is not a man who is not stirred by the motion of it. … It is like a vast tide of life moving very slowly but steadily.'
>
> Philip Gibbs, official British wartime reporter

During August and September, Allied forces pushed the Germans back nearly 40km (25 miles) on an attack frontage of 113km (70 miles) – eradicating the gains of Ludendorff's Spring Offensives. Shown are the Siegfried (1), Wotan (2), and Hermann (3) Stellung of the Hindenburg Line.

clear that the first phase of the Allied offensives had come to an end. Allied forces, on a front of nearly 113km (70 miles), had achieved a remarkable string of victories and had pushed the Germans back nearly 40km (25 miles), eradicating the gains of Ludendorff's Spring Offensives. The sense of accomplishment, however, was tempered by the fact that the Allies now faced the most formidable defensive network ever constructed on the Western Front.

As Haig and Foch paused to consider how best to assail the Hindenburg Line, the British Government very nearly lost its heart. While enthused by the recent string of victories, Lloyd George believed that the BEF did not have the strength to break the Hindenburg Line, and despaired that an attack on the mighty German defensive position would devolve into another Somme or Third Ypres. Hoping that Haig and Foch would call a halt to operations along the Western Front, pending the arrival of more American troops, Lloyd George had Wilson send Haig a telegram warning the commander-in-chief that the War Cabinet 'would become anxious if we received heavy punishment in attacking the Hindenburg Line without success'. The telegram angered Haig who recorded in his diary:

'The object of this telegram is, no doubt, to save the Prime Minister in case of any failure. So I read it to mean that I can attack the Hindenburg Line if I think it right to do so. The C.I.G.S. and the Cabinet already know that my arrangements are being made to that end. If my attack is successful, I will remain on as C. in C. If we fail, or our losses are excessive, I can hope for no mercy!'

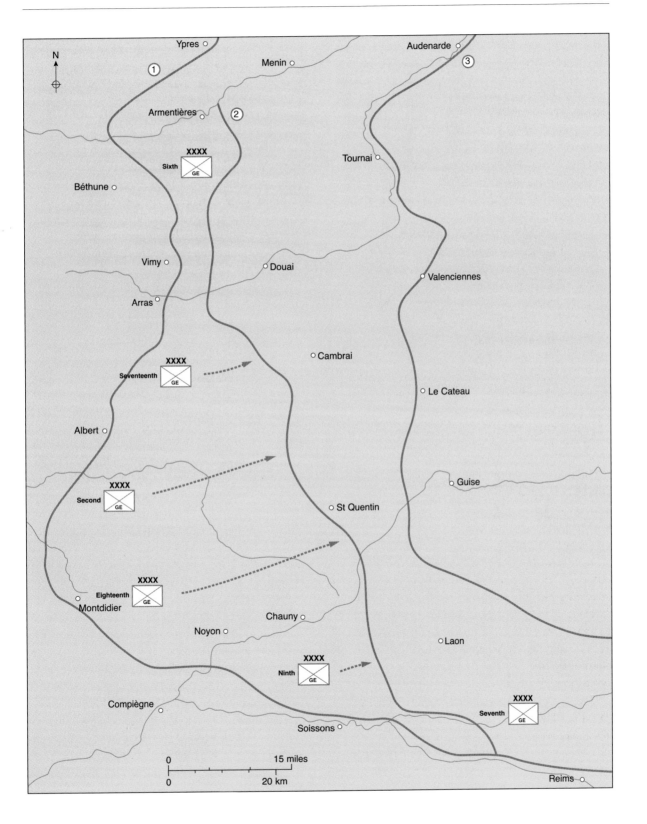

With the mutinies a thing of the past, a column of French soldiers, cheered by the recent string of Allied victories, moves to the front lines near Amiens. This regiment is moving up to take its position in the line between Amiens and Montdidier.

Convinced of the need to press the offensive, in early September Haig took his case directly to the new Secretary of State for War, Lord Milner, who instead of supporting an offensive warned Haig that costly attacks would only compromise Britain's position if the war lingered. After their meeting, Milner reported to Lloyd George that he 'had grave doubts whether he had got inside of D.H.'s head', and that Haig was 'ridiculously optimistic'. Wilson agreed and argued that the War Cabinet would have to, 'watch this tendency & stupidity of D.H.' Believing that Haig's optimism had once again gotten the better of him, and fearing a repetition of the Somme, Lloyd George tried for the last time to shift British forces away from the

Western Front, which would have allowed the war there to become a rather American affair. However, events in France and Flanders soon proved the Prime Minister wrong and pre-empted his planning.

PLANNING FOCH'S GRAND OFFENSIVE AND THE FUTURE OF THE AEF

In his arguments with his own government, Haig had found an ally in Foch; both men believed that the opportunity to win the war was at hand and hoped to force the issue through continued attacks, while Clemenceau and Lloyd George, on the other hand, argued for conservation of strength in a war that they deemed would last into 1919 or even 1920. With the bit between their teeth, Haig and Foch both concluded, not without some rather acrimonious debate, that a converging attack by all Allied forces on the German salient in central France aimed at the critical communications hub of Mézières provided the best opportunity to dislocate German defences and provide a quick victory. In obtaining approval for their grand offensive, the formidable team of Foch and Haig steamrolled over opposition from sceptical politicians in France and London only to find that the greatest challenge to their scheme came from an unexpected source, General Pershing.

The spring and summer of 1918 had been an incredibly difficult time for the commander of the American Expeditionary Force. Pressured by Washington to form a coherent and independent American army, his increasingly desperate Allies also bombarded Pershing with pleas to send whatever forces he could to the front to stem the German tide during Ludendorff's Spring Offensives. American divisions answered the call, especially during the confused fighting in the Marne Salient, delaying Pershing's long-hoped-for separate American command. Of less notice, but perhaps of even greater

importance, was the fact that, at the request of the British and French militaries, which were in desperate need of men, the US had shipped only infantry and machine-gunners to France, which left Pershing critically short on logistics, transportation and artillery. Regardless of the political and logistic difficulties, however, on 10 August, Pershing had achieved his goal with the activation of the American First Army.

Although dependent on the French and British for artillery and transport, Pershing wanted his force to play a major role in the ongoing offensives against the Germans, and after considerable deliberation opted for an assault on the German salient south of Verdun

German soldiers pose with a captured French 155mm gun. The 155mm was a standard design used by the French, and later the US Army, during World War I. Later known as the 'Long Tom', it was upgraded and carried on in service throughout World War II.

at St Mihiel. Pershing hoped that the French could lock German defending units in place at the base of the salient, while American attacks on its shoulders caused the entire German position to collapse, leading to a general advance on Metz. On 17 August, Foch had given Pershing permission to prepare for offensive operations around St Mihiel, and even promised six French divisions to aid in the undertaking. Two weeks later, though, Foch unveiled his new plan in a meeting with Pershing, and informed the American commander that the proposed US drive on St Mihiel was to be cancelled since it diverged from the planned general Allied offensive toward Mézières. Instead, Foch proposed that, as part of the general advance, the American First Army be split up to take part in assaults in the Meuse-Argonne region and in Champagne under command of French generals.

Pershing angrily rejected the proposal, stating, 'This virtually destroys the American army we have been trying so long to form.' Fearing for the future of his planned grand offensive Foch pressed the issue further and Pershing responded, 'Marshal Foch, you have no authority as Allied commander-in-chief to call upon me to yield up my command of the

A US officer in his command post. Lacking experience, logistical and communication difficulties would continue to dog the US war effort through the remainder of the conflict.

The American Browning machine gun. Capable of firing 450–600 rounds per minute, the water-cooled Browning only entered service on 26 September 1918.

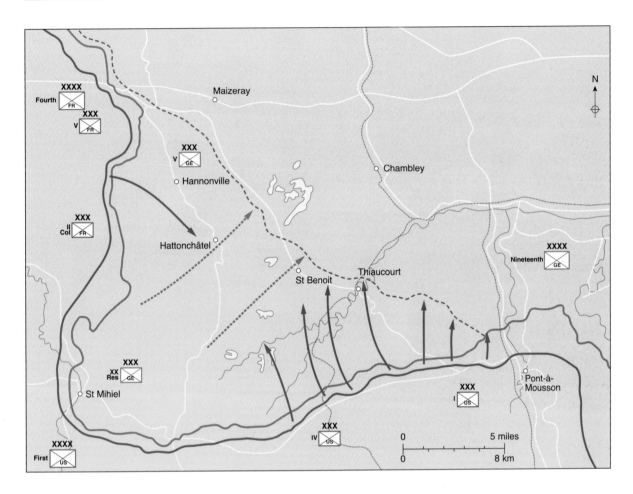

Maizeray

Chambley

Hannonville

Hattonchâtel

St Benoit

Thiaucourt

St Mihiel

Pont-à-Mousson

First

The reduction of the St Mihiel Salient, a successful operation that gave Pershing a false sense of the capabilities of the AEF. Many of the German formations were actually in the process of attempting to withdraw from the salient when the Americans attacked.

American army and have it scattered among the Allied forces where it will not be an American army at all.' Adamant, Foch stood up from the table and said, 'I must insist upon this arrangement.' 'Marshal Foch, you may insist all you please,' Pershing retorted, 'but I decline absolutely to agree to your plan. While our army will fight wherever you may decide, it will not fight except as an independent American army.' Foch left the meeting exasperated and threatened to take the matter directly to President Wilson.

On 2 September, after Pétain had attempted to mediate the dispute, Foch and Pershing met again and agreed upon a compromise. Foch allowed Pershing to choose whether US forces, acting independently, would play their role in the grand offensive by attacking in the rough terrain between the Argonne Forest and the Meuse River, or in easier

terrain west of the Argonne. Due in part to its proximity to existing American supply depots, Pershing chose the Meuse-Argonne. Foch then pressed Pershing to abandon his offensive at St Mihiel, but the American commander remained adamant. Although he realized full well that shifting American troops and supplies from the area of St Mihiel to the Meuse-Argonne would be a difficult undertaking for the untested staff of the AEF, Pershing, without consulting his superiors, made matters immeasurably worse by insisting that American forces first fight a battle at St Mihiel and

US troops advancing during their first major offensive operations in the Battle of St Mihiel. Although the US First Army fought admirably in the battle, it was against a disorganized enemy and harder tasks awaited the AEF in the Meuse-Argonne.

then shift northwards to prosecute an offensive at the Meuse-Argonne. The twin efforts would tax the abilities of American logisticians beyond their limits.

The final scheme, as agreed to by Foch, Haig and Pershing, was an example of true coalition warfare. The American effort to reduce the St Mihiel Salient, though subsidiary to the main attack, would come first, on 12 September. Only two weeks later, leaving the Americans precious little time to shift their forces more than 97km (60 miles) northwards, on 26 September American and French units would launch what Foch presumed to be the main attack between the Meuse River and Reims aimed at the seizure of Mézières, some 80km (50 miles) distant. The next day the British First and Third armies would assault simultaneously and cross the Schelde Canal towards Cambrai. On 28 September, a composite force of Belgian, British and French units, known as the Group

of Armies in Flanders (GAF), would strike toward Roulers. Finally, on 29 September, the British Fourth Army, supported by the French First Army on its right, would attack into the teeth of the main Hindenburg Line system along the St Quentin Canal.

ST MIHIEL

As the American First Army gathered its strength in preparation for the single largest American military undertaking since the Civil War, Ludendorff concluded that the St Mihiel Salient was too vulnerable to defend, and, on 8 September, ordered his troops there to withdraw to the defences of the Hindenburg Line. Due to delays, though, General Max von Gallwitz, in command of German forces in the area, had only just begun the complicated operation when, on 12 September, 16 American divisions struck on both flanks of the salient. Supported by the fire of 3010 artillery pieces, of which 1681 were manned by Americans and 1329 by the French, American forces crashed through the thinly held German front lines. Although some German formations resisted the advance, most simply tried to complete their withdrawal from the salient before the advancing Americans cut them off. By 16 September, the American First Army had scored a remarkable victory, reducing the St Mihiel Salient and capturing 15,000 German prisoners and 450 artillery pieces at the cost of only 7000 US casualties.

To Pershing, St Mihiel vindicated both his long fight to found an independent American military force and his tactical belief in more open methods of warfare. In his final report on the battle Pershing wrote:

'The material results of the victory achieved were very important. An American army was an accomplished fact, and the enemy had felt its power. No form of propaganda could overcome the depressing effect on the morale of the enemy of this demonstration of our ability to organize a large American force and drive it successfully through his defenses. It gave our troops implicit confidence in their superiority and raised their morale to the highest pitch.

'For the first time wire entanglements ceased to be regarded as impassable barriers. ... Our divisions concluded the attack with such small losses and in such high spirits that without the usual rest they were immediately available for employment in heavy fighting in a new theater of operations.'

Although the reduction of the St Mihiel Salient had been an important victory, observers within the French, British and even the American military noted that it had come against a German force bent on retreat, and that a skilled and more experienced army might have performed even better. General Robert Lee Bullard, eventually promoted to command the American Second Army, remarked: 'St. Mihiel was given an importance which posterity will not concede it. Germany had begun to withdraw. She had her weaker divisions, young men and old and Austro-Hungarians. The operation fell short of expectations.'

In the afterglow of St Mihiel, though, Pershing must have thought that attacks in World War I were not as difficult as the French and British experience of

Even without the aid of trenches, German defenders, as these pictured firing their *minenwerfer* at St Mihiel, could inflict heavy casualties on attacking forces through the skilful use of blocking positions and machine guns.

past years had led him to believe. Confident in his abilities and in the readiness of his army, Pershing began to shift forces northwards to the Meuse-Argonne, where, in the next American offensive, the Germans would choose to stand and fight – altering Pershing's opinion of World War I.

THE MEUSE-ARGONNE

The shift of American forces from St Mihiel to the Meuse-Argonne front was a massive undertaking, but in 10 days, under the direction of Colonel George C. Marshall, US and French forces succeeded in

transferring some 428,000 men, 90,000 horses, 3980 artillery pieces and 816,466 tonnes (900,000 tons) of supplies, all under great secrecy. With the French Fourth Army on his left flank, Pershing, on a 32km (20-mile) front, gathered I, III and V corps and enjoyed an eight-to-one superiority in men and a ten-to-one superiority in artillery over the defending Germans. In light of his recent success at St Mihiel, the American commander planned to break through three successive belts of German defences and advance 16km (10 miles) all in one great push, after which the American First Army would halt for only a short period before pressing on toward Mézières.

Pershing's planning, though, was hopelessly optimistic, especially considering the fact that the AEF basically remained an untried force, with four of the nine divisions slated to take part in the opening assault

The slow advance of French and American forces during the Meuse-Argonne campaign from September to November 1918. The Americans in particular struggled in the face of a well organized defensive system and determined opposition from German forces.

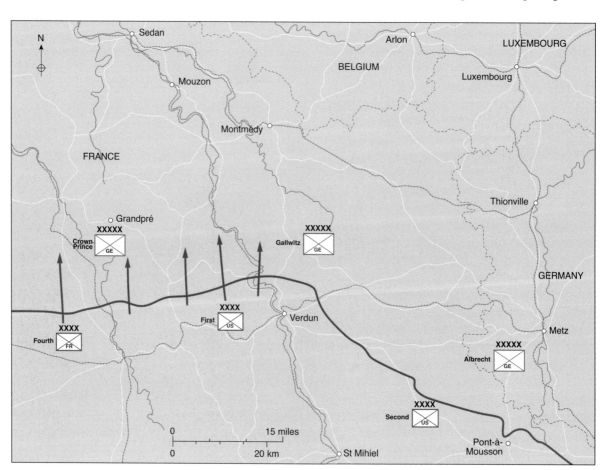

The Colt New Service revolver, a .45-calibre handgun of which 150,000 were produced during World War I. This weapon was originally introduced in 1909 after the US Army's experiences in the Philippines. It was improved for wartime use as the M1917.

having had no previous combat experience. Also the Germans expected an attack in the area, having their suspicions confirmed by French deserters, and prepared a defence in depth based on a system of machine-gun nests and strongpoints that were now so familiar to British and French forces, but were new to the Americans. General Hugh Drum, Pershing's chief of staff, commented concerning the German defences, 'This was the most ideal defensive position I have ever seen or read about. Nature had provided for flank and crossfire to the utmost in addition to concealment.' As evidenced by Drum's remarks, the terrain also worked against the attackers, canalizing any advance into gaps between the Meuse River, the Montfaucon Hills and the Argonne Forest. General Hunter Liggett, in command of the American I Corps, termed the area a 'natural fortress

German troops digging fortifications in the Argonne region. After initial successes, the Franco-American advance became bogged down by the the difficult ground and the tenacity of its German defenders.

... beside which the Wilderness in which Grant fought Lee was a park'.

After a short artillery barrage, on 26 September, the American First Army and French Fourth Army launched the Meuse-Argonne Offensive. Shocked by the sheer scale of the bombardment and badly outnumbered, the German defenders initially wavered, leading to an advance by Allied forces of nearly six kilometres (four miles). Spearheaded by the American 79th Division, filled with soldiers mainly from the Washington DC area, the advance plunged into the Montfaucon Hills, only to stall amid a wilderness of German strongpoints. Without the benefit of battlefield experience, American units often advanced in waves, and played to the strengths of the German defensive system as their British and French allies had in years past. Suffering from severe communication problems, American units also often became intermingled, causing untold confusion. Although some units renewed their forward movement on 27 September, the attack had fallen apart so completely that the German commander, General von Gallwitz, later remarked that, 'on the 27th and 28th we had no more worries'.

The Lost Battalion

On 2 October 1918, as part of the Meuse-Argonne offensive, elements of six companies of the 308th Infantry Regiment, one company of the 307th and two companies of the 306th Machine Gun Battalion (about 600 men in all) outpaced the other advancing forces only to find themselves surrounded and cut off near Charlevaux Mill. Major Charles Whittlesey, as the senior officer present, took command of the composite group, which became known as the lost battalion.

Caught in a shrinking perimeter without water, and under constant attack by the Germans, the situation for Whittlesey and his men quickly became desperate. Making matters worse, on the second day of their ordeal, the lost battalion also came under fire from friendly artillery. With no means of direct communication, Whittlesey resorted to the use of his last remaining carrier pigeon, Cher Ami, releasing the bird with the message, 'Our own artillery is dropping a barrage directly on us. For heaven's sake stop it.' Whittlesey was crestfallen when the bird merely flew into the branches of a nearby tree and perched. After a few minutes, a private clambered up the tree and scolded the bird until it flew off. Cher Ami lost a leg and an eye en route, but eventually reached divisional headquarters with its message, and received the Croix de Guerre from the French Government.

Even though the American barrage was stopped and the 50th Aero Squadron attempted the first air resupply in battle, the men of the lost battalion were in desperate straits, with supplies running low and the dead and wounded piling up all around.

A photograph depicting the members of the ill fated 'lost battalion'.

Demonstrating the bravery of the men, one private, who was shot through the stomach, was informed that his groaning would only attract more enemy fire. The private replied, 'It pains like hell, but I'll keep as quiet as I can.' He made no sound and died 30 minutes later.

It was the afternoon of 8 October before an attack by the American 82nd Division led to a link-up with the lost battalion. Having refused several German demands of surrender, Whittlesey and 193 other survivors, most of them wounded, made their way to safety after 104 hours without food or medical attention. One who witnessed their return recorded: 'I couldn't say anything to them. There was nothing to say, anyway. It made your heart jump up in your throat just to look at them. Their faces told the whole story of the fight.'

Attempting to take the measure of its new foe, the German Fifth Army quickly produced an assessment of American forces, and forwarded the document to an anxious Ludendorff. While praising the bravery and stamina of the individual American soldier, the document judged American staff and liaison work to be 'inadequate'. Interrogations of American prisoners revealed most to be 'naïve in military and political matters', who followed their officers in an effort to crush 'German militarism'. The interrogations also revealed that the difficulties experienced in the fighting at the Meuse-Argonne had come as a surprise to the untested Americans, who had previously seen the war as a 'happy picnic'. Although Ludendorff took heart at the relative inexperience and rather amateurish tactics of the American First Army, he also realized both that Pershing would learn from his mistakes and that the sheer weight of American numbers would quickly become a telling factor. Sensing that the advance in the Meuse-Argonne area was the centrepiece of the Allied attack plan, and fearing a steady improvement on the part of his American foe, Ludendorff ordered six additional German divisions to the area in an effort to blunt the offensive.

Meanwhile, the scene behind the lines of the American First Army was one of utter confusion. Traffic jams snarled the roadways, one lasting for 12 hours, which made supplying units in the field nearly impossible. Facing stiffening German resistance, with his own staff nearing a logistical breakdown, and with his grandiose plan in tatters, Pershing halted the offensive on 29 September to regroup and prepare for a renewed assault. Incensed that the lynchpin effort of his grand offensive had met with such little success, Foch placed much of the blame on the failures of the French Fourth Army, which had so much more

experience than the Americans. Clemenceau, though, had no such charity toward Pershing and his men, having visited the American headquarters on 29 September, only to get caught up in the massive traffic jam behind the American lines. Convinced that the American staff was incompetent, and that its failings would not only cost French lives but also prolong the war, Clemenceau launched into a criticism of the American commander that nearly led to a breakdown of Allied command.

SUCCESS IN THE NORTH

While the Franco-American assault at the Meuse-Argonne sputtered, to the north the BEF achieved a much greater level of success. On 27 September, Currie's Canadian Corps and elements of Byng's

American Doughboys pick their way through the heavily wooded terrain of the Argonne, which served to shatter the cohesion of Allied advances in the area. The American failure to press through was met by a barrage of criticism from Allied politicians.

British Third Army assaulted the formidable German defensive system anchored on the Canal du Nord outside of Cambrai. Under cover of a punishing and accurate barrage, the Canadians clambered through and over the obstacle of the partly filled canal, and assaulted the German defensive system that lay just beyond. Unlike the Americans in the Montfaucon Hills, the Canadians and British had often faced the strongpoints that typified the German defensive system, and utilized specially trained and equipped engineer units both to destroy centres of resistance and maintain the advance. Although the units of Byng's Third Army often lagged behind the hard-charging Canadians, together both forces surpassed their final goals, and in many places reached the Schelde River. After only two days of fighting the Canadian Corps and the British Third Army had driven a wedge 19km (12 miles) wide and 10km (six miles) deep into the German defences, captured 10,000 prisoners and made Cambrai useless as a railhead for the Germans.

As Ludendorff struggled to rush reserves to the Meuse-Argonne and to Cambrai, on 28

The German 37mm anti-tank gun was introduced at the end of the Great War as a counter to the Allied use of armour. The weapon fired a 455g (one-pound) armour-piercing explosive shell, which could penetrate 15mm ($\frac{3}{5}$in) of armour at 200m (220 yards).

German Propaganda

Conscious that they were losing the war, the Germans turned to more desperate forms of propaganda, some aimed at what they hoped would be a weak point in the Allied structure – the place of African-Americans in the US Army. One German leaflet dropped to a segregated black unit read:

'Hello boys, what are you dong over here? Fighting the Germans? Why? Have they ever done you any harm? Of course some white folks and the lying English-American papers told you that the Germans ought to be wiped out for the sake of humanity and Democracy. What is Democracy? ... Do you enjoy the same rights as the white people do in America, the land of freedom and Democracy, or are you rather treated over there as second class citizens? Can you get into a restaurant where white people dine? Can you get a seat in a theatre where white people sit? Can you get a seat or a berth in a railroad car, or can you even ride in the South in the same streetcar as white people? ... Now all this is entirely different in Germany, where they do like coloured people; where they treat them as gentlemen. ... Don't allow ... [the Americans] to use you as cannon fodder. ... Throw ... [your weapon away] and come over to the German lines. You will find friends who will help you.'

Regardless of the German efforts, though, there were not any significant numbers of desertions from African-American units.

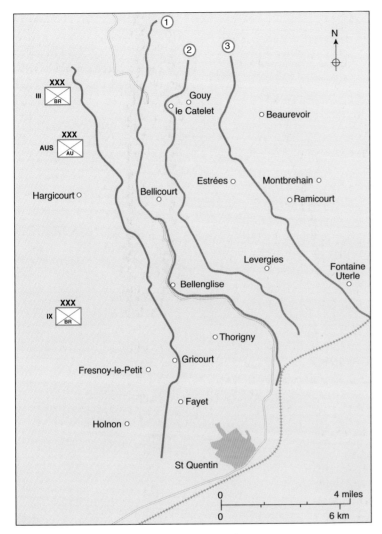

The British Fourth Army's assault on the Hindenburg Line on 29 September 1918. Rawlinson's aim was to break through the main line (1), the support system (2) and, finally, the reserve system (3).

more territory in one short battle than it had in the entire Third Battle of Ypres, seizing the entire Passchendaele Ridge and threatening Roulers.

The avalanche of Allied offensives unhinged Ludendorff, who suffered some form of mental breakdown. He had reason to be worried, for in August alone the Germans had lost 228,100 men, of whom 110,000 had deserted. The number of divisions in the German Army had fallen from a high of roughly 200 in March to only 125 by September, of which only 47 were deemed fit for combat. The Allies, by comparison, fielded 211 divisions and could count on the arrival of more and more American soldiers as the war continued. At a meeting of the German general staff, Ludendorff, recovering somewhat from his episode, informed all present that the German Army was, 'finished; the war could no longer be won; rather the final defeat was probably inescapably at hand'. With the burgeoning strength of the AEF, Ludendorff opined that the Allies would soon gain 'a great victory, a breakthrough in grand style'. In an effort to save his beloved military from inevitable and catastrophic defeat, Ludendorff advised the Kaiser to, 'request an armistice without any hesitation'. Although Ludendorff could hardly have believed it at the time, the worst was yet to come.

BREAKING THE HINDENBURG LINE

The final, and most important, portion of the Allied offensive fell to Rawlinson's Fourth Army, aided by the French First Army, and involved an assault against the might of the Hindenburg Line along the St Quentin Canal. The German defences in the area were the

September, the GAF, based around the strength of the British Second Army, launched its assault on the familiar battlefields of Flanders outside Ypres. Unable to achieve surprise due to German observation of the battlefield from the ridges surrounding Ypres, the ten divisions of Plumer's Second Army, aided by Belgian forces under the command of King Albert, weathered a German counterbarrage before going over the top. After the assault, the five understrength German defending divisions quickly gave way, which allowed British and Belgian forces to advance 14km (nine miles) in two days, taking over 2000 prisoners. For Plumer the victory was cathartic, with his force taking

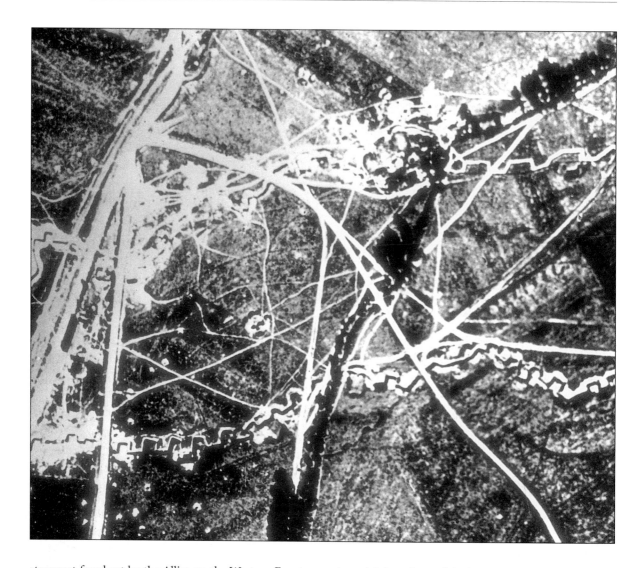

An aerial view of part of the formidable German Hindenburg Line defensive system, which Ludendorff had hoped would hold throughout the winter – a hope dashed by Rawlinson's Fourth Army on 29 September successfully crossing the St Quentin Canal.

strongest faced yet by the Allies on the Western Front, and were believed by many to be impervious to both tank and infantry assault. The southern portion of the German lines was anchored on the obstacle of the St Quentin Canal, which was 11m (35ft) wide, contained mud of over two metres (six feet) in depth and was guarded by barbed-wire-studded sheer banks of nearly 15m (50ft) in height. Rows of concrete pillboxes, in three distinct lines, stood guard on both the east and west banks of the canal, forming a total defensive network of over 5486m (6000 yards) in depth.

Although the defences seemed nearly impregnable, there were reasons for optimism within the Fourth Army. On the northern portion of the front, the St Quentin Canal ran through the 5486m (6000-yard) Bellicourt Tunnel, which essentially provided British planners with a broad, ready-made bridge. While the Germans had recognized the tunnel sector as the potential Achilles heel of the defensive network and had prepared accordingly, Rawlinson still hoped to make the sector his main avenue of advance.

Additionally, while attacking and defending forces for the coming battle were roughly equal in number, the morale of the badly battered German forces was sagging. The BEF also had captured detailed plans for the defences of the St Quentin Canal area, prompting Rawlinson's chief of staff to remark, 'It has fallen to the lot of few commanders to be provided with such detailed information as to the nature of the enemy's defences.'

Highlighting the increasing importance of Dominion forces to the BEF, General Monash and his staff at the Australian Corps undertook much of the tactical planning for the coming battle. One problem, though, was that much of the Australian Corps was not available for the operation, having been withdrawn from the front after days of exhausting battle. In need of two strong divisions to replace the Australian 1st and 4th divisions, Monash chose the American 27th and 30th divisions, the last two American divisions serving with the BEF. Impressed with the strength and eagerness of the US units, Monash remained concerned about American operational readiness, and accordingly placed the Americans under overall control of the Australian Corps.

Monash's plan called for the American divisions to advance, under cover of a heavy artillery barrage and aided by tanks, over 3658m (4000 yards) into the German defensive system in the tunnel sector, and then for two Australian divisions to leapfrog through the breech created in the German defences by the Americans. Rawlinson, though, argued both that Monash's plan would result in a vulnerable advance on too narrow an attack frontage, and that it was overly reliant on almost untested American units.

Women and War

World War I proved to be a watershed in the lives of women in many western nations. The Victorian ideal for middle- and upper-class women involved home life, and caring for their husbands and families. However, the voracious demand of World War I for military manpower resulted in women replacing men in much of the workforce, taking jobs ranging from working in munitions factories to tilling the soil. In Britain alone, World War I saw two million women join the workforce for the first time. Although at the close of the conflict many women lost their jobs to returning soldiers, ideas about women and their place in society had already been changed. With material needed for military uniforms, women got by with less fabric, and those involved in factory work for the first time began to opt for trousers rather than dresses. Many young women earned a real wage for the first time during the war, and lived on their own or with other single women, experiencing previously unheard of levels of independence. Some of the more daring women took to smoking in public and even frequented pubs, something unheard of in the Victorian world.

From joining the workforce to wearing trousers, World War I greatly impacted the lives of women in the combatant nations.

Accordingly, Rawlinson extended the attack frontage, adding an assault by IX Corps across the St Quentin Canal. The commander of IX Corps, Lieutenant-General Walter Braithwaite, had made the extension of the attack possible by suggesting that his men could cross the canal by using lifebelts, portable boats and ropes and ladders. Although Rawlinson judged the scheme to be risky, he concluded that a single division, the 46th, just might be able to force its way across the canal using such methods and believed that its attack might catch the Germans unaware.

The bombardment that accompanied the attack of British, Australian, American and French forces on 29 September, though only roughly equal in weight to that of the first day of the Somme, was both accurate and lethal, silencing German defences in many areas of the front. In the north, however, the attack almost

British troops assaulting a battered German strongpoint in the Hindenburg Line. The Fourth Army, spearheaded by the Australian and American divisions of the Australian Corps, had forced a way through the much-vaunted German defensive position in a single day.

immediately stalled. The American 27th Division, like most units taking part in the attack, had been involved in a variety of smaller operations designed to seize important tactical features in the run-up to the main offensive. However, the 27th had failed to reach its jumping-off point, and its divisional commander feared that pockets of American troops were holding out, marooned in German lines. Fearing for the lives of his stranded men, the 27th commander insisted that the artillery barrage begin 914m (1000 yards) to the east of the start line, meaning that, when the men of the 27th went over the top at 5.50am, they faced untouched German defences. Although the unit fought bravely, it quickly became entangled with the Australian 3rd Division, which was meant to leapfrog through American gains. With little artillery support, the confused and intertwined units failed to advance into the main system of the Hindenburg Line.

Further south, though, the American 30th Division achieved a much greater level of success. Without the same concerns that plagued the 27th Division's commander, the artillery support for the 30th Division was devastating and seemingly shocked many of the German defenders in the area into relative inaction. By noon the Americans had taken Bellicourt and were even advancing into the supporting defences behind the main Hindenburg Line system. Although the 5th Australian Division successfully passed through the advance units of Americans, little else was gained that day, with the Australians facing concerted German counterattacks and enfilade fire from German lines on their left flank, where the American 27th and Australian 3rd divisions had failed to keep pace.

The main advance of the day fell to the British 46th Division, which had taken part in the attack only at Rawlinson's insistence. The artillery support provided

> '**Tomorrow we are to take part in the greatest and most important battle that we have yet been in, for we are to assault the Hindenburg Line, the famous trench system which the Germans have boasted is impregnable.**'
>
> Captain Francis Fairweather, Australian Corps, 28 September 1918

by IX Corps for the assault was overwhelming: on one 457m (500-yard) stretch of front, there were 54 18-pounder field guns firing two rounds per minute, and 18 4.5in field howitzers firing one round per minute. While the 46th Division moved forwards, then, every minute 126 shells were falling on the 457m (500-yard) attack frontage in advance of the infantry. The damage done by the bombardment also collapsed the banks of the St Quentin Canal, making it easier for the men of the 46th to scramble down and to rush across the water obstacle utilizing their flotation devices. Bursting out of a thick fog, the men of the 46th Division caught the German defenders, who thought that the canal provided them with an impregnable defensive line, by surprise.

Reeling with shock, the German defenders fell back behind the canal, where the offensive halted for three hours while the artillery pounded away at the next German lines and fresh British reserves joined the attack. At 11.20am, the attack began anew and units of the 46th punched through the main Hindenburg Line by 3pm, allowing the British 3rd Division to pass through and assault the supporting lines. By nightfall it had become apparent that the Fourth Army had achieved a stunning victory. In one day American, Australian and British troops had broken through the Hindenburg Line and the Hindenburg Support Line, overthrowing the most important German defensive system on the Western Front. Advancing to a depth of 5486m (6000 yards) on a frontage of 9144m (10,000 yards), the Allied forces not only had ruptured the German defences but also had captured 5100 prisoners and 90 artillery pieces. In a truly international battle, the Fourth Army had achieved one of the greatest successes of the war on the Western Front. With the Allies advancing everywhere, and with their greatest system of defences, upon which they had staked so much hope, breached, the German military realized that the end of the conflict was near.

As the German Army continued its fighting retreat, morale among the German troops reached a new low. Fresh units moving toward the front were even greeted by the fabled Prussian Guards with cries of 'strike breakers' and 'war prolongers'. Although the German Army did not dissolve into a state of mutiny, the signs that it was nearing the end of its ability to resist were everywhere. The most compelling evidence of an impending collapse of military discipline could be found in the crowds of shirkers and slackers milling behind the German lines – loose groupings of soldiers estimated to number between 750,000 and one million for the last two months of the conflict. Facing

German troops near Reims. Although the Germans fought fiercely in defence of the Hindenburg Line and the Meuse-Argonne, the continuous Allied advances led many to a sense of desperation.

continued battering by strengthening Allied forces, and considering the increasingly fragile nature of his own military, Major von Leeb of Army Group Crown Prince Rupprecht, spoke for many when he stated, 'The campaign has been lost, the military mistakes [made] have now come home to roost'.

On 1 October, Ludendorff chaired an operational review of the war that not only reached a conclusion similar to that of von Leeb but also had chilling differences. With his hopes for holding at the Hindenburg Line dashed in a single day by Rawlinson's offensive, Ludendorff opened the meeting with a statement that stunned those present into silence: 'The OHL and the German Army are finished'; the war could no longer be won; rather, the final defeat was probably inescapably at hand. Bulgaria had fallen, and both Austria-Hungary and Turkey were at the very end of their ability to resist, leaving Germany alone to face the might of nearly three million fresh American troops. Ludendorff then

admitted the sagging morale of the German army, remarking that he could 'no longer rely on the troops'. With defeat looming on every front, Ludendorff announced that he was going to advise the Kaiser to 'request an armistice *without any hesitation*'.

Amid protests from the assembled staff officers, Ludendorff drove his point home with conviction, repeating his refrain that further 'prosecution of the war was senseless'. Ludendorff then went on to demonstrate an amazing motivation for his conclusions – the war had to come to a 'quick end' to salvage the institution that he most loved, the German Army, from destruction. Instead of blaming his own failed tactics, or indeed the military itself for Germany's impending defeat, Ludendorff blamed the German nation, which he believed had been found wanting under the pressures of war. Instead of fighting to the end and being destroyed in the process, the German Army, which Ludendorff believed to be the heart of the German state, had to survive and eventually redeem the shattered German body politic. Closing the briefing Ludendorff made his motivations clear, suggesting that the Kaiser be asked to bring to power '*those circles which we mainly have to thank* that things have come to this'. In other words Ludendorff hoped that the liberals and socialists would be brought into power to bear the burden and the blame for bringing the failed war to an end. Ludendorff concluded, '*They can now clean up the mess for which they are responsible.*'

Several of the staff officers present broke down into tears as the enormity of the moment became clear – Germany had been defeated in World War I and all of the sacrifice and loss had been in vain. Amid the tears, though, nobody could have realized the powerful connection between Ludendorff's words and another, greater, war that would soon engulf the world. Ludendorff had laid the foundations for the 'stab-in-the-back' legend that was to dominate German

General Erich Ludendorff. As First Quartermaster General, Ludendorff effectively controlled Germany's military planning on the Western Front. Although his great Spring Offensives had been tactical masterpieces, their lack of strategic coordination possibly cost Germany the conflict.

politics in the inter-war period; a legend that was fundamental to the rise to power of Adolf Hitler. Central to the legend was the idea that the German Army had not been defeated in World War I. It was holding out steadfastly in France and in Russia, only to have the home front collapse amid a welter of communist- and socialist-inspired uprisings. The gallant German Army had been stabbed in the back by men and women not brave enough to join the fight for survival. The myth would prove a valuable tool in the hands of demagogues; however, it was just that – a myth. Under hammer blows from the Allies, the German Army was being comprehensively defeated. As Ludendorff knew, its only hope for survival was to quit the war before its destruction was complete. Instead of fighting on for its honour, the German Army chose to capitulate, putting its own survival before that of the nation.

CHAPTER 7

The Armistice

As Germany slowly imploded, the Allies pressed ever onwards on the Western Front, forcing the German Government to sign an armistice, which brought the Great War to a close on 11 November 1918. With their army still in the field in France, though, many Germans did not admit a true military defeat, dooming the world to fight a second world war 20 years later.

Max von Baden took over as Chancellor of Germany on the evening of 3 October, and, due in large measure to the pessimism of Ludendorff, within 48 hours he had sent a formal note to President Wilson through Swiss intermediaries which read: 'The German government requests the President of the United States to take in hand the restoration of peace, acquaint all the belligerent states of this request, and invite them to send plenipotentiaries for the purpose of opening peace negotiations.' The diplomatic note then went on to mark Wilson's own Fourteen Points (see over) as a basis for negotiations and concluded, 'With a view to

After years of bloody warfare, the signing of the armistice on 11 November 1918 was the cause for jubilation among Allied ranks, the culmination of four long years of struggle on the Western Front.

avoiding further bloodshed, the German Government requests the immediate conclusion of an armistice on land and sea.'

Needing time to consider the implications of the German note, Wilson's initial reply simply requested clarification of Imperial Germany's acceptance of the Fourteen Points. The President's measured response was a cause for celebration among the ruling class of Germany, many of whom dared to hope that they could play Wilson off against Lloyd George and Clemenceau to achieve a more lenient peace, one that might even allow Germany to retain German-speaking areas of the Ukraine and Alsace Lorraine. Among the French military, however, Wilson's response touched off a furious reaction. Fearing that America would withdraw from the conflict before a true victory had been achieved, one French officer asked his American liaison, 'Does your President realize with what swine he

American President Woodrow Wilson, whose Fourteen Points placed him at odds with the leaders of France and Britain, who were more stern in their demands for peace with Germany.

The Fourteen Points

Outlined by President Woodrow Wilson in a speech on 8 January 1918, the Fourteen Points were designed both to end World War I and to prevent future conflicts. Although France and Britain rejected aspects of the Fourteen Points, Wilson's principles became a guiding force behind the Versailles negotiations. The Fourteen Points included:

• Open covenants of peace; no secret agreements.
• Freedom of the seas
• The removal of economic barriers
• Guarantees of the reduction of armaments
• Adjustment of all colonial claims, with the interests of the subject populations being equal with the claims of governments
• Evacuation of all Russian territory
• Restoration of Belgian sovereignty

• Restoration of all French territory including Alsace Lorraine
• Readjustment of Italian frontiers along national lines
• Opportunity for the autonomous development for the people of Austria-Hungary
• Evacuation of occupying forces from Romania, Serbia and Montenegro, with relations of the Balkan states to be decided along lines of nationality
• Opportunity for autonomous development for non-Turkish peoples within the Ottoman Empire. The Dardanelles to be free for all shipping
• Creation of an independent state of Poland with access to the sea
• Formation of a general assembly of nations with the aim of affording mutual guarantees of political independence and territorial integrity to great and small states.

is dealing? They'll fool him if he is not very, very canny.' Another French officer opined that it was 'unthinkable' to deal with the Germans so long as they occupied French or Belgian soil. On 14 October, though, Wilson sent his first detailed response to the German call for negotiations, the tenor of which dashed German hopes and allayed French fears. The American response demanded 'absolutely satisfactory safeguards and guarantees of the maintenance of the present military supremacy of the armies of the United States and the Allies in the field', and vowed to leave conditions of any armistice to the 'judgment and advice of the military advisors of the Government of the United States and the Allied Governments'.

Although a measure of cold water had been thrown on the German hopes for a lenient negotiated peace, Ludendorff had once again regained a measure of composure after the shock of the British Fourth Army's overthrow of the Hindenburg Line. To the south the Franco-American drive in the Meuse-Argonne remained stalled, while to the north the advance of the GAF had also ground to a halt. Although Rawlinson's men continued to press forwards, the flanks of the great Allied offensive had ceased to advance, and Ludendorff no longer feared an immediate military catastrophe. In a meeting with Prince Max, Ludendorff stated that it had become apparent that the strength of the enemy offensive was 'falling off'. Ludendorff then went on to add that under the new strategic circumstances Germany could continue the war for another year by withdrawing to more defensible lines and wrest a more favourable peace from the Allies in 1919.

With both wings of his grand offensive stalled, a furious Foch both sought a solution to the tactical dilemma and attempted to prod those whom he felt

German defenders in the open fighting that came to typify the final, semi-mobile phase of World War I on the Western Front. Increasingly, aircraft became used in a ground-attack role in the final months of the war, a process made easier for the Allies by the creation of the Royal Air Force in April 1918.

were most responsible for the delay. Clearly surprised that the British Fourth Army, which enjoyed the least in the way of numerical superiority and had faced the strongest German defences, had become the de facto spearhead of the Allied offensive, Foch tried to get his own French forces moving faster and sent a scathing note to Pétain, which read: 'Yesterday ... we witnessed a battle that was not commanded, a battle that was not pushed, a battle that was not brought together … and in consequence a battle in which there was no exploitation of the results obtained.'

While Foch levelled criticism at his own forces, others were quick to single out the American First Army, which had been slated to play the major role in the attack but instead had succumbed to both logistic and tactical difficulties, as the cause of the delay. On 1 October Haig commented:

'Reports from Americans (west of Meuse) … state that their roads and communications are so blocked that the offensive has had to stop and cannot be recommenced for four or five days. What very valuable days are being lost! All this is the result of inexperience and ignorance on the part of … [the American staff] of the needs of a modern attacking force.'

For his part Sir Henry Wilson made his feelings clear regarding American failings in a diary entry: 'The state of chaos the fool [Pershing] has got his troops into down in the Argonne is indescribable.' In a later diary entry Wilson called Pershing a 'vain ignorant weak ASS'.

Clemenceau and Pétain also saw Pershing's handling of American forces as 'risking disaster' and placed great pressure on Foch to lessen the American's control over the battle and even threatened to complain about the situation directly to President Wilson. Because of the increasing pressure, on 11 October Foch sent General Maxime Weygand to Pershing's headquarters with a letter relieving him of command. Pershing refused to comply and instead drove to Foch's headquarters for direct talks. In the meeting, which threatened to unhinge Allied unity, Foch got right to the point and said to

A lieutenant in the Tank Corps in France, wearing protective face gear for use in the dangerous interior environment of the late model British tanks. Enemy small-arms fire could cause splinters to fly off the inside of the armour plating.

The final Allied advances on the Western Front from late September through to the armistice. As generalissimo of the Allied forces, Marshal Foch organized a series of interconnected offensives that kept the Germans under pressure the length of the Western Front.

Pershing, 'On all other parts of the front the advances are very marked. The Americans are not progressing as rapidly'. Pershing replied that his army faced both stern German resistance and difficult terrain. Foch countered that he judged those under his command only by results and added, 'I am aware of the terrain. You chose the Argonne and I allowed you to attack there.' With Franco-American cooperation hanging by a thread, in the end Pershing and Foch put their differences aside and agreed to the formation of the Second American Army, under the command of General Robert Lee Bullard, a move that both elevated Pershing to the level of an army group commander and was designed to lessen the staff and logistic problems that plagued American forces.

RENEWING THE ALLIED ASSAULT

While he dealt with the diplomatic difficulties of conducting a coalition war, Foch also had to reinvigorate the Allied offensive and keep the Germans from pulling back and creating coherent lines of defence near to the Franco-German border. After considering various plans, Foch settled on a scheme of three converging offensives, in which the GAF would renew its drive towards Ghent, while Franco-American forces advanced on the right of the Allied line in the direction of Mézières. In a tacit acknowledgement of the success gained by British forces, and the corresponding lack of forwards movement by French and American units, Foch made a British attack in the centre of the Allied lines aimed at Maubeuge the centrepiece of his new grand offensive.

Plainly pleased that the BEF was now considered the most reliable Allied military force, Haig directed Byng's Third Army and Rawlinson's Fourth Army to attack in concert

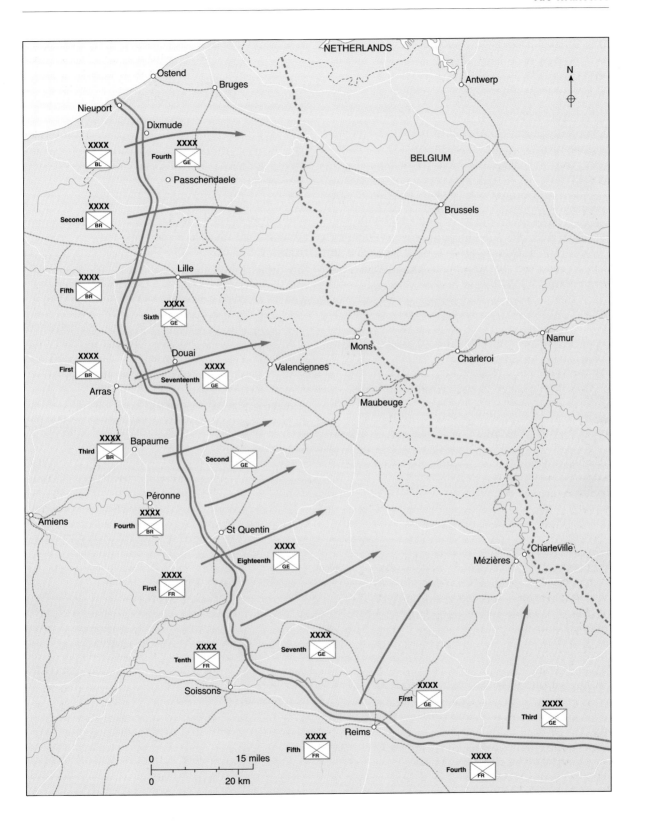

near Cambrai. Utilizing the heaviest artillery barrage since their successful attack of 27 September, British and Dominion forces went over the top on 8 October against only a smattering of defensive artillery fire from the outmatched Germans. Supported by tanks, the men of Third Army punctured the defences of the German Beaurevoir Line, advancing 4572m (5000 yards) and capturing over 2700 prisoners. On the British right flank, supported by the French First Army, Rawlinson's force advanced 5486m (6000 yards) on most of its front, took the villages of Serain and Méricourt and captured 4000 prisoners and 40 guns. The fact that the German prisoners were identified as having come from 15 different divisions was taken by British intelligence officers as further indication of the administrative collapse of the German Army.

The defeat at Cambrai was a heavy blow for Ludendorff, for the Allies had rekindled their forwards

The Australians, here shown advancing, and the Canadians were renowned as among the best shock troops in the BEF during the battles of the Hundred Days. Both were organized into their own corps and used to spearhead many of the BEF's set-piece attacks.

movement before he had been able to establish a coherent defensive line. Recognizing that the BEF advance had made Cambrai untenable, Ludendorff ordered a withdrawal in the region to hastily constructed new defences dubbed the Hermann Position. With the Canadian Corps leading the way, the British Third and Fourth armies harried the retreating Germans until 13 October when the lines solidified along the Selle River.

As the BEF's advance in the centre slowed, Foch unleashed Allied forces on both the left and right wings of the line, in an attempt both to keep the Germans guessing and retain the all-important initiative. In the north the GAF, spearheaded by Plumer's British Second Army, crashed through the German lines on 14 October with an ease that the historian of the British 36th Division remarked, 'would have seemed impossible a year ago'. Although the British received concentrated fire from a few machine-gun nests, much of the German Fourth Army's infantry offered only cursory resistance to the onrushing attackers. By evening, the British Second Army had advanced nearly six kilometres (four miles)

As the front lines crumbled around them, many Germans continued to fight bravely, while others for the first time began to surrender in record numbers. On the home front civil unrest was increasing, while the German Navy was edging towards mutiny in its home ports.

on a broad front and had captured 6000 prisoners and 50 artillery pieces. With the continuing support of the Belgians, who a British staff member remarked had 'fought magnificently', Second Army resumed its advance with equal vigour the following day.

As the GAF surged forward, Ludendorff chose again to trade space for time in an effort to keep his doomed military from fighting at too great a disadvantage. Abandoning the Belgian coast, a strategic goal that the British had sought in vain for nearly five years, on 15 October, the Germans withdrew to the natural defensive barrier of the

Schelde River, joining the Hermann Position near Valenciennes. Farther south, German forces withdrew in advance of a suspected French offensive to the Hunding and Brunhild positions between Guise and Rethel.

While the GAF made great gains in the north, on 14 October, the French and newly reorganized American forces launched an attack in the Meuse-Argonne area that finally captured Romagne, the goal that Pershing had set as the main objective for the first day of his 26 September offensive. Ludendorff still saw the Franco-American axis of advance to be critical and threw his best remaining units into the defence of what was known as the Kriemhilde Line. Making the importance of holding the line in the Meuse-Argonne clear, Ludendorff ordered General Max von Gallwitz, the army group commander in the area, to 'put into

German Naval Mutiny

Perhaps stung that it had done only little in a war its creation had done much to cause, the leadership of the German High Seas Fleet sought to reclaim its honour by facing the British Grand Fleet in battle as World War I neared its end. Admiral Rheinhard Scheer did his best to convince his sailors to fight stating, 'An honourable battle by the fleet – even if it should be a fight to the death – will sow the seed of a new German fleet in the future.' Unwilling to die to reclaim the honour of their superior officers, the sailors chanted, 'We do not want to put to sea, for us the war is over.' Five times the order went out for the High Seas Fleet to put to sea; five times it was ignored. Stokers on board ships that were already at sea even put the fires out in their boilers. A thousand mutineers were arrested, and, on 27 October, Admiral Franz von Hipper remarked simply, 'Our men have rebelled.' By 3 November, the mutinies had spread beyond the fleet, with 3000 mutinous sailors linking up with disgruntled workers to raise the red flag of revolution in Kiel. Although the governor of Kiel, Admiral Wilhelm Souchon, had eight of the mutineers killed, the unrest only spread. On 4 November, thousands more sailors, factory workers and up to 20,000 garrison troops joined the uprising. Within days, the mutiny had spread to Lubeck, Hamburg, Bremen and Wilhelmshaven, heralding a wave of unrest that convinced even the most diehard militarists that Germany had lost World War I.

the fighting front every unit that is at all fit for use in battle'. Thus, although Pershing saw the seizure of Romagne as an event the importance of which could 'hardly be overestimated', Foch was once again left to fume that the Americans, along with the French Fourth Army, struggled to make further headway.

Incensed that Pershing had once again botched the offensive, Clemenceau fired off an angry letter to Foch demanding change. The letter railed:

'You have watched at close range the development of General Pershing's extractions. Unfortunately, thanks to his invincible obstinacy he has won against you as well as your immediate subordinates. The French Army and the British Army, without a moment's respite, have been daily fighting for the past three months … but our worthy American allies, who thirst to get into action and who are unanimously acknowledged to be great soldiers, have been marking time ever since their forward jump on the first day, and in spite of heavy losses, they have failed to conquer the ground assigned to them as their objective. No one can maintain that these troops are unusable; they are merely unused.'

Clemenceau urged Foch to inform President Wilson of Pershing's failings and to make a 'final decision' regarding the American general. Wisely, though, Foch chose to ignore Clemenceau's letter, as the Allied advance along the entire front gathered steam.

As the GAF pursued the retreating Germans in the north, and the French and American forces in the Meuse-Argonne fought an attritional bloodbath, Rawlinson made ready to breach the German defences in the centre of the Allied line along the Selle River.

> 'It is on the unconquerable resistance of the Verdun front that depends the fate of a great part of the western front, perhaps even of our nation.'
>
> General Georg von der Marwitz

Although the river itself was not an imposing obstacle, Rawlinson thought that the German defensive positions behind it were solid enough to necessitate a pause in the battle to allow the British Fourth Army to bring forward its artillery and logistic support. Rawlinson's caution ensured that, on the day of the attack, Fourth Army could call on covering fire from

33 field artillery brigades, plus 20 brigades and 13 independent batteries of heavier guns. Besides ample firepower support, Rawlinson had reason for optimism, for British intelligence reported that the German defenders only consisted of four exhausted and two comparatively fresh divisions. Unbeknownst to Rawlinson, though, Ludendorff had rushed reinforcements to the scene and Fourth Army in fact faced five fresh and four fairly fresh German divisions, meaning that the troop strength in the fight for the Selle River would be roughly equal.

At dawn on 17 October, Fourth Army went forward into the attack, against much stronger than expected German resistance. Leading the attack, the South African Brigade and the American II Corps, now a truly veteran unit that had seen continuous action as part of the Fourth Army, initially made only fitful gains against uncut barbed wire and ferocious German counterattacks. South of the headwaters of the Selle, though, IX Corps, supported by twice as many tanks, forced the German defences to an initial depth of 4114m (4500 yards) and flanked the German lines farther to the north. By the evening, the British Fourth Army, aided by the French First Army, had broken the German defences of the Hermann Position and had captured more than 5000 prisoners. In two

From left to right, David Lloyd George of Britain, Vittorio Orlando of Italy, Georges Clemenceau of France and Woodrow Wilson of the United States, gather to discuss peace terms at the Paris Peace Conference.

more days of intense fighting the Allied forces pushed to a depth of 8229m (9000 yards) on a frontage of 11km (seven miles) and reached the Sambre River and the Oise Canal.

MOVING TOWARDS AN ARMISTICE

As the Germans fell back ever further, the Allied leaders for the first time really dared to think that the end of the war was near. For his part Foch advocated stern armistice terms, which amounted to unconditional surrender on the part of the Germans. Clemenceau quickly intervened, though, and put Foch in his place, reminding the commander-in-chief that,

As the clock ran down on the war, at 11am on 11 November 1918, several Allied units vied for the honour of firing the last shot of the conflict. The gun pictured is 'Calamity Jane' of the 11th Field Artillery, which fired the last US artillery round of the war.

'Your business is war, and everything that pertains to the peace … belongs to us [the government] and only us.' On 19 October, Lloyd George asked Haig for the first and only time regarding his opinion on armistice terms. Haig, who had rightly been accused of being overly optimistic in the past, sounded a note of caution at the 11th hour due to the unexpectedly ferocious German defence of the Selle River and replied:

'The German Army is capable of retiring to its own frontier, and holding that line if there should be any attempt to touch the honour *of the German people and make them fight with the courage of despair. … The French and American Armies are not capable of making a serious offensive* now. *The British alone might bring the enemy to his knees. But why expend more British lives – and for what? … I therefore advise that we only ask in the armistice for what we intend to hold, and that*

we set our faces against the French entering Germany to
pay off old scores.'

While the Allies struggled with their first thoughts
concerning how to end the war, events rushed towards
a climax in Germany. Talks concerning an armistice
had been ongoing in fits and starts since Hindenburg
and Ludendorff had demanded an armistice at the end
of September following the Allied breaking of the
Hindenburg Line.. However, Germany's last
remaining hope, that the United States would
advocate a lenient peace treaty, was dashed by the
receipt of a note on 23 October from President Wilson
demanding that Germany convert itself into a
parliamentary democracy before an armistice could
be granted. Wilson made it quite clear that if the
United States had to deal with the 'military masters

The 240mm trench mortar, with its plunging fire, proved a
devastating weapon, especially during the trench warfare
phase of the Western Front. First introduced by the French
in 1915, this example is operated by the US Army in 1918.
Much of the US equipment came from the French.

and monarchical autocrats of Germany', then, 'it must
demand not peace but surrender'.

Aghast at the American demand, Hindenburg and
Ludendorff, without consultation, published an army
order reading:

'Wilson's answer is a demand for unconditional
surrender. It is thus unacceptable to us soldiers. It proves
that our enemies' desire for our destruction, which let
loose the war in 1914, still exists undiminished …
Wilson's answer can thus be nothing to us … but a
challenge to continue our resistance … when all our

Foch and Peace

The Allied generals who fought World War I had only little say in the peace process. For his part, Haig willingly stepped away from matters that he believed were better left to politicians. Foch, on the other hand, became more and more agitated at concessions given by Clemenceau in the negotiations at Versailles, concessions that had been bought with French blood. Believing that Germany remained a threat, and suspicious of the League of Nations, Foch resorted to outright insubordination to make his point, stating in the press:

'Having reached the Rhine, we must stay there. Impress that upon your fellow countrymen. … We must have a barrier. … Democracies like ours, which are never aggressive, must have strong natural frontiers. Remember that these seventy millions of Germans will always be a menace to us. … They are a people both envious and warlike What was it that saved the Allies at the beginning of the war? Russia. Well, on whose side will Russia be in the future? … And next time, remember, the Germans will make no mistake. They will break through into Northern France and will seize the Channel ports as a base of operations against England.'

Foch, though he avoided being fired, was unable to alter the peace process, causing him finally to remark, 'All of Europe is in a complete mess. Such is the work of Clemenceau.'

enemies know that no sacrifice will achieve the rupture of the German front, they will be ready for a peace which will make the future of our country safe for the great masses of our people.'

Prince Max, and the Kaiser himself, saw Ludendorff's unilateral announcement as an act of gross insubordination. The next day the Kaiser reprimanded Ludendorff, both for the release of the army order and for his recent wild fluctuations of judgement concerning the military situation. Chastened, Ludendorff resigned. Hindenburg also offered his resignation, but the Kaiser urged him to stay. In Ludendorff's place the Kaiser appointed General Wilhelm Groener, who had the unenviable task of rushing to headquarters from the Eastern Front to oversee the conclusion of a failed war.

As Groener struggled to come to grips with his new task, events on the Western Front rushed towards a conclusion. While the French worked to outflank the Hunding Position, and British forces pursued the Germans to new defensive positions in the north, on 31 October, Foch made ready to launch a climactic offensive involving attacks by all major Allied forces. In the centre of the Allied lines, two corps from the French First Army broke through German defences and occupied Guise. Further north the British First Army, spearheaded by the Canadian Corps, launched an assault on 1 November on the hastily constructed German defensive lines around Valenciennes. Facing only light resistance, and capturing several thousand demoralized German prisoners, the Canadians broke through the defences with ease, forcing a German withdrawal from the defensive line formed by the Schelde River.

FINAL ACTS

The most important and cathartic victory, though, fell to the maligned American Expeditionary Force and its embattled commander. The AEF had entered the war as an untested military; however, it had survived its baptism of fire during the bitter struggle in the Meuse-Argonne. The AEF had finally become a veteran fighting force, numbering 1,867,623 men, with more arriving every day. At 3.30am on 1 November, a massive two-hour artillery barrage heralded the AEF's final assault, in which Pershing's men finally broke the stubborn Kriemhilde Line, and joyously began to pursue the defeated enemy. The Germans, though, fought with tenacity and skill in their withdrawal, which F. Scott Fitzgerald later described by saying that the Germans, 'walked very slowly backward a few inches a day, leaving the dead like a million bloody rags'.

Between 1 and 7 November, American and French forces advanced 39km (24 miles) on both sides of the Meuse River, with the French finally capturing Mézières. The Battle of Meuse-Argonne was, at the time, the largest battle ever fought by the United States Army, involving 1,250,000 men in 22 divisions. In 47 days of continuous battle, US forces had suffered 26,277 dead and 95,786 wounded. However, the Americans had given as good as they got, in the final week of fighting alone inflicting 100,000 casualties on the Germans, while capturing 26,000 prisoners, 874 artillery pieces and 3000 machine guns. Pershing's faith in his men, and his long struggle to found an independent American military

force had been vindicated. Although the AEF had to suffer through a steep learning curve, and did not play the most important role in the final offensives on the Western Front, its presence in battle, its burgeoning size and tenacity were all critical factors in both giving strength to the battered Allies and in demonstrating to the beleaguered Germans that their war was lost. As a result, Pershing was correct in his judgement that the Meuse-Argonne Offensive was 'one of the great achievements in the history of American arms'.

Marshal Ferdinand Foch, who, as Supreme Allied Commander, was the architect of the victorious Allied campaign of 1918. He signed the Armistice with Germany at 5am on the morning of 11 November in his railway carriage near Compiègne.

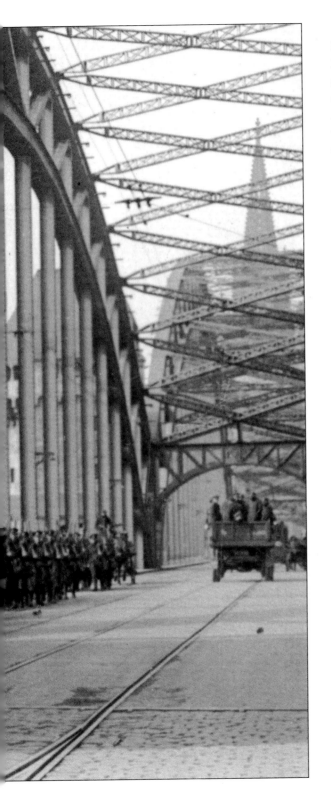

The final great Allied offensive on the Western Front in World War I fell to the British Third and Fourth armies along the Sambre River. It was somehow fitting that Rawlinson's force, which had done so much to begin the Allied string of victories at Amiens, should have the honour of finally breaking the back of the German Army. With its soldiers and officers now quite adept at fighting the newly mobile

> ## 'I was woken up with a wire that hostilities would cease at 11am. There were no great demonstrations by the troops, I think because it was hard to realize the war was really over.'
>
> Captain Westmacott, 24th Division, BEF

form of battle that pervaded the final days of World War I, the men of the BEF went over the top at 5.30am on 4 November, under the cover of an especially strong artillery barrage. Facing German defenders who obviously knew that the war was already decided, the British Third and Fourth armies advanced over 16km (10 miles) in two days, taking 10,000 prisoners while suffering only light casualties. The Germans in the area were now in full flight, and the end of the war was at hand.

When General Groener had arrived at Spa on 30 October to take over the German high command, he had immediately taken stock of both the military situation on the Western Front and the political situation on the German home front. By the time of his arrival a serious mutiny had broken out among the sailors of the German High Seas Fleet, who, after years of inaction, refused to take part in a final 'death ride'

British troops enter Cologne, Germany, as part of the peace agreement ending World War I. The occupation force was known as the British Army of the Rhine and was under the command of General Sir Herbert Plumer, formerly commander of Second Army.

against the British Grand Fleet. The mutiny quickly spread to 11 northern cities, including Bremen and Hamburg, and troops sent to suppress the mutineers instead joined them. As unrest spread across the nation, Groener toured the front and discovered that the military situation was untenable. Groener informed the German Chancellor, Prince Max, that, to avoid total military catastrophe, an armistice was required by Saturday 9 November, and that even 11 November might be too late.

Prince Max, though, realized that Wilson and the Allies would never deal with the Kaiser, and sent a representative to Spa, where the Kaiser had taken refuge with the German high command, to suggest his abdication. In fury the Kaiser responded:

'All the dynasties will fall along with me, the army is left leaderless, the front line troops disband and steam across the Rhine. The disaffected gang together, hang, murder, and plunder – assisted by the enemy. That is why I have no intention of abdicating … I have no intention of quitting the throne because of a few hundred Jews and a thousand workmen. Tell that to your masters in Berlin!'

The Kaiser, though, had greatly overestimated his worth and standing in his own empire, for he had long ago become secondary to the needs of the military at war. The military and the nation now required an

The final armistice line of the Great War on the Western Front. The fact that Allied forces had not yet entered Germany added credence to the myth that Germany was not defeated on the battlefield, but was instead stabbed in the back by homegrown enemies.

armistice to survive, and chose no longer to stand behind the oaths that bound them to an ancient regime. After polling his officers regarding the situation, Groener informed the Kaiser, 'The Army will march home in peace and order under its leaders and commanding generals, but not under the command of Your Majesty for it no longer stands behind Your Majesty.' Crestfallen, on 10 November the Kaiser boarded his cream and gold train, which carried him into exile in the Netherlands, ending 504 years of Hohenzollern rule in Prussia and Germany.

Meanwhile, on 8 November a German armistice delegation, headed by Matthias Erzberger, had met with Foch where it received terms, tantamount to unconditional surrender, which allowed the German Army to go home with its rifles, and its officers with their swords, but demanded the handing over of all of its artillery and most of its machine guns. The proposed agreement also required the Germans to pull back to their frontier and to allow the Allies bridgeheads over the Rhine, while leaving the British naval blockade in place. Shocked by the harsh terms,

Mourning

For millions of parents, children and siblings, the end of World War I meant not joy, but only profound grief over the loss of a loved one. After her youngest son was killed in battle, German artist Kaethe Kollwitz not only wrote of her grief to her surviving son but also carved the sculptures that would later be placed in the Flanders cemetery where her son was buried:

'Why does work help me in these times? It is not enough to say that it relaxes me very much. It is simply that it is a task that I may not shirk. As you, the children of my body, have been my tasks, so too are my other works. Perhaps that sounds as though I meant that I

would be depriving humanity of something if I stopped working. In a certain sense – yes. Because this is my post and I may not leave it until I have made my talent bear interest. Everyone who is vouchsafed life has the obligation of carrying out to the last item the plan laid down in him. Then he may go. … If it had been possible for father or me to die for him so that he might live, how gladly we would have gone. For you as well as for him. But that was not to be. I am not seed for the planting. I have only the task of nurturing the seed placed in me. And you, my Hans? May you have been born for life after all! You must have been, and you must believe in it.'

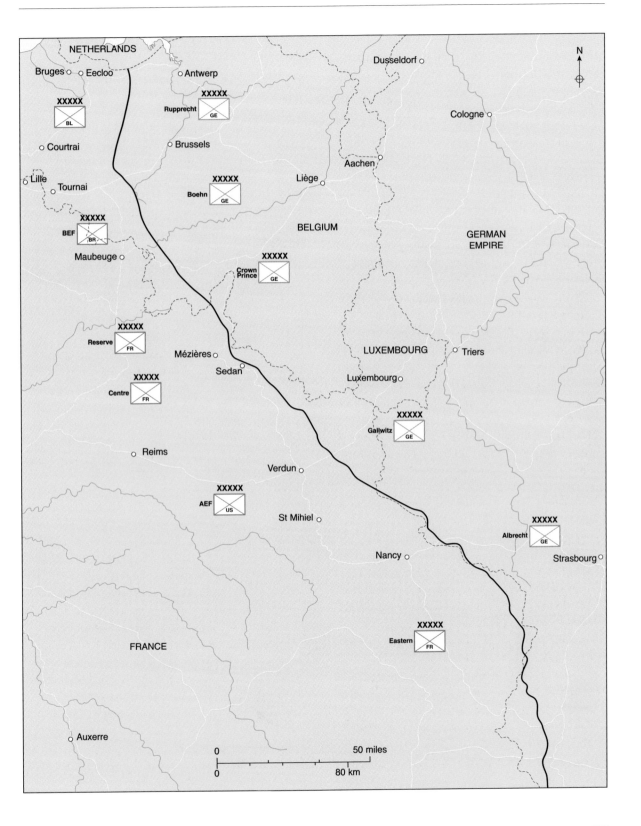

N

NETHERLANDS

Bruges ○　○ Eecloo　　　○ Antwerp　　　　　　Dusseldorf ○

XXXXX
Rupprecht | GE

XXXXX
BL

○ Courtrai　　　　　○ Brussels　　　　Cologne ○

Lille ○ ○ Tournai　　　　　　Liège ○　　Aachen ○

XXXXX
Boehn | GE

XXXXX
BEF | BR

BELGIUM　　　　GERMAN
EMPIRE

○ Maubeuge

XXXXX
Crown
Prince | GE

XXXXX
Reserve | FR

LUXEMBOURG　　○ Triers

○ Mézières　　　　Luxembourg ○

XXXXX
Centre | FR

Sedan ○

○ Reims

XXXXX
Gallwitz | GE

Verdun ○

XXXXX
AEF | US

St Mihiel ○

XXXXX
Albrecht | GE

Nancy ○　　　　　　Strasbourg ○

XXXXX
Eastern | FR

FRANCE

○ Auxerre

0 _____ 50 miles
0 _____ 80 km

the delegation returned to report the terms to the German Government. The abdication of the Kaiser, and the proclamation of the new German Republic, left the matter of armistice terms in the hands of the Social Democratic government of Friedrich Ebert, which, under severe pressure to end the war and to halt the collapse of the German body politic, saw no option but to accept what it saw as the draconian terms.

The German armistice team returned to meet with Foch aboard his railway carriage in the Forest of Compiègne, and, at 5.05am on 11 November, signed the armistice, which went into effect at 11.00am. At

Adolf Hitler

Born in 1889, the son of a minor Austrian customs official, Hitler moved to Vienna in 1908 to pursue a career as an artist. Rejected for admission to the prestigious Viennese Academy of Fine Arts, Hitler eked out a meagre living through the sales of his artwork and soon became involved in radical fringe political movements, which mixed anti-Semitism and strident German nationalism. Seeking both to rekindle his artistic career and to immerse himself more fully in German right-wing politics, in 1913 Hitler moved to Munich, where he was caught up in the events leading to World War I. After rushing to join the army upon the outbreak of war, in November 1914, Hitler took part in the First Battle of Ypres, where he won the Iron Cross Second Class for bravery. Reflecting on the difficulties of trench warfare, in January 1915 Hitler wrote to an acquaintance:

Adolf Hitler (back row, centre), like many German World War I veterans, could not come to terms with Germany's defeat.

'I think so often of Munich and each of us has but one wish … that those among us who have the luck to see our homeland again will find it purer and cleansed from foreign influence, so that by the sacrifice and agony which so many hundreds of thousands of us endure every day, that by the river of blood which flows here daily, against an international world of enemies, not only will Germany's enemies from the outside be smashed, but also our domestic internationalism will be broken up.'

After recovering from wounds received in battle on 7 October 1916, Corporal Hitler returned to the front for the remainder of the war, during which time he often served in the dangerous position of a runner. Hitler took part in the German Spring Offensives of 1918, receiving an Iron Cross First Class for an incident in which he captured four French prisoners with only his pistol for protection. As the war turned against Germany, Hitler fought on with determination and was shocked to learn of strikes and riots on the German home front. He wrote that he wondered what the army was fighting for 'if the homeland itself no longer wanted victory? For whom the immense sacrifices and privations? The soldier is expected to fight for victory and the homeland goes on strike against it!'

As the war neared its end, on 14 October 1918 Hitler was blinded in a gas attack near Ypres and evacuated to a military hospital in Pasewalk, Germany. When he learned of the armistice ending the Great War, Hitler turned his face to the hospital wall and wept bitterly. Galvanized by his experiences in World War I, Hitler would devote himself to undoing the Treaty of Versailles and punishing those whom he believed to be responsible for Germany's defeat.

American troops, who had done so much to tip the balance of the war in favour of the Allies and help weather the storm of the Spring Offensives, celebrate the end of the conflict. The United States lost 126,000 dead in World War I, and over 200,000 wounded.

the designated time, the guns of the Western Front fell silent, and World War I had come to an end. Nearly 10 million men died in World War I – 3.6 million from the Central Powers and 5.7 million from the Allied and Associated Powers. During the war Russia lost 2.3 million men, France 1.9 million, Britain 900,000, Italy 450,000 and the United States 126,000. Regardless of the cost, many on the Allied side believed that the war had ended too soon, that an incomplete defeat of Germany would inevitably lead to trouble in the future. Perceptively, Pershing remarked:

'We shouldn't have done it [the armistice]. If they had given us another ten days we would have rounded up the entire German army, captured it, humiliated it. … The German troops today are marching back to Germany announcing that they have never been defeated. … What I dread is that Germany doesn't know that she was licked. Had they given us another week we'd have taught them.'

As it happened, Pershing was correct. Ludendorff and others utilized the stab-in-the-back legend quite effectively in the inter-war years, a legend that played well in a nation that had paid so much and had received so little in return. The myth that the German army had not been defeated, coupled with the imperfect Treaty of Versailles, consigned Europe to the grim fate of fighting World War II.

FURTHER READING

Asprey, R., *The German High Command at War* (New York, William Morrow, 1991)

Bidwell, S. and D. Graham, *Fire-Power* (Boston, Allen and Unwin, 1982)

Blake, R., *The Private Papers of Douglas Haig* (London, Eyre and Spottiswoode, 1952)

Bruce, A., *An Illustrated Companion to the First World War* (London, Michael Joseph, 1989)

Churchill, W., *The World Crisis* (New York, Scribner's, 1992)

Doughty, R., *Pyrrhic Victory: French Strategy and Operations in the Great War* (New York, Belknap, 2005)

Farwell, B., *Over There: the United States in the Great War, 1917–1918* (New York, Norton 1999)

Gilbert, M., *First World War* (London, Weidenfeld and Nicolson, 1994)

Herwig, H., *The First World War* (London, Arnold, 1997)

Jünger, E., *The Storm of Steel* (New York, Zimmerman, 1985)

Liddle, P., *Passchendaele in Perspective* (London, Leo Cooper, 1997)

Lyons, M., *World War I* (New York, Prentice Hall, 1999)

Middlebrook, M., *The Kaiser's Battle* (London, Allen Lane, 1978)

Moyer, L., *Victory Must Be Ours* (New York, Hippocrene, 1995)

Neiberg, M.S., *Foch: Supreme Allied Commander in the Great War* (Washington, Potomac, 2003)
—— *Fighting the Great War: a Global History* (Cambridge, MA, Harvard, 2005)

Prior, R. and T. Wilson, *Command on the Western Front* (Oxford, Blackwell, 1992)

Shaffer, R., *America in the Great War* (New York, Oxford, 1991)

Sheffield, G., *Forgotten Victory* (London, Headline, 2005)

Weintraub, S., *A Stillness Heard Round the World*, (New York, Oxford, 1985)

Wiest, A., *Passchendaele and the Royal Navy* (Westport, Greenwood, 1995)
——, *Haig: the Evolution of a Commander* (Washington, Potomac, 2005)

Wilson, T., *The Myriad Faces of War* (Cambridge, Polity, 1988)

INDEX

Subheadings are arranged in alphabetical order. Page numbers in *italic* denote illustrations. Page numbers in **bold** denote information boxes.

PICTURE CREDITS

AKG Images: 19(top)

Art-Tech/Aerospace: 60, 62, 63, 68, 78, 92, 95, 98, 99, 146, 158, 159, 194, 206

Art-Tech/MARS: 30, 34, 44, 57, 97(top), 130, 131, 132, 135(top), 141, 152, 163, 166, 168, 174, 187

Cody Images: 10, 13(top), 24(top), 26, 27, 28, 38, 41, 43, 85, 100, 102, 105, 107, 112, 115, 121, 175, 177, 189(bottom), 191, 196, 213, 214, 218

Corbis: 8, 124, 142, 190, 210

Mary Evans Picture Library: 16(bottom), 167

E. W. W. Fowler: 40(bottom), 66, 79, 110, 111, 211

Getty Images: 53, 75

Getty Images/Popperfoto: 51, 74, 86, 87, 90, 106, 118, 200

Library of Congress: 1, 11, 35, 52, 70, 71, 91, 114, 129, 139, 195, 202

Bertil Olofsson/Krigsarkivet: 6, 18, 31, 39, 54, 58, 61(top), 65, 76, 81, 82, 93, 94, 108, 134, 135(bottom), 138, 148, 151, 155, 170, 179, 183, 198, 199, 207

Photos 12: 16(top), 22, 37, 49, 50, 143, 145(bottom), 171, 182

Suddeutsche Zeitung: 19(bottom), 46, 122, 126, 128, 147, 154, 156, 165, 203

TopFoto: 59, 140

US Department of Defense: 117, 119, 125, 178, 184(top), 186, 209, 219

Artworks

Amber Books: 116, 120, 189(top),

Art-Tech/Aerospace: 17, 24(bottom), 29, 61(bottom), 89, 97(bottom), 104, 137, 157, 173

Art-Tech/John Batchelor: 20, 40(top), 48, 184(bottom), 192

Art-Tech/De Agostini: 13(bottom), 32, 72, 133, 145(top), 161, 204

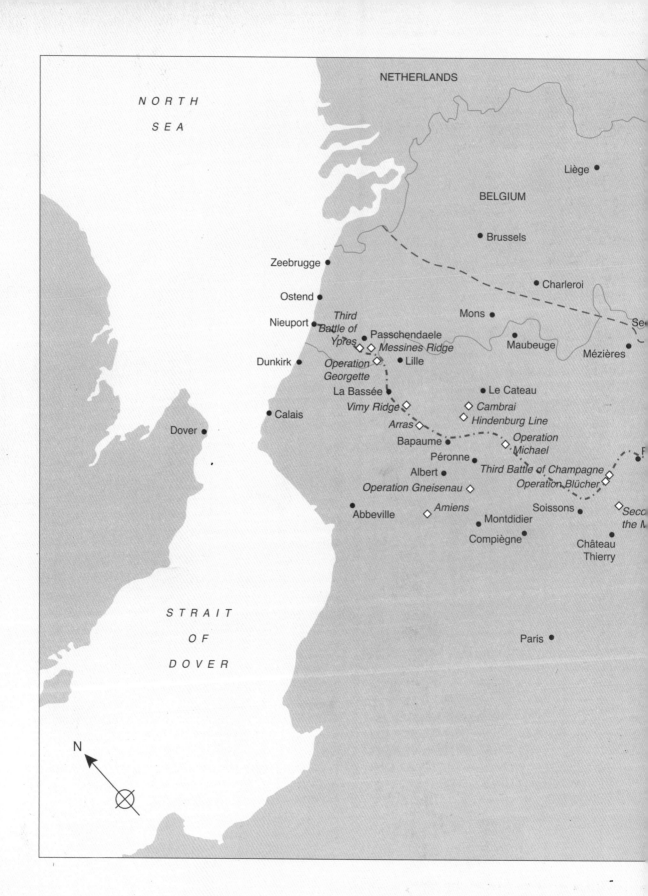

NORTH
SEA

NETHERLANDS

Liège •

BELGIUM

• Brussels

Zeebrugge •

• Charleroi

Ostend •

Nieuport •   *Third*   Mons •   Se
              Battle of
              Ypres   Passchendaele •   Maubeuge •   Mézières
                    ◇ ◇ *Messines Ridge*
Dunkirk •   *Operation* ◇ • Lille
          Georgette ◇
          La Bassée •   • Le Cateau
              Vimy Ridge ◇   ◇ *Cambrai*
Calais •   ◇ *Hindenburg Line*
          Arras ◇   *Operation*
Dover •   Bapaume •   ◇ *Michael*   F
              Péronne •   *Third Battle of Champagne*
              Albert •   ◇   ◇
          Operation Gneisenau ◇   *Operation Blücher*
                                        ◇
Abbeville •   ◇ *Amiens*   Soissons •   ◇ *Seco*
              Montdidier •   *the M*
          Compiègne •   Château
                          Thierry

STRAIT

O F

D O V E R

                          Paris •

N
⊗